THE NEW MIDDLE AGES

BONNIE WHEELER, *Series Editor*

The New Middle Ages is a series dedicated to transdisciplinary studies of medieval cultures, with particular emphasis on recuperating women's history and on feminist and gender analyses. This peer-reviewed series includes both scholarly monographs and essay collections.

PUBLISHED BY PALGRAVE:

Women in the Medieval Islamic World: Power, Patronage, and Piety
  edited by Gavin R. G. Hambly

The Ethics of Nature in the Middle Ages: On Boccaccio's Poetaphysics
  by Gregory B. Stone

Presence and Presentation: Women in the Chinese Literati Tradition
  by Sherry J. Mou

The Lost Love Letters of Heloise and Abelard: Perceptions of Dialogue in Twelfth-Century France
  by Constant J. Mews

Understanding Scholastic Thought with Foucault
  by Philipp W. Rosemann

For Her Good Estate: The Life of Elizabeth de Burgh
  by Frances A. Underhill

Constructions of Widowhood and Virginity in the Middle Ages
  edited by Cindy L. Carlson and Angela Jane Weisl

Motherhood and Mothering in Anglo-Saxon England
  by Mary Dockray-Miller

Listening to Heloise: The Voice of a Twelfth-Century Woman
  edited by Bonnie Wheeler

The Postcolonial Middle Ages
  edited by Jeffrey Jerome Cohen

Chaucer's Pardoner and Gender Theory: Bodies of Discourse
  by Robert S. Sturges

Crossing the Bridge: Comparative Essays on Medieval European and Heian Japanese Women Writers
  edited by Barbara Stevenson and Cynthia Ho

Engaging Words: The Culture of Reading in the Later Middle Ages
  by Laurel Amtower

Robes and Honor: The Medieval World of Investiture
  edited by Stewart Gordon

Representing Rape in Medieval and Early Modern Literature
  edited by Elizabeth Robertson and Christine M. Rose

Same Sex Love and Desire among Women in the Middle Ages
  edited by Francesca Canadé Sautman and Pamela Sheingorn

Sight and Embodiment in the Middle Ages: Ocular Desires
  by Suzannah Biernoff

Listen, Daughter: The Speculum Virginum and the Formation of Religious Women in the Middle Ages
  edited by Constant J. Mews

Science, the Singular, and the Question of Theology
  by Richard A. Lee, Jr.

THE LITERARY SUBVERSIONS
OF MEDIEVAL WOMEN

Jane Chance

THE LITERARY SUBVERSIONS OF MEDIEVAL WOMEN
Copyright © Jane Chance, 2007.

First published in 2007 by
PALGRAVE MACMILLAN™
175 Fifth Avenue, New York, N.Y. 10010 and
Houndmills, Basingstoke, Hampshire, England RG21 6XS
Companies and representatives throughout the world.

PALGRAVE MACMILLAN is the global academic imprint of the Palgrave Macmillan division of St. Martin's Press, LLC and of Palgrave Macmillan Ltd. Macmillan® is a registered trademark in the United States, United Kingdom and other countries. Palgrave is a registered trademark in the European Union and other countries.

ISBN-13: 978–1–4039–6910–1
ISBN-10: 1–4039–6910–8

Library of Congress Cataloging-in-Publication Data

Chance, Jane, 1945–
    The literary subversions of medieval women / by Jane Chance.
       p. cm.—(New Middle Ages)
    Includes bibliographical references and index.
    ISBN 1–4039–6910–8 (alk. paper)
      1. Literature, Medieval—Women authors—History and criticism.
    2. Women and literature—Europe—History—To 1500. I. Title.

PN682.W6C53 2007
809′.9335220902—dc22
                                              2007060090

A catalogue record for this book is available from the British Library.

Design by Newgen Imaging Systems (P) Ltd., Chennai, India.

First edition: August 2007

10 9 8 7 6 5 4 3 2 1

Printed in the United States of America.

"Diversification threatens a subversion of the tradition."
—Mary Wollstonecraft

CONTENTS

ACKNOWLEDGMENTS

Various individuals have helped midwife this book into being, through invited lectures and symposia and conferences about medieval women during which I first aired a portion of what became a chapter in this book, through answers to my queries, or through encouragement and support. Among them are Anne Clark Bartlett, Phyllis R. Brown, Juliette Dor, Deanna Evans, Sister Julia Bolton Holloway, Jane Jeffrey, Lesley Johnson, Betty Joseph, Judith Kellogg, Christina Lee, Colleen Lamos, Linda A. MacMillan, Cristina Mazzoni, Katharina M. Wilson, and Jocelyn Wogan-Browne.

Thanks also go to the following institutions: the National Endowment for the Humanities, for the Summer Institute for College Teachers on medieval women that I directed in 1997 in which various ideas crystallized; the Institute for Advanced Studies in the Humanities at the University of Edinburgh for a Visiting Research Fellowship during which I researched the influence of St. Catherine of Siena in Great Britain in the late Middle Ages; and Rice University, particularly Fondren Library, for its terrific interlibrary loan and document delivery department, and the English Department, whose Graduate Program has supported my work on this book with continuing student research assistance and whose chair, Helena Michie, granted funds for copyediting assistance and an index.

For their specific aid I would also like to thank several Rice English graduate students: Ronit Berger, my research assistant for the spring of 2000; Jill Delsigne, who so carefully gathered bibliographic items in fall of 2004; Benjamin Saxton, who rechecked documentation and citations in fall of 2005; Cassandra de Kanter, who compiled a list of works cited in spring of 2006; Jen Carey, who rechecked other citations in fall of 2006; and Ryan Kehoe, who helped read the copyedited MS in spring of 2007. I am further indebted to the anonymous Palgrave reader for many fine suggestions for improvement, to Bonnie Wheeler, series editor extraordinaire, for her encouragement and support, and to the editing staff at Palgrave for their helpfulness. For indexing, I appreciate Blythe Woolston's excellent work.

Portions of several chapters of this study have been delivered as conference papers and guest lectures. An early version of chapter 2 was presented at the International Interdisciplinary Conference on "Medieval Medicine: Texts, Practices, Institutions" organized by the Department of Cyrillo-Methodian Studies, the University of Sofia (Bulgaria), the Institute of History, the Croatian Academy of Sciences, Zagreb (Croatia), and the Orthodox Theologian Faculty at the University of Veliko Turnovo (Bulgaria) and sponsored by the Open Society, Rila Monastery, Bulgaria, on 30 August 2000. Chapter 2 was also invited as a guest lecture in the Medieval Seminar Series of the Institute for Medieval Studies at the University of Nottingham, England, on 10 March 2005. A shorter version of chapter 3 was presented in a session on "Ideology in Arthurian Romance" at the International Triennial Congress on Arthurian Studies, University of Utrecht, Utrecht, Netherlands, on 25 July 2005. Small portions of chapters 4 and 5 originated in a conference paper in a session on "Responses to the Beguines" at the Conference on New Trends in Feminine Spirituality: The European Impact of the Holy Women of Liége held at the Université de Liège, Liège, Belgium, 12 December 1996. Additionally, two papers have derived from chapter 4: one, on Marguerite Porete, delivered in a session on "Gender and Innovation in Medieval Literary Women," at the Forty-First Annual International Congress on Medieval Women, Medieval Institute, Western Michigan University, Kalamazoo, MI, on 4 May 2006, and one, on Marguerite Porete and Christine de Pizan, delivered at the Sixth International Colloquium on Christine de Pizan, University of Paris-Denis Diderot, Paris, France, on 20 July 2006. An early version of a portion of chapter 5, on St. Catherine of Siena, constituted the Annual Medieval Lecture at the University of Texas, Austin, on 1 December 1994; a portion on Margery Kempe was presented at the Forty-Second Annual International Congress on Medieval Studies, Medieval Institute, Western Michigan University, Kaloamazoo, MI, on 12 May 2007.

Permission to reprint selected pages of material previously published—substantially updated and revised and reassembled for this volume—has been obtained from the publishers for the following, in order of first appearance in this volume:

"Speaking *in propria persona:* Authorizing the Subject as a Political Act in Late Medieval Feminine Spirituality," in *New Trends in Feminine Spirituality: The Holy Women of Liége and Their Impact*, edited by Juliette Dor, Lesley Johnson, and Jocelyn Wogan-Browne (Turnhout: Brepols, 1999), 274–77, 284–87 [266–90].

"St. Catherine of Siena in Late Medieval Britain: Feminizing Literary Reception through Gender and Class," *Annali d'italianistica: Women Mystic Writers* 13 (1995): 166, 175–80, 182–85, 186–89 [163–203].

CHAPTER 1

INTRODUCTION: THE DISCURSIVE
STRATEGIES OF THE MARGINALIZED

How might postcolonial theory illuminate the psychology of female alterity? Caught between two cultures, one dominant and controlling and one passive and controlled, women suffer marginalization similar to that of the colonized because of gender difference. That is, alterity arises because of a tension between the subject and what Judith Butler has termed a "constitutive outside" that anticipates the position of the colonized within postcolonial theory. According to Butler, "The subject is constructed through acts of differentiation that distinguish the subject from the constitutive outside, a domain of abjected alterity (conventionally associated with the feminine, but clearly not exclusively)."[1] So also, as members of a single culture, those colonized experience being conquered or inhabited by another culture, or they emigrate into a new and alien culture; either way, the marginalized are displaced into minor status. Raphael Patai, in *The Arab Mind*, defines this state precisely as one of failure of cultural identification:

> "Marginality" denotes the state of belonging to two cultures without being able to identify oneself completely with either.
>
> An individual becomes "marginal" if, after having been born into a culture and enculturated into it in a more or less normal fashion, he becomes exposed to another culture, is attracted to it, acquires a measure of familiarity with it. . .and strives to become a full-fledged carrier of it—an endeavor which, in most cases, never completely succeeds. The marginal man suffers from his inability to feel completely at ease or "at home" in either culture. . . .Marginal man is marginal, not because he is unable to acquire the intellectual thought processes of the culture to which he wants to assimilate, nor because he is unable to free himself of the thought processes of the culture on which he has

turned his back. He is marginal because *emotionally* he is unable to identify with either of the two cultures.[2]

Similarly, women identify with the marginalized culture of the feminine in which they feel most at home, most familiar, but that identification carries with it dissonance, alienation within a patriarchal culture that insists on continuing primacy. In a note later in her same essay, Butler uses the analogy of the colonized and the colonizer for the relation between the feminine subject and the domain she inhabits—an analogy borrowed from Albert Memmi's *The Colonizer and the Colonized*. In this situation, at the "height of the revolt," according to Memmi, "the colonized still bears the traces and lessons of prolonged cohabitation (just as the smile or movements of a wife, even during divorce proceedings, remind one strangely of those of her husband)."[3] For Butler, the analogy of the trace of the husband's presumed domination of (or at least influence upon) the wife identifies "the feminization of the colonized," or the colonized as feminine, "where the colonized is presumed to be the subject of men, *and* the exclusion of the women from the category of the colonized subject."[4] While the boundary between the colonizer and the colonized endlessly reduplicates, through the binary opposition of male/female it also simultaneously encodes a limitless process of female marginalization.

Butler's example from Memmi also offers an opportunity for a fresh approach to gender difference as an example of the alterity produced by colonization. In commenting on an awareness of the broader significance of the postmodern condition in particular, Homi K. Bhabha, in *The Location of Culture*, remarks on the "epistemological 'limits' of ethnocentric ideas" as the "enunciative boundaries of a range of other dissonant, even dissident histories and voices—women, the colonized, minority groups, the bearers of policed sexualities."[5] Marginalization by gender, nation, race, and class within a culture, ongoing and never ending, results in the loss of articulation of meaning in everyday life and, therefore, requires continuing opposition, or subversion.[6] For Butler, the constitution of the subject by power does not "cease at the moment the subject is constituted, for that subject is never fully constituted, but is subjected and produced time and again."[7] In line with this explanation, Bhabha suggests that, for minorities, the "social articulation of difference" requires a "complex, on-going negotiation" to attempt to legitimize "cultural hybridities that emerge in moments of historical transformation."[8] What Bhabha means by "cultural hybridities" are "these 'in-between' spaces" that "provide the terrain for elaborating strategies of selfhood—singular or communal—that initiate new signs of identity, and innovate sites of collaboration, and contestation, in the act of defining the idea of society itself." Because "interstices" map over and even displace "domains of difference," they are important for the negotiation of "the intersubjective and collective experiences of nationness, community interest, or cultural value."[9]

Out of a whole consisting of "parts" of difference, whether racial, class, or gender, then, subjects can form either within the interstices or beyond the whole, according to Bhabha. But as subjects how do they oppose the act of marginalization? Bhabha himself poses the following question, from which a postcolonial feminist theory might appropriate a beginning: "How do strategies of representation or empowerment come to be formulated in the competing claims of communities where, despite shared histories of deprivation and discrimination, the exchange of values, meanings and priorities may not always be collaborative and dialogical, but may be profoundly antagonistic, conflictual and even incommensurable?"[10] An example of resistance that Bhabha provides as an answer, even if extreme, exists in slave resistance through homicide, infanticide, and self-mutilation, as presented by Elizabeth Fox-Genovese in *Within the Plantation Household*.[11] Implicit within this answer is the potentiality for empowerment, by necessity, to be antagonistic. But does this antagonism hold for feminism as well? Here Bhabha, in defining the role of feminism in the clarification of society as patriarchal and gendered, reveals its approach as "making visible the forgetting of the 'unhomely' moment in civil society" to trouble "the symmetry of private and public which is now shadowed, or uncannily clarified, by the difference of genders which does not neatly map on to the private and public but becomes disturbingly supplementary to them."[12] What is private should be the home, which may be displaced or relocated for the colonized—and, therefore, "unhomely"—but that may also be true for the alien public domain; because of gender difference, the private home for women also can constitute an ironically "unhomely" space.

While Bhabha is most concerned with national difference and concomitant social expressions of the locations of culture, within the context of postcolonial theory, a minor literature may also express difference—of gender, race, and class. Gilles Deleuze and Félix Guattari observe, in *Kafka: Toward a Minor Literature*, that a minor literature (that is, not the literature from a minor language but a minority literature within a major language, such as Czech Jews writing in German) is in its singularity political and possibly revolutionary. The three features of a minor literature are, first, a means of recuperating territory ("The impossibility of not writing because national consciousness, uncertain or oppressed, necessarily exists by means of literature"); second, a wholly political nature; and, third, a collective value, in that in a minor literature the "scarcity of talent" makes even one author's enunciation take on a "collective, and even revolutionary, enunciation."[13]

A minor literature need not necessarily apply only to displaced peoples within a culture. Medieval women inscribed a minor literature in several senses, regardless of whether "minor" reflects the writing of a minority, which medieval women certainly were; or writing in a major language, such as Latin, in which their contributions were relatively fewer in number than those of ecclesiastical male writers, although recent scholarship has demonstrated how plentiful they were[14]; or writing in a linguistic tradition that was both patriarchal and gendered and, therefore, by necessity representative of their authority in a minor voice within that language.

Women writing in the Middle Ages encountered two languages in their attempt to write, because "writing" during most of the early and high Middle Ages meant "in Latin," the so-called lingua franca. Certainly medieval women writers were not necessarily literate, that is, they might not have been able to read Latin, much less write in it, which was particularly true for women authors beginning with the affective tradition of the mendicant movement in the thirteenth century, dependent as it was on itinerancy and the oral tradition of preaching. However, even if women authors were able to write in Latin, this lingua franca did not necessarily function for them as a passport for entry into an elite fraternal community in which all members shared one language and equal status. Instead, Latin served as a barrier to that oneness of community and as a constant reminder of their gender difference and their status as second-class citizens. For medieval women authors, belonging to two cultures almost invariably meant attaining a position as a monastic or beguine within a male-dominant church—they were colonized or policed as a subgroup by a hierarchy of priests and confessors, bishops, archbishops, and popes.

Beyond the falsity of Latin as a lingua franca for literate women, the Latin language in the Middle Ages built into itself an implicit misogyny, and a concomitant gender difference, through the patriarchy that controlled the writing process. The words for "man" and "woman," "male" and "female," easily sum up the gender differences upon which such medieval misogyny both culturally and theologically rested. According to Isidore of Seville (ca. 570–636) in his monumental and much-copied *Etymologiae*, the ancients called women *vira*, female for *vir* (man), rather than *femina* (female), a word related to that portion of the *femores* (thighs) that signifies her biological difference.[15] Isidore explains that "the two sexes are differentiated in the strength [*fortitudine*] and weakness [*imbellicitate*] of the bodies," so that man (*vir*) boasts a greater force (*vis*) than woman (*femina*): "hence also the word 'strength' [*virtus*]—or, man is so named because he controls woman [*feminam*] forcefully [*vi*]. In contrast, woman [*mulier*] gets her name from 'softness' [*mollitie*], or as it were 'softer,' *mollier*, with a letter taken away or changed."[16] What is "taken away" in women—to acknowledge the misogynistic tradition inherited later, in the twentieth century, by Freud—is the penis of the male as much as "a letter," as if the words for the nature of woman define her ontology on the basis of her sexuality and corporal form. Yet the physical difference between men and women as defined by Isidore supports a social purpose, for weak women must obey strong men in order that the species be reproduced: "Thus there is the greatest strength [*virtus*] in man [*viri*], and less in woman [*mulieris*] so that she might be forbearing to man; otherwise, if women were to repel them, sexual desire might compel men to desire something else or rush off to another sex."[17] Further, Isidore adds, she is also *femina* (female) from the Greek, *fos* (burning force), given her intense sexual desire, a function of her lust, greater than that of man, and akin to the animals, so that excessive love (*amor*) in antiquity is gendered female when applied to the male through the use of the word *femineus* (effeminate).[18]

The perceived domestic and sexual roles of men and women in the Middle Ages also manifest a gender difference, ultimately reinforced by the Fall of Man, that strips women of agency: according to Isidore, the active role of the father (*pater*), the head of the family (*paterfamilias*), in procreation represents an accomplishment (*patratio*); his semen leads to conception and then growth (*crementum*), making men creators (*creatores*).[19] But the mother (*mater*) has a passive role, Isidore notes, borrowing from Aristotle: from her something is made, as if from matter (*materia*), "while the father is the cause."[20] As the first woman, Eva (in English, Eve) is indeed "life" (*vita*), but also, when Isidore reorganizes the letters of her name, "woe" (*vae*).[21] The origin of being born, coming to life, Eve also causes death through the fall of Adam, and, hence, "because woman is often the cause of man's welfare," she is the also the "cause of his disaster and death (which is called woe [*vae*])."[22]

The misogyny of the church fathers, buttressed as it was by the Latin language in gendering the female to represent corporal desire, restricted male access to women and, therefore, women's autonomy, especially when women occupied ecclesiastical roles. This cultural construction pervades the pronouncements of the church fathers, who echo St. Paul. St. Jerome (ca. 342–420), seizing upon Paul's declaration in 1 Corinthians 7 that "it is good for a man not to touch a woman," acknowledges in *Adversus Jovinianum* that "by mere touch the peculiar nature of man and woman is perceived, and the difference of sex is understood."[23] The necessity to flee from women, or from their carnal bodies, according to Jerome, prevents men from being burned by their touch. Best, then, says St. John Chrysostom (ca. 347–407) in *Homily 9 on St. Paul's Epistle to Timothy*, for women to be modest and decorous in dress, appearance, and, most importantly, speech, and, drawing on Paul's Epistle to the Corinthians, also for women to "learn in silence" and not speak in the church, that is, not speak "of spiritual matters."[24] Certainly Paul, and John Chrysostom after him, wants women not to teach but only to learn, for "[in] this way they will show submission by their silence."[25] The nature of females is to be talkative; through speech they deceive as Eve did Adam, say both Paul and John Chrysostom. And with this, Paul and John Chrysostom arrive at the punch line: woman was created for man, who was formed first, and therefore man should rule over her.[26] Specifically, Jerome finds, woman's inferior steadfastness and lack of perseverance suggest she should not preach; thus, "the evangelical role is assigned to men."[27]

Throughout antiquity and the Middle Ages, antifeminism leaked into all forms of writing—ecclesiastical, theological, legal, scientific, medical, philosophical, and, most especially, literary, as R. Howard Bloch defines the "register" in his essay "Medieval Misogyny" (1987).[28] Whatever the perceived nature of woman in the Middle Ages—as quarrelsome, proud, demanding, or anxious in her speech—for Bloch, "the reproach against women is a form of reproach against language itself—'that which is said by the mouth.' "[29] Irrational when speaking, she *becomes* language itself, so much so that "the misogynist speaks of the other in terms that bespeak otherness, and this through the voice of the other."[30] Further, for women to represent themselves, to have agency, was regarded so pejoratively that it was perceived as a type of insanity: according to Stephen Harper, "Since female autonomy was abhorred as unnatural and even mad, the causal connection between madness and indiscipline was reverted, so that insane women were described as 'ungovernable' or 'unrulable.' "[31] Debates about women surfaced in every country in the Middle Ages, from Anglo-Saxon England to early modern Spain,[32] but they were always propelled by the misogyny of the church, and a masculine church at that.

Given this early and continuing tradition of a colonized culture of medieval women, what surprises is that women authored their own texts at all, and, when they did write, created a voice of their own, not reflective of the patriarchal culture in which they inscribed. Yet fairly recently, beginning primarily in the twentieth century, scholarship on medieval women has corrected misogynistic scholarly stereotypes that accompanied the earliest editions and treatments of medieval women writers. More detailed studies have grouped women by nationality, city, or community as a determinant influence and appropriate form of classification.[33] In beginning to understand medieval women's networks of reception and dissemination as part of their own literary tradition, scholars have also examined the ways in which women influenced others' writing[34] and commissioned, inherited, or bequeathed books by others.[35] Approaches to the individual writer have, finally, singled out the medieval woman writer as a distinctive and worthy literary, historical, and religious subject, whether Hrotsvit of Gandersheim in the tenth century or Anna Comnena in the eleventh-twelfth centuries[36]; Heloise or Hildegard of Bingen in the twelfth century[37]; or, in the fourteenth and fifteenth centuries, among a host of others, Christine de Pizan,[38] the mystics, and Margery Kempe[39] or the Paston women and the Rožmberk sisters.[40] Most importantly, medieval women writers have been read more postcolonially in relation to intercultural situations and the problem of national boundaries. For example, scholars have recently examined gender difference in twelfth-century poet Marie de France through the lens of postcolonialism.[41] With the emergence of print culture in early modern France and England, debates over female literacy and the rise of nationalism came to involve women writers such as Marguerite de Navarre, Christine de Pizan, Elizabeth Cary, and Aphra Behn.[42]

Within the general tradition of literary criticism on medieval writers, it has not always been clear how women writers fit into the canonical (which is to say, patriarchal) literary traditions. As Susan Schibanoff reminds us, "What is still crucial for us to examine now is how and why some female readers resist immasculation and others succumb to it, for our literary texts and traditions remain largely male-made."[43] Some recent scholars have amply rehearsed the necessity for literary subversion on the part of medieval women writers, who created their own "spaces for self-expression within a masculine literary tradition."[44] Feminized resistance to patriarchal domination surfaces most explicitly in the gendering of genre. Medieval women authors for the most part ignored the favored masculine literary genres of the heroic epic poem,[45] didactic or learned poetry, and social satire. Heloise in the twelfth century took up the epistle, as did a range of women who were both royal and secular.[46] Her contemporary Marie de France popularized the Breton lay, or short courtly romance, and the fable.[47] The thirteenth-century *trobairitz* appropriated the courtly vernacular lyric from the troubadours.[48] In the fourteenth and fifteenth centuries, Marguerite Porete, St. Catherine of Siena, Julian of Norwich, and Margery Kempe turned to the mystical and confessional, or autobiographical, work.[49] Around the same time, borrowing from Boccaccio, Dante, and Petrarch, Christine de Pizan made the allegorical visionary poem her own.

Recent feminist criticism, in its attempt to identify the woman writer's voice in the Middle Ages, has additionally theorized the very nature of language itself as double (aside from the two languages of Latin and the mother tongue), a vehicle for gender acculturation that privileges patriarchy and silences women and, therefore, of course, whatever individual voice might be designated as other and authentically female. Monique Wittig observes that when women characters enter texts, they do so through crablike speech, moving sideways,[50] a description in itself a handy tool for recognizing heteroglossia, a technique offered by Laurie Finke in *Feminist Theory, Women's Writing.* Finke opts for a theory of "complexity," based on chaos theory, in the cultural productions of society—such as individuals, genders, class identities, and written texts—which "maintain and refashion them."[51] Rejecting the monolithic voice of patriarchy, Finke defines a methodology sensitive to the historical moment and place, "as well as to the heterogeneity of socioeconomic formations, the intersecting and competing interests of different groups, and the hegemonic practices that work to smooth over or to suppress these conflicts."[52] Accordingly, Finke's feminist theory of complexity—dialogic, double-voiced, reflective of the culture and the self, as denoted in Bakhtin's concept of "heteroglossia"—means that "another's speech in another's language" has to express "(the speaker's) intentions, but in a refracted way."[53] Second, the theory has also to acknowledge history as the product of a suppression of conflict and discord, overpowered oppositions—put elegantly, the "textuality of history and the historicity of textuality."[54] And third, its chief characteristic is what Finke calls the "noise" of history, referring to Michel Serres's concept of "anything that survives as part of the message, but which was not part of the message when sent," that is, what Alice Jardine defines as alterity, that which is "troped" feminine.[55] Another metaphor, used by Finke, is Michel de Certeau's term "poaching," that is, "those strategies that parasitically undermine hegemonic cultural practices and enable the disempowered to manipulate the conditions of their existence. . . . Poaching is neither straightforward conformity nor rebellion but a dialogic and destabilizing encounter between conflicting cultural codes."[56]

How to recognize heteroglossia in the marginalized texts of the Other is more difficult, primarily because "double-voiced" language, for Finke, "calls into question the fiction of authoritative or monologic discourse," with any expression "always inhabited by the voice of the 'other,' or of many others, because the interests of race, class, gender, ethnicity, age, and any number of other related 'accents' intersect in any utterance."[57] As a result, for the women writers throughout the history of literature—Finke compares thirteenth-century *trobairitz* and women mystics with the feminist discourses of Mary Wollstonecraft and the fiction of Kate Chopin in the nineteenth and twentieth century—the words of the oppressor have to be turned against the oppressor himself to empower the marginalized Other or, in the words of Bakhtin, "take[n] into new contexts, attach[ed] to new material, put. . .in new situations in order to wrest new answers from it, new insights into its meaning, and even wrest from it new words of our *own* (since another's discourse, if productive, gives birth to a new word from us in response)."[58]

The strategies thus far identified by feminist critics as used by medieval women share a denominator in their implicitness within the text, varying in nature from encoding to ventriloquism and "bodytalk." Encoding embeds the text strategically with literary codes such as symbolic images and rhetorical features such as understatement, elision, irony, and hyperbole to effect a "poetics of silence."[59] Ventriloquism endows women's female characters with concealed means of exercising power.[60] Such female characters exhibit a "bodytalk" ("resistant doubled discourse"): one discourse both social and cultural and reflective of repressive gender systems; the other discourse the embodied female voice that disrupts and riots.[61] As a means of challenging gender structures in medieval society, the women writers' male protagonist—by analogy with female characters constructed by men, who exhibit a trace of difference—might be deployed in the gendered, passive and silenced, position of the female to embody her critique of a patriarchal social system.[62] However, these means of subversion—*écriture féminine* as a "philosophically-disruptive stylistics" (in the phrasing of Sharon Kinoshita)—have not always been as clear, primarily because the literary strategies of medieval women writers have themselves been read through the same pernicious pattern of cultural difference.[63]

The problem in dealing with heteroglossia rests, then, upon the detection of the identity of the voice(s) involved, as Matilda Bruckner has fruitfully suggested in analyzing the "fictions of the female voice" in *trobairitz* lyrics. Women troubadours, she has argued, channeled their own voices through the voices of many others. The very fact that they wrote signifies an empowerment: Bruckner notes that "while silence becomes the metaphor of a suppressed female other, women's *prise de parole* signifies an act of power, a self-empowerment that announces their entry into language and the public spheres of social interaction, whether in oral or written exchanges."[64] But when are women troubadours speaking in their own "voice" and when in a "borrowed" voice? Or do they speak through a "double voice" (that is, the male idea of female speech, in addition to whatever their own individual may be)? Bruckner finds that "by manipulating that system and its contrasting voices, the *trobairitz* invented their own distinctive and quite varied fictions of the female voice."[65] How, then, do we recognize the authentic voices of medieval women writers, fictionalized to include the male version or a "borrowed" voice, which then becomes their own? Or their own voice, preserved side-by-side with the patriarchal voice? And how did women adapt "speaking in their own voice" to the gendered spaces in which and from which they wrote, especially women who stepped out of their enclosures (both literal and figurative)?

Two examples of how female readers and writers resist immasculation—from medieval texts by widely distanced women, Hildegard of Bingen (1098–1179) in the twelfth century and Christine de Pizan (1364–1430?) in the fifteenth century—suggest the polarized extremes of subversive literary strategy represented by the early and later medieval. Hildegard regenders misogynist texts implicitly, in her Latin treatise, without explicit acknowledgment. In contrast, Christine de Pizan explicitly and dramatically counters misogyny, in the form of a text by a male ecclesiast, by valorizing female experience through fantasy and allegory to displace patriarchy entirely. But she does so through mimicry, in a gesture dramatized by occlusion of the masculine space.

Hildegard of Bingen, in her unusual and innovative study of natural philosophy, cosmology, and embryology, *Cause et cure* [Causes and Cures] (ca. 1151–58), feminizes her adaptation and encoding of misogyny through corporalization of the male. By "feminization" I mean that Hildegard implicitly rereads conventional biblical texts and Aristotelian philosophical theories to regender, redefine, and reaffirm the unhomely female as much as she deconstructs and displaces the male. Initially, beginning with the Creation, Hildegard explains the Fall of humankind conventionally, as triggered by Eve rather than by Adam, because of Eve's greater weakness as a female. But then Hildegard acknowledges through a logical next step that, if Adam had fallen first, the severity of his transgression—given his greater strength and responsibility—would have been impossible to mollify.[66] Further, given his greater role, Adam's Fall results in a serious and negative bodily change (similar to one, we remember from Genesis, usually associated with women in their condemnation to suffer during childbirth): Adam secretes the poisonous foam of semen caused by the breath of the serpent; this semen produces the black bile of depression—the melancholic humor—which Hildegard analyzes psychologically as a sadness that cuts off hope in God.[67] This corporalization of the Fall in the male in its tragedy for both men and women leads to a masculine despair characterized by irascibility and rage. Further, Adam's dark condition derives from his creation from clay to flesh, which connects him with earth so that from working it he can produce fruit. In contrast to this consequence of the Fall for Adam, Hildegard empowers the lesser Eve by giving her greater agency: because female Eve was taken from flesh and remained flesh, God allots a more "artificiosum opus" [artful work] to her, consequently, one that can be performed with her hands: "quasi aerea est" [She is airy, as it were].[68] The subsequent conception of children by Adam and Eve, accordingly and more positively than usual in the conventional patristic sources, proceeds through consent—actually, free will—by both parties and depends on *delectatio* [pleasure], which "serpens in pomo primo homini insufflavit" [the serpent blew into the primal human by means of the apple].[69] Following up on this gender alterity in origin, one of Hildegard's most interesting and original theories of human conception—one more given to female choice than are those in many ecclesiastical and scientific discourses on the subject—relates to the feelings each partner has for the other: a man of strong semen and love for the woman, coupled with a woman feeling appropriate love for the man, produces an intelligent and virtuous male child, whereas if the woman lacks this love for him, a weak, immoral male child will be conceived.[70] Conversely, a man of thin semen who loves a woman as she loves him will produce a virtuous female, whereas if she does not love him and he does not love her, a bitter female will be born; if neither loves the other but the man has strong semen, a bitter boy will be born.[71]

In my second example of feminized resistance to misogynistic texts, poet and scholar Christine de Pizan explicitly overturns the monologic voice of the patriarchy in the ad feminam charges of the real (nonfictional) Mathéolus in his *Lamentations* (translated into French by Jean LeFèvre and probably read by her in that version), through a clever elision in the narrative that uses the private space, the home, to confuse and trouble gender roles. The opening to the *Livre de la Cité des Dames* [Book of the City of Ladies] (1405)—well known to Christine scholars because of its dramatic encounter between the unidentified narrator and a book about women written by a male cleric—yields insights into the discursive strategy of mimicry in the interiority and exteriority employed by the conscious artist de Pizan. What is being appropriated here is space and time usually marked as his by the literate clergyman or scholar, but here, eventually, identified as hers—that is, the marginalized woman notary, scribe, and poet who must preserve her family's survival through her words. "Christine" mimics (say) Jean Gerson but deliberately delays the speaker's own identification with her sex to indicate how location specifies gender difference. In this reading, then, throughout the passage de Pizan marks the narrative to display her protagonist as wealthy enough to have servants cooking for "him" and leisure time to read, write, and think for "his" own pleasure and benefit. Her preparation of the narrative is so carefully constructed, her hand so light, it is only after repeated readings that the reader appreciates that this scene is hardly conventional for a woman living in Paris in the year 1405.

Christine tells us in the first sentence that this one day, while seated in a study, her narrator has paused in the reading of books and the mulling over their authors' opinions—the "maniere que j'ay en usage et a quoy est dispose le excercice de ma vie" [practice that has become the habit of my life]—to read some lyric poetry for "joyeuseté" [pleasure].[72] What medieval author outside a monastery or royal library, much less a woman, had the opportunity to study expensive books all day (or even to own them)? What cleric has had the leisure to sample lyric poems for the sheer joy of it? From the location of the scene we guess that this is a male scholar—and an important one. The narrator has so many books, some provided for safekeeping, that there is readerly choice among them, whether for study or for pleasure, at a time when manuscripts were so costly that they often took a year or two to be produced. Selecting a book by Mathéolus, the narrator smiles, a gesture of recognition that conveys a sense of well-being, for to smile is to enjoy the luxury of appreciating this author as a fellow writer and scholar, a member of a select coterie. The book is about "reverence des femmes" [respect for women], apparently not entirely unusual, because it is "entre les autres livres cellui parloit" [like other books it discussed]. The narrator, for whatever the reason, finds it amusing to read about women, perhaps because the subject is diverting or entertaining. At this moment, the narrator's mother summons the speaker to another location to eat dinner. It is the woman, the mother-nurturer, who prepares food behind the scenes, in private, and the scholar who, after reading all day in the study—a masculinized and equally private space, even if for more public production of new manuscripts—eats. Even though the narrator's work has been disrupted, he—still no identification of the narrator as female—will take up the book the next day, with the days open before him like blank sheets of paper for his leisure use.

The contrast between the subject and the subject's mother very clearly sets up a dichotomy between agency and nonagency, between the scholar—usually a man who spends his life reading and writing—and women as an object, matter for a text usually written and read by a man, or a food-preparer, that which men write about in the margins. Space in the narrative is private, expansive, and expensive, marked by leisure and productivity. The self of the narrator fills up the space, or at least the mind, which becomes the room of de Pizan's text. We are inside, presumably, a man's head.

But when the narrator returns the next day and finds the book by Mathéolus irritating because it is fallacious and poorly written, the subject puts it aside. What follows is a sequence that reflects the narrator's mind in the process of thinking: "mais la veue de ycellui livre" [just the sight of the book] jogs the memories of other "clercs" who have expressed "tant de deableries et de vituperes de femmes" [{so many} devilish and wicked thoughts about women].[73] As thoughts of these other learned men crowd the narrator's memory, he concludes that "tous parlent par une mesmes bouche" [they all speak from one and the same mouth], and that they all agree that "les meurs femenins enclins et plains de tous les vices" [the behavior of women is inclined to and full of every vice].

Only at this point, late in the introductory passage, does the mind thinking identify itself as a "femme naturelle" [natural woman], because it is *as a woman* that the narrator begins to research the evidence from the authority of her own experience rather than from books—that is, to compare both her own character and behavior, and then the character and behavior of many of the women she has known, against what august scholars in general have concluded about women. Although her experience tells her these pronouncements are incorrect, her respect for books as authoritative and learned discourse compels her judgment to agree that they must be true. At this point she sinks into self-contempt for herself and "tout le sexe femmenin si comme se ce fust monster en nature" [the entire feminine sex, as though we were monstrosities in nature].[74] That is, she sinks into despair, as defined above by Hildegard, a masculine state, which can only be rectified through the epistemological resuscitation offered by the faculty of reason associated with man— here, however, the allegorical female personification of her Reason—accompanied by two other abstractions, Justice and Righteousness. The narrator like a man loses her head, succumbs to irrationality, and must be reminded through history and example of how good, in fact, women are. Ironically, it is only at this moment that she behaves the way that clerical authorities presume women do— irrationally, unable to perceive truth accurately without male guidance. Christine's joke here is that her narrator rescues herself through female guidance, without reliance on any male authority. She thus counters ecclesiastical "authority" through the authority of her own individual experience and reading. That is, she discovers from within herself the female allegorical personifications of Reason, Justice, and Righteousness—who are all female, who all remind Christine's persona of other female examples of virtues and wisdom, and who all chide her for momentarily allowing despair over the alleged evil of women to sink in.[75] Perspective, Christine might conclude, is the first principle behind learning to read texts by women differently and with respect for their experiential authority.

How fragile is the secure, even authoritative, masculine position appropriated by the woman scholar, for it can be dislodged by the culture in which she lives, abetted principally by herself. Indeed, that culture insists and persists in reminding her of her very fragility and inability. The plight of medieval women writers might well be compared with that of modern political prisoners who must stand firm in response to the prison system's attempts to wrest "recantations" of their allegiances, which might then be published in newspapers as a means of demoralization of the opposition.[76] As Barbara Harlow acknowledges, "When to talk, when not to talk, when to recognize, when to deny: the critical tension between 'freedom of expression' and the 'right to remain silent' and their overdetermination by the circumstances of history and the exigencies of political struggle inform the institutional narratives of discursive encounter in political detention between the state and its contestants."[77] If the medieval woman is a prisoner, she herself also represents the jailer within the prison system of culture. The luxe study in which de Pizan's narrator pursues her goal of knowledge fades into a jail in which the narrator herself appropriates the methods of torture of the interrogators. Mimicry is not always enough.

The discursive strategy de Pizan employs to defend her narrator is the allegory of the city of women, a fantasy citadel that combines the visual image of a moated, gated castle with the retrieval of women's history (actually, legend and hagiography)—which produces for her the inhabitants of the city—and the text of the *Book of the City of Ladies*. De Pizan's genre of fantasy (visionary allegory) allows her to create her own space, not that of the male scholar alone in his study. Note that in the third book of *City of Ladies* St. Christine of Tyre—De Pizan's namesake—is similarly imprisoned in a patriarchal tower by her father to protect her beauty and, later, in a dungeon by a judge, both of whom torture and dismember her because she resists their demands to worship pagan idols.[78] Significantly, St. Christine continues to speak (and to counsel these men to worship God), even though her tongue has been pulled out by its roots. Projecting herself into this wildly hyperbolic saint's life, Christine finally allows herself to resist patriarchal and imperial demands and remain strong within the prison. Interestingly, given the overwhelming sense of male domination in the tale, a mob of women collectively tries to protect the saint at one point, angry because these cruel men have so abused this young girl; their strength frightens her pagan judge to the extent that he agrees to worship her god, thinking she means the god Jupiter. Her resistance to his continuing verbal admonishments and her prayers to God to overturn and demolish the pagan idol convert three thousand men and drive the tyrannical judge out of his mind.

This study, in identifying medieval women writers as literary artificers who created their own feminized authority and convention through subversive voices that contested patriarchy's monologic voice, nevertheless fits into and extends previous studies of medieval women as having a historicized literary tradition separate from that of male writers. It posits a practical means of identifying the ways in which marginalization—in its derivation from postcolonial theory as intersected by feminism—mirrors cultural difference, specifically, the broadening of gender difference to include differences in location of culture and their manipulation in intertextuality. Assuredly, the concept of two cultures indicated by a patriarchal Latin literature and the native tongue also implies a relationship between the colonizer and the colonized. In addition, and more historically, like male ecclesiasts and scholars, women writers also may have themselves emigrated to another country in which their place of origin was regarded as alien (certainly the case with Marie de France, who may have spent most of her life as an abbess in England, or Christine de Pizan, born in Venice but living most of her life in Paris). As tertiaries they may have grown up to be different from others in their families, like St. Catherine of Siena, who left home to pursue a vocation of begging and service to the poor in urban environments, or they may have been accused of and stopped from preaching (or in some other way refused to obey a prohibition demanded by the church or society, which put them at odds with the culture to which they marginally belonged, like Flemish Marguerite Porete, whose resistance led to her burning at the stake in Paris). Or women may have had to travel alone, without male accompaniment, outside their home, in order to perform what they thought of as "God's work" (Margery Kempe comes to mind), or they may have had unusual "out of world" experiences that made them seem alien to others (for example, Christina Mirabilis, who appeared to have come back to life after death before performing some of her extraordinary acts, such as perching on the roof).

In these senses, all three of the characteristics of a minor literature as defined by Deleuze and Guattari crop up in the writing of medieval women as a minority, always expressed through the collective value of feminization: in rewriting history, especially of the church; in refashioning masculine behavior toward women; in restructuring church hierarchies so that women and their talents have a place; and in granting to women the right to speak, even if it is ordinary female speech (gossip, conversation, words addressed to other women). In all cases language, even Latin, is their medium: Saxon Hrotsvit of Gandersheim wrote in Latin and not in Old High German, but unlike those more canonical male writers of the Middle Ages, her works exist in a single manuscript little known in her own day outside her own convent of Gandersheim and, later, the abbey of Emmeram that housed it for so many centuries before it was discovered. Both Marie de France and Marguerite Porete wrote in French instead of Latin but by doing so appeared both political and revolutionary, the former, because she took on the major subject of Arthurian chivalry (commonly appropriated by male writers), and the latter, because she crafted a new church, of female souls. Like Geoffrey Chaucer or John Lydgate—or St. Catherine of Siena—Margery Kempe dictated her story in Middle English to two scribes. Yet she did so in the third person, as if she were a character, intentionally defined as a "creature" to highlight her status as an alien within the masculinized culture she inhabited outside the home.

The Literary Subversions of Medieval Women will define a medieval feminist pattern of literary strategies of subversion in which women writers, resisting the repressions of a patriarchy that demanded a silencing of the female voice, express their alterity within the dominant tradition by rewriting conventions and, thereby, establishing authority as female. In order to feminize conventions, they familiarized themselves with contemporary master narratives, either by reading or oral dissemination, often through intertextual and intercultural means. In terms of the postcolonial definitions established by Deleuze and Guattari and Bhabha, women writers demonstrate their gender difference—their marginalization—through resistance to the patriarchy, which takes varied forms.

The medieval woman writer displays both the historicized moment of the truth of her culture and her position within it, that is, her own unique voice and her means of cultural subversion as illustrated by the literary figure she employs. But what is essential in these deliberately subversive techniques—but not necessarily in the historical woman writer herself—is some particular manifestation of her discomfort toward and consciousness of the repressive and monolithic antifeminist tradition of her culture. That she could not speak openly, critically, and thereby slip into the stereotypical role of the female set by the church as disruptive and riotous is also clear. A female writer could not afford to have her work dismissed by the church or court and therefore be erased, as the example of Marguerite Porete testifies.

To legitimize their authority, medieval women construct such unhomely spaces within their writing to subvert an alien and colonizing public culture. To dismantle the authority of the patriarchal voice, they reincode or relabel masculinized binaries so that the female dominates the male; they invert gender roles of characters to valorize the female, or immasculated, role; they create alternate idealized feminist societies and cultures, or utopias, through fantasy; or they authorize female triviality—the unhomely female space—to provide autonomy. While these methodologies often overlap in practice, they illustrate how cultures impinge on languages to create a minor literature for women as displaced.

Specifically, Saxon canoness Hrotsvit of Gandersheim appropriates from and feminizes patriarchal sources from other nations for her own culture in reflection of a cross-cultural identity politics and a personalized church. Breton Marie de France, who may have been an illegitimate royal daughter, inverts both male and female gender roles in her adoption of a language—the French vernacular—to subvert a patriarchal culture in which she must mediate. Beguine Marguerite Porete fantasizes a society and culture in which female epistemologies triumph over their patriarchal and scholastic equivalents. Finally, Catherine of Siena and eccentric Margery Kempe model stigmatized female difference as exemplary and holy to create a space for preaching as "conversation"—gossip, the province of women.

This study begins with chapter 2, "St. Agnes and the Emperor's Daughter in Saxon Hrotsvit of Gandersheim: Feminizing the Founding of the Early Roman Church," in which the tenth-century Saxon woman canon Hrotsvit of Gandersheim uses the figures of St. Agnes and the pagan emperor's convert daughter to celebrate virginity and the triumph of feminized softness over masculine strength. Most likely using books brought across the channel with an imperial bride, Hrotsvit borrows from the two-part Anglo-Saxon saint's life by Ælfric, abbot of Eynsham, in which Agnes heals the corporal and spiritual diseases that afflict Constantia, the daughter of the Roman emperor Constantine, who also appears in a central role in this legend. Because the power of St. Agnes in the Old English version of her legend stems from her role as a *female* healer of other women's bodies, particularly virgins such as Constantia, Hrotsvit also deploys Agnes in her own Latin legend of the saint, *Passio Sanctae Agnetis Virginis et Martyris*, or *The Passion of the Blessed Virgin and Martyr Agnes*. But Hrotsvit then separates Constantia from the legend and celebrates her as central, instead, to her own Latin conversion drama, called by both Hrotsvit and by modern (male) editors *Gallicanus I* and *II*. In *Gallicanus I* Constantia herself imitates Agnes by similarly "healing" (converting) the Roman general's daughters Artemisia and Attica, spiritually rather than physically. Hrotsvit's double usage of Agnes, literally, in a Latin legend and, more analogically, in a Latin play becomes key to the theological unity of Hrotsvit's entire corpus, in that the legend actually occupies the final position among the legends in the unique manuscript of Hrotsvit's works. Appropriately, the *Gallicanus* play occupies the initial position among the plays that follow the legends, a signal medial position within Hrotsvit's canon that similarly celebrates the figure of Agnes, female saint, virgin, and healer, in the supreme role as *salvator* in imitation of Christ within what might be termed Hrotsvit's construction of a feminized Roman church. Against the colonizing Romans' imperialism, indeed, within that very patriarchy, emerges the spiritual victory of the colonized feminine.

In chapter 3, "Marie de France versus King Arthur: Lanval's Gender Inversion as Breton Subversion," we see how Marie de France constructs a feminized and powerless male hero, Lanval, in her twelfth-century Breton lay of the same name. His alien nature—he is from the foreign land of Brittany—matches his similarly unconventional inability to manage the English chivalric and masculine duties of valor and the indoor and courtly virtues of courtesy and feudal homage to a lady. Otiose, escapist, horseless Lanval has to be transported by visions to another domain, one ruled by a fairy queen whose strength lies in magic and Celticized power. Insubordinate and insolent to King Arthur and his unnamed queen, presumably Guinevere, whose disloyalty to her own lord Lanval unmasks, Marie's antihero is rescued repeatedly by acts of feminized fairy grace. Ultimately Lanval projects forward Marie de France herself, whose own power resides in her ability to write truth—as she notes in her prologue—and thereby to reveal God's grace through the modest gifts bestowed on a mere woman. Male failure and female heroism reflect her signature protofeminism in this brief vernacular Breton lay like no other Arthurian romance. If King Arthur is uncharitable and Queen Guinevere promiscuous, feminized Lanval is, perhaps, right to reject the English world of chivalric values for the more virtuous, even noble realm of faerie led by a true queen.

In chapter 4, "Marguerite Porete's Annihilation of the Character Reason in Her Fantasy of an Inverted Church," Marguerite Porete of Hainaut, who was burned at the stake in 1310 for continuing to advance ideas from and for copying her heretical work, *Le Mirouer des simples ames anienties et qui seulement demourent en vouloir et desir d'amour* [Mirror of Simple Annihilated Souls and Those Who Only Remain in Will and Desire of Love], repudiates the clerical (and masculine) privileging of reason—found, for example, in the allegories and treatises of Alan of Lille and Hugh of St. Victor—and, instead, opts for the journey home to Dame Amour and to annihilation and nothingness for "simple souls" like herself. In viewing God the Holy Spirit as a feminized Love, Porete (very much like twelfth-century Hildegard of Bingen) substitutes love as the transformative force that allows the embodied soul—the soul while still in its earthly body—union with God. Porete, accordingly, also affirms the nobility of certain souls and offers the possibility of grace outside the mediation of the church (a transgression that made *Mirror of Simple Souls*, along with its vernacular language, especially dangerous). By turning the church upside down (or inside out), Porete in her Holy Church the Greater creates a feminized utopia through tropes of inverted education and class distinction that dismantle conventional patriarchal hierarchies of society and church mandated by law and practice.

In chapter 5, "Unhomely Margery Kempe and St. Catherine of Siena: 'Comunycacyon' and 'Conuersacion' as Homily," we encounter the most outrageous and clever example of gendered literary subversion in Margery Kempe (b. ca. 1373, but flourishing in the early 1420s)—despite her contemporaries' charges of heresy and witchcraft and twentieth-century scholars' characterizations of her as crazy. Through eccentricity and obnoxious and exaggerated gender difference, Margery in her *Book* uses "comunycacyon" and "conversacion" in her fables and homilies in order to appear powerless and marginal as a loquacious married woman. Such illusions allow her to trump the charges of Lollardy and heresy leveled against her and, under cover, as it were, to accuse male clerics and church officials of similar lapses. The homely, made unhomely, empowers the colonized feminine. In the sense that her cross to bear in loving and serving Christ was her own eccentricity and difference from others, Margery resembles the eccentric twelfth-century beguine Christina Mirabilis, whose astonishingly antisocial behavior was celebrated in the life written down by Thomas de Cantimpré. As an additional possible model for Margery's life, St. Catherine of Siena displays similar kinds of aberrant behavior. Like Margery, Catherine hailed from a commoner's family; she similarly "conversed" and "communicated" with both men and women, but she also became a Dominican tertiary who displayed the stigmata, preached sermons, authored the *Dialogue* (by dictating them to confessor Raymond of

Capua, the head of the Dominicans in Italy), and counseled a pope. Common to all three women—Margery, Christina, and Catherine—is their class background in the third estate and the idea of alterity as sanctified, which explains why Margery, in particular, has been so misunderstood by scholars. Especially characteristic of Catherine and Margery is their realization of Christ as a bridge across difference for those colonized by class and gender.

The conclusion, chapter 6, "Toward a Minor Literature: Julian of Norwich's Annihilation of Original Sin," presents an example of the transmission of a tradition in a minor literature marked by an equally minor mode of feminization and subversion in its theology. Just as Porete essentially repudiates original sin through her doctrine of the annihilation of the soul without mediation by clergy, the late English anchorite and mystic Julian of Norwich (fl. 1373) rejects the concept of a humanity debased by original sin, through a feminized theology dependent on Trinitarian maternality. Julian safely and without major consequence (as far as we know) rehearsed Poretian concepts at a historical moment very different from the heresy-sensitive early fourteenth century, but in doing so suggests a way in which a female canon of difference might have operated in the Middle Ages. To an extent, medieval clerics and scholars permitted and even encouraged the reception of women's writing wherever this double marginalization—female to female—occurred. Also boosted through Julian's mystical process is the authority of women: if anyone can be touched by God, even the most ignoble and deficient of beings, such as a woman, the power of God's grace and efficacy must be all the greater. In contrast, in cases like that of the earlier Porete—seemingly working alone and writing originally—the authority of women remained solely a feminized phenomenon, creating resistance and obfuscation or erasure by male authorities.[79]

What is new in this study, then, depends upon a twofold assumption. First, the complex and innovative literary subversions offered by individual women writers from the tenth to the fifteenth centuries vary, depending on the genre, purpose, and subject of the literary work and the individual subjectivity of the writer; and, second, types of and approaches to literary subversion over the six centuries differ from century to century, within each century, country to country, and cannot be generalized to define a monolithic "female literary tradition," any more than the canonical (male) literary tradition can be so summed up or categorized. What gendered rhetorical strategies Hrotsvit of Gandersheim and Marie de France offer as subversion of patriarchy in the tenth and twelfth centuries are not the same as the more openly feminist techniques that displace patriarchy altogether in the utopian visions of Marguerite Porete, St. Catherine of Siena, Christine de Pizan, or Julian of Norwich in the fourteenth and fifteenth centuries.

Appropriation, feminization, gender inversion, fantasization, modeling—the movement is always to valorize that which is regarded as marginal and pejorative, the feminine as the trace of gender difference, to recuperate a place in society, even if artificial and literary. It is the reimagining of cultural position and space that brings to the foreground that which has been shunted to the margins, but that imaginary can depend on drawing away from patriarchal insistence on the feminine corporeal within the church, turning upside down gender roles and cultural expectation for members of a select aristocracy, rejecting the current hierarchies of society as untruthful and shackling, or moving within a band of dismissed marginality to surprise with a new alterity. Rewriting history, rewriting culture, refashioning society and the ways of experiencing reality, and creating spiritual value in the trivial and unimportant ways of female difference are all ways these women reinvigorate the feminine.

CHAPTER 2

ST. AGNES AND THE EMPEROR'S DAUGHTER IN SAXON HROTSVIT OF GANDERSHEIM: FEMINIZING THE FOUNDING OF THE EARLY ROMAN CHURCH

One of the most popular saints in England in the eighth to the tenth centuries, the Roman martyr St. Agnes (291–304) was lauded in Latin works about virginity written by Aldhelm (640?–709) and the Venerable Bede (673–735).[1] Aldhelm's influential *Prosa de virginitate*, of which fourteen English manuscripts exist, was "popular in England and the continent until Viking invasions put an end to native learning in the last half of the ninth century," according to Scott Gwara; interest in Aldhelm's work revived in the 920s, along with "a new movement in 'hermeneutic' Latin that lasted, in some centers, beyond the turn of the twelfth century."[2] St. Agnes's virginity may have been responsible for the inclusion of material from her vita, as well as that of St. Agatha, in English liturgical ceremonies after the tenth century in which nuns professed their vows.[3] Widely circulated, St. Agnes's vita is narrated in Latin and Anglo-Saxon in Bede's *Martyrology*, the anonymous ninth-century *Old English Martyrology*, and Ælfric's later Old English *Lives of the Saints* (ca. 996–97).[4]

Most likely St. Agnes represented a model for female monastics and converts at a time when the English church was still in its founding stages. Why Anglo-Saxon hagiographers singled out St. Agnes as an exemplar of virginity in the eighth–tenth centuries may have been related to her *aemulatio Christi* in a role that advocates both physical (or literal) virginity and spiritual (or figurative) "virginity." In her legend her healing power cures leprosy (a medieval consequence and sign of sexual promiscuity)[5] as her staunch faith in God cures the spiritual "disease" of paganism (specifically, belief in the Roman gods). Reflective of these double roles for Roman Agnes, the Old English legend by Ælfric the Grammarian (ca. 955–1020), abbot of Eynsham (near Oxford), in its two parts presents Agnes as healing both the physical and spiritual diseases that afflict Constantia, the daughter of Roman emperor Constantine the Great (ca. 285–337).

Rather curiously, both Agnes and Constantia, through their relationship in Ælfric, appear to play significant symbolic and teleological roles in the works of the Saxon canon Hrotsvit of Gandersheim (ca. 935–1000). Characters Agnes and Constantia literally connect Hrotsvit's eight Latin legends and her six dramas in the unique manuscript of her complete works,[6] as hinted in the past, briefly and without elaboration, by Katharina M. Wilson: "The initial linkage between the legends and the dramas is effected by the person of Agnes, heroine of the last legend, at whose grave and at whose intercession Constantia, heroine of the first legend, is healed from the double evil of leprosy and paganism."[7] Hrotsvit may have been drawn to both Agnes and Constantia because of their perseverance in remaining chaste and also because their legends celebrate the triumph of female weakness over masculine strength. In the preface to her dramas in the Emmeram codex, Hrotsvit announces female virginity and the triumph of female weakness over male strength as the key themes in her dramas, clearly an explicit statement of her construction of a minor literature: she will use her "facultatem ingenioli" [little talent] to laud the "sacrarum / castimonia virginum" [chastity of sacred virgins] rather than "turpia lascivarum / incesta feminarum" [the shameless acts of lascivious women] presented in Roman Terence's fiction. She explains that "quanto blanditiae amentium ad illiciendum promptiores, tanto et superni adiutoris gloria sublimior / et triumphantium victoria probatur gloriosior, / praesertim cum feminea fragilitas vinceret / et virilis robur confusioni subiaceret" [the more seductive the unlawful flatteries of those who have lost their sense, / the greater the Heavenly Helper's munificence / and the more glorious the victories of triumphant innocence are shown to be, / especially / when female weakness triumphs in conclusion. / And male strength succumbs in confusion].[8] Because she is writing for her "sapientes. . .fautores" [learned. . patrons]—most likely her previous teachers at Saint Emmeram, including Archbishop Bruno of Cologne, as her letter to them that follows the preface to the dramas indicates[9]—her explicit desire to foreground the triumph of

(Christian) female virginity over (pagan) men of strength appears justified and yet also subversive, given the Christian power of the female protagonists in her plays.

In this chapter I offer an explanation of why and how Hrotsvit uses Agnes to link the legends with the plays, through her changes in her crucial source of Ælfric's Old English legend that lead to the feminization of conversion from paganism to Christianity in the early Roman church at a time when the Roman Empire moved to colonize and dominate those along or outside its significant borders—whether borders of territory, religion, or gender. What attracted Hrotsvit to Ælfric's treatment of Agnes may have been the saint's virgin martyrdom as a native Roman, herself oppressed by Roman imperialism. Like Sicilian saints Lucy and Agatha, Agnes shared their political situation as subjects of Roman colonization. "As Christians and as women," according to Andrea Rossi-Reder, "they represent a distinctly oppressed group subject to the same disdain, neglect, and ill treatment as those native saints of other countries occupied by Rome."[10] The differing treatment of Roman Agnes by Ælfric and Hrotsvit mirrors their respective gendered understandings of Bhabha's "nationness." For Ælfric, the growth of an English church came, as Rossi-Reder reminds us, during renewed Danish attacks on the nation. "The female saint is symbolic of the *patria*, and the highly sexualized bodily sufferings she endures mirror the imperialistic violations exacted upon her country: she is both land and native people."[11] While Ælfric may have been particularly attracted to a legend that marks the founding of an *English* church, Hrotsvit prefers in her own last legend and first play to empower exemplary saint Agnes and pagan convert Constantia within a Roman and patriarchal context—the Roman Empire. In Ælfric's two-part Old English legend, Agnes's own "constantia" enables her to heal Constantia's body, which leads to Constantia's conversion to Christianity through Christ and is then followed by the conversion of her father, Constantine the Great, and other virgins, through a church dedicated to Agnes. Because Constantine the Great was crowned emperor in York in 306, his conversion initiates the first steps in the founding of the Church in western Europe. In contrast, Hrotsvit accomplishes her empowerment of the two women, martyr and convert, within a climate of masculine oppression—nation gendered—by appropriating Christ's healing role for both these virgins. They heal *like* Christ, not more passively *through* him, via ecclesiastical agency.

Like the other early English treatments of St. Agnes, including that of Ælfric, Hrotsvit's celebrates the saint's virginity and martyrdom in an appropriately titled Latin legend, *Passio sanctae Agnetis virginis et martyris*, or *The Passion of the Blessed Virgin and Martyr Agnes*. Last in the series of legends in the manuscript of Hrotsvit's works, the life of St. Agnes as an exemplar of virginity unifies all of Hrotsvit's legends.[12] Although scholars have recognized the indebtedness of Hrotsvit's legend of St. Agnes to earlier Latin treatments—the pseudo-epistle of St. Ambrose and the metrical *Vita* by Prudentius and the one by Pope St. Damasus, preserved in the *Acta sanctorum*[13]—they have not yet identified as a possible source Ælfric's late-tenth-century Old English saint's life of Agnes. Hrotsvit separates Constantia from St. Agnes in Ælfric's legend and, as well, their chief roles—respectively, as a converted pagan, object of *conversio*, and a converting Christian, subject of *imitatio Christi*. As a consequence, the Saxon scholar makes Constantia central instead to her first legend and her first, two-part, conversion drama, called by Hrotsvit and modern (male) editors *Gallicanus I* and *II*. Hrotsvit then also makes Agnes central to her last legend, immediately prior to the *Gallicanus* in the manuscript. That is, a kind of rosary effect operates.

Through these thematically linked and analogous works, Hrotsvit feminizes the founding of the early church in Europe, despite Roman imperialism located both in home and nation, given Constantia's familial situation. In developing this argument, I first examine Ælfric's legend of St. Agnes and Constantia and conclude with their roles in Hrotsvit's first legend and *Gallicanus I* and *II*. Of special interest here is how Ælfric's legend of St. Agnes's conversion of the emperor's daughter offers a previously unidentified source as well for Hrotsvit's play *Gallicanus*.[14] In this first play in the unique manuscript, Constantia and the other major characters all share a relationship, direct or indirect, with the saint (even though St. Agnes does not appear in person in the play).[15] Where Hrotsvit's treatment of St. Agnes in *Gallicanus* differs from that in her legend lies in how Constantia herself in *Gallicanus I* imitates Agnes—who has herself imitated Christ—by similarly "healing" (converting) the general Gallicanus's daughters, Artemia and Attica, through a series of spiritual chain reactions. This amplifies and genders the second part of Ælfric's legend, when Constantia asks her father, Constantine, to build a church dedicated to St. Agnes that will lead other young women to pursue a vocation as Christian virgins; young women then flock to her tomb. The intertextuality of the

Latin Hrotsvit play and Ælfric's Old English legend is remarkable because St. Agnes is not explicitly linked with the conversion of Constantia in either of the two carefully distinguished parts of *Gallicanus*. Further, conversion of the character Ter(r)entianus in both the Old English legend and in Hrotsvit's play *Gallicanus* itself represents the means of healing the madness of Terrentianus's son (a kind of acting out in a dysfunctional family).

St. Agnes, Virgin Healer of the Emperor's Daughter in Ælfric's Old English Legend

Before proceeding, we need to interrogate the plausibility of transcultural borrowings from Anglo-Saxon to Saxon. Certainly a connection between Anglo-Saxon England and Saxony had existed from the eighth century, when missionaries were sent to Saxony from England. In addition, early Latin biographies exist: for these two missionaries; the abbot of the first monastery in Germany; St. Leoba (d. ca. 780), the abbess of Bischofsheim (the latter biography written ca. 836 by Rudolf of Fulda); and St. Willibald (ca. 700–81), one of the first archbishops. St. Willibald's Latin biography, the eighth-century *Hodoeporicon*, was said to be written by an "unworthy sister of [Anglo-] Saxon origin," Huneberc of Heidenheim.[16] Because of the subsequent copying and transmission of native manuscripts to Saxony during this period, which was furthered through Saxon marriages with royal Anglo-Saxon women, it is more likely for the following reasons that Hrotsvit was familiar with Ælfric than that Ælfric was familiar with Hrotsvit.

First, regardless of whether Hrotsvit knew the Old English legends of the *Martyrology* or of Ælfric, it is now understood, according to Christina Lee, that her contemporary Eadgyth (or Editha) of Wessex, Athelstan's half sister and wife of the Saxon Holy Roman Emperor Otto I, brought with her from England to Saxony in late 929 or 930—at the time of her marriage—various devotional tracts; others were bestowed upon Athelstan by Otto I.[17] That Hrotsvit admired Eadgyth is apparent from her references to her as the "highest descendant of kings," meaning, specifically, her alleged and beneficial ancestral connection with Northumbrian king St. Oswald.[18] Second, apparently Hrotsvit's works were not copied, making it unlikely that Ælfric knew her work directly. The only known manuscript of Hrotsvit's entire corpus is the eleventh-century Emmeram-Munich Codex that was discovered at the monastery of St. Emmeram, Ratisbon, in 1495, and now held at the Munich library (Clm 14485, fols. 1v–150v). Third, I have recently argued for Hrotsvit's thematic indebtedness to the Old English poem *Elene* in this same Latin play *Gallicanus*: the religious epic *Elene* introduces Constantine the Great and his mother Helena, as founder of the English Church through her discovery of the True Cross.[19]

Fourth and most importantly, as a canoness Hrotsvit lived most of her life from youth at an abbey in Saxony that was renowned as a center of multicultural learning because of its connections with the imperial court, which makes it likelier that foreign manuscripts might have landed there. Hrotsvit belonged to what is known as a free abbey, that is, beholden to the king and not the Church, although in 947 Otto I emancipated the abbey further from rule by the crown when he authorized the abbess to maintain a court of law and an army, coin money, and represent the abbey in the imperial diet.[20] The tenth-century abbey was a center of learning like others of its day with which it held ties (Fulda, Corvey, Herford, and St. Emmeram) and a place of harbor for many learned foreigners and kindred of the imperial house.[21] When in 965 the rule by royal abbess once again was decreed, Gerberga II (940–1001), under whom Hrotsvit served and wrote, was consecrated by Bishop Otwin of Hildesheim, and the abbey commenced a period of prosperity during which it became further known for its intellectual and cultural significance.[22] Gerberga II, daughter of Henry of Bavaria and a niece of Otto I, was one of Hrotsvit's two known teachers; the abbess is thought to have trained Hrotsvit in the Roman and patristic writers and the trivium. Certainly Hrotsvit knew rhetorical figures found in Donatus, Isidore, and the Venerable Bede.[23] Another advantage for Hrotsvit was the introduction to Byzantine culture through the wife of Otto II, who frequently spent holy days at Gandersheim.[24] Through the transmission of Byzantine Greek arts and culture, including embryonic church drama and hagiography, Hrotsvit acquired knowledge of and interest in Eastern subjects, as demonstrated by at least four of her legends and four of her dramas.[25]

What similarities do the two treatments of Agnes, Anglo-Saxon and Saxon, share? Ælfric's Old English legend of St. Agnes, like Hrotsvit's own Latin legend, celebrates the constancy of the Roman girl's love for Christ and her defense of her literal virginity from attempts to sexualize her body within an oppressive Roman colonialism bolstered by paganism. After Ælfric's Agnes refuses to marry the son of Simpronius, the prefect of the city, because of her love for the bridegroom Christ, the prefect offers her the choice either of consecration of her virginity to the pagan goddess

Vesta or sacrifice of her virginity in the house of the prostitutes. When Agnes rejects the one alternative because of its idolatry, she is stripped of her clothing and sent to the house of the prostitutes to await the coming of the prefect's son. On the way, her hair grows sufficiently to cover her nakedness and God sends her a "scinende tunecan" [shining tunic].[26] Eventually martyred for her alleged sorcery (at the age of thirteen, on 21 January 304, during Diocletian's persecution), Agnes thereafter appears in a vision to Constantia, the ill daughter of the emperor Constantine, who has prayed at St. Agnes's tomb (on the Via Nomentana) in Rome for healing from "egeslice wunda" [monstrous wounds] (which we understand as leprosy).[27] In a move to heal Constantia's physical and spiritual "wounds," the saint offers the emperor's daughter the choice of virginity as an antidote to sexual license (the sign of which is leprosy), that is, as an alternative to the life of the prostitute.

However, Ælfric does not allow Agnes to convert Constantia directly, as she does in Hrotsvit's legend, but merely to educate her in the existence of Christ as the Savior. When Constantia is healed through belief that "se hælend" [the Savior, literally, the Healer]—"ge-hælen mæge" [can heal] both her "sarra wunda" [sore wounds] and her paganism—and "se hæðen-scipe wanode . and godes geleafa weox" [heathenism waned and belief in God waxed]—she and her father are baptized, and (in accord with Agnes's suggestion) Constantia takes up the veil.[28] As a result of Constantia's example, other women convert and are healed at Agnes's tomb in the church built by Constantia and her father.

> and manega oðre mædenu . þurh hire mærlican ge-bysnunga .
> forsawon woruld-lustas . and wurdon criste gehalgode .
> Ða bæd constantia . constantium hire fæder .
> þæt he þære eadigan agne . ane cyrcan aræde .
> and hire sylfre ane ðrúh . þære hét gesettan .
> Þes hlisa asprang þa on eallum ðam leod-scipe .
> and coman fela untrume to þære halgan byrigene .
> and wurdon gehælede . þurh ða halgan agnen .
> Ða romaniscan mædenu manega eac ðurh-wunodon
> on clænum mægðhade . for cristes lufe .
> æfter agnes gebysnunga þe þær bebyrged ís .

[Through her illustrious example, many other maidens renounced worldly pleasures and were consecrated to Christ. Constantia asked her father Constantine to raise up a Church for the blessed Agnes and commanded that a coffin be placed there for herself. Fame of this spread through all the region, and many ill people came to the holy tomb and were healed by

Saint Agnes. *Afterward, many Roman maidens remained pure in maidenhood also for the love of Christ, according to the example of Agnes, who is buried there.*][29]

In the Old English legend the two basic choices offered to St. Agnes by Simpronius—the temple of Vesta or the house of prostitutes—represent antithetical social roles for young Roman women in a patriarchal society, those of the virgin pagan priestess and the sexually active prostitute. Why Vesta? Because the Roman goddess Vesta guarded the hearth and thereby preserved the family and home, or earthly civilization, her temple accordingly also symbolized the role of wife. Whether in service to Vesta and the imperial Roman ideal of the family or to the prostitutes as a sexualized body, Agnes would serve men, violating one or another type of virginity. The prostitute offered an alternative to a career as wife, but serving through her body rather than through her nurturing of family members and the orderly running of household affairs; and the priestess, serving a goddess, an alternate to a role as martyred Christian virgin, but serving the patriarchal state religion and thereby violating the purity of Agnes's spiritual bond to Christ. In this respect it is interesting to note that Ambrose in Milan compared the virgins of Christ with those of Vesta in his late-fourth-century letter concerning virgins to his sister Marcellina, to the disadvantage of vestal virgins because of the term limits placed on those admitted to the service of the goddess. This comparison may have influenced both Ælfric and Hrotsvit in that Aldhelm based his treatise on virginity on Ambrose's letter.[30] In both legends Agnes rightly refuses to sacrifice her *spiritual* or *figurative* virginity by becoming a vestal virgin because she is already the bride of Christ. Instead, she acquiesces to being led *physically* or *literally* naked (but spiritually pure) to the house of the prostitutes, where God miraculously covers her, as a reward, first, with her own hair and, then, with a shining tunic.

The real threat to Agnes in the Old English legend has always been to her spiritual rather than to her sexual virginity,[31] namely, the threat of belief in the pagan gods, although Ælfric expresses this through emphasis upon Agnes's body. This "dis-ease," likened to madness psychologically and spiritually, correlates to the physical wounds that appear on Constantia's leprous body when she comes in the night to petition Agnes at her tomb. The saint spurns the controlling frame of the prefect's choices by opting for spiritual virginity—and therefore sanity, or health. That is, if the consequence of belief in the gods—*daemones*—is demoniacal possession, then the antidote to paganism is, appropriately, Christianity (specifically, virgin martyrdom, or eternal symbolic virginity as Christ's bride). Thus, St. Agnes appropriates the role of Christ in her act of resurrecting (with angelic help) the once lustful but now dead son of Simpronius and subsequently converting his father to Christianity. Given the double roles played by St. Agnes and the double concept of her virginity in the two-part Old English legend, it is no accident that Agnes, in the second part, heals the diseases of both body and soul (or mind) that afflict Constantia. Madness as demoniacal possession (and therefore the converse, of faith in Christ as healing) is a topos that frequently marks the dramatic conflict in the saint's life and can be gendered female as a marker for cultural difference, as female different from male, as Barbara Newman has recently demonstrated.[32]

Agnes's specific antagonism to the worship of Roman gods predominates in both legends, Ælfric's Old English one and also Hrotsvit's Latin one. In accord with her choice, when Agnes in Ælfric rejects Vesta and the role of wife but chooses the role of prostitute, she intends to cede her literal virginity out of respect for the greater power of spiritual virginity. This resistance to the pagan accords with the concept of Christ refusing to battle the pagan gods, at least according to the apocryphal book of Nicodemus, until Christ's Harrowing of Hell, after his Crucifixion. The Old English conversion of Constantia comes about because of the efficacy of her prayers to a female (Agnes) martyred for her purity of body and soul and because of Agnes's Christian faith. Constantia's conversion does not occur because of any vision—epiphania— of a cross (as with her father Constantine, in Elene) or a Christ-figure (as is the case with the general Gallicanus in Hrotsvit's play).[33] Indeed, even Constantine's conversion comes about not because he is in despair in the midst of battle and seeks help from above but because of the influence and importance of his daughter, Constantia.[34]

If Agnes's virginity is the locus of the spiritual drama in the Old English legend, it is a sacral, sexual virginity shared by pagan Vesta and her vestal virgins in Roman religion—the choice Agnes rejects because it would violate her spiritual virginity and constancy to Christ as his bride. That Hrotsvit intends this choice as reflective of a pagan and, specifically, Roman imperialism is clear from the details of Vesta's cult dominated by the sexual practice of virginity. As fostered by the vestal virgins, the cult of Vesta placed her temple on the edge of the city in the Roman forum (outside the Palatine city) and timed her festival, the *Vestalia*, for mid-June, when donkeys were adorned with garlands.[35] Even the donkeys have some connection with protection of Vesta's virginity: in Ovid's *Fasti* 6.319–48, the braying of an ass awakens Vesta and thereby prevents her rape by Priapus, Roman god of gardens and fertility.[36] In support of the concept of material virginity, according to the philosophic (Stoic) explanation in Ovid's *Fasti*, Vesta signifies ungenerative fire, a "living flame" that does not produce or accept seeds, semen. In Stoic philosophy, fire, as one of the four elements of matter, was the only element not present in bodies, although it often acted as a catalyst. Ovid asks:

> cur sit virginibus, quaeris, dea culta ministris?
>   inveniam causas hac quoque parte suas.
> ex Ope Iunonem memorant Cereremque creatas
>   semine saturni, tertia Vesta fuit;
> utraque nupserunt, ambae peperisse feruntur,
>   de tribus impatiens restitit una viri.
> quid mirum, virgo si virgine laeta ministra
>   admittit castas ad sua sacra manus?
> nec tu aliud Vestam quam vivam intellege flammam,
>   nataque de flamma corpora nulla vides.
> Iure igitur virgo est, quae semina nulla remittit
>   Nec capit et comites virginitatis amat.

[You ask why the goddess is tended by virgin ministers. Of that also I will discover the true causes. They say that Juno and Ceres were born of Ops by Saturn's seed; the third daughter was Vesta. The other two married; both are reported to have had offspring; of the three one remained, who refused to submit to a husband. What wonder if a virgin delights in a virgin minister and allows only chaste hands to touch her sacred things? Conceive of Vesta as naught but the living flame, and you see that no bodies are born of flame. Rightly, therefore, is she a virgin who neither gives nor takes seeds, and she loves companions in her virginity.][37]

Adding to the support of Vesta's sexual virginity, Vesta's temple always contained an ever-burning fire, but without any effigy of either the goddess or the fire.

Yet, to signify the hearth's architectural and cultural core in the Roman family as guardian of the hearth and therefore as nurturing deity of female domesticity, Vesta in Ovid's *Fasti* is also equated with Earth and the earthly role of the chaste wife at the hearth, in the vestibule and the first room of the house. Ovid writes, "Tellus Vestaque numen idem" [the Earth and Vesta {are} one and the same deity].[38] Ovid etymologizes "Vesta" as coming from *ve* and *stare*, "to stand apart," thereby understanding *vestibulum* as coming from Vesta: because the hearth emanates heat through flame, it is associated with *focus* from *foveo*, "to cherish" or "to warm."

> stat vi terra sua: vi stando Vesta vocatur,
>   causaque par Grai nominis esse potest
> at focus a flammis et quod fovet omnia, dictus;
>   qui tamen in primis aedibus ante fuit.
> hinc quoque vestibulum dici reor: inde precando
>   praefamur Vestam, quae loca prima tenet.
> ante focos olim scamnis considere longis
>   mos erat et mensae credere adesse deos.

[The earth stands by its own power; Vesta is so called from standing by power (*vi stando*); the reason for her Greek name may be similar. But the hearth (*focus*) is so named from the flames, and because it fosters (*fovet*) all things; yet formerly it stood in the first room of the house. Hence, too, I am of the opinion that the vestibule took its name; it is from there that in praying we begin by addressing Vesta, who occupies the first place: it used to be the custom of old to sit on long benches in front of the hearth and to suppose that the gods were present at table.][39]

Vesta's seemingly contradictory relationship with fire (sexual virginity) and earth (figurative or spiritual "virginity," that is, the purity of intentionality and constancy in earthly family stability—an oxymoron) is explored as an earthly version of heavenly perfection in early medieval commentaries on Martianus Capella. In the dual (Latin and Old High German) glosses of Hrotsvit's contemporary Notker Labeo (d. ca. 1022), Vesta as granddaughter of Rhea and daughter of Ops (the earth and its four elements), the wife of Saturn (time), is the "nourisher" (literally, "wet-nurse") because philosophers say earthly fire nourishes the heavenly: "Nutrix autem. . .quia ferunt philosophi terreno igni caelestem nutriri" (from Remigius, *In Martianus* 33.18),[40] with the added gloss, "Uuánda celestis ignis (ist óbe ethere. Únde úetherem.) únde dáz chédent philosophi mít temo érdfiure gezúgedôt uuérden" [For *celestis ignis* (is above *ether* and around *ether*) and the philosophers designate that as being nourished with the earth-fire].[41] How the earthly fire supports and manifests the celestial fire—as if one and the same—is philosophically an idea Hrotsvit appears to borrow in her reconstruction of Agnes's agency in the spiritual regeneration of others.

That Hrotsvit was aware of the importance of Agnes's spiritual virginity in her repudiation of the choice to become a Vestal Virgin exists in the coincidence of the date of Vesta's festival, roughly mid-June, with the day of the martyrdom of Christians Paul and John, on 7 June, in Hrotsvit's play *Gallicanus II*. Ælfric may not have known of this, but the details of Vesta's holiday were preserved in Ovid's *Fasti*—one of the first Ovidian works of the Middle Ages to merit glosses in the commentary traditions, most especially in the Saxon monasteries of the tenth and eleventh centuries contemporary with that of Hrotsvit.[42]

Hrotsvit of Gandersheim's *Salvator* Agnes in the Latin Legend and Apostolic Constantia in *Gallicanus I* and *II*

Hrotsvit's changes in Ælfric's Agnes in part 1 of his legend are primarily twofold. Where Ælfric gives us an Agnes who does not convert Constantia but merely points her to the choice of belief in Christ, Hrotsvit in her legend provides the saint with an active role as a type of Christ (*imitatio Christi*) in converting Constantia. Hrotsvit's Agnes calls on Christ to resurrect the son and father when Agnes's suitor suddenly dies as he approaches the brothel to consummate his lust, followed in death by his father.[43] This resurrection occurs with angelic help, and thereafter both he and his father convert to Christianity.[44]

Hrotsvit also portrays Agnes as one joined to Christ as if by marriage. She emphasizes Agnes's passionate, militant betrothal to Christ the Spouse, "Nitens, servata bene virginitate beata / Spernere carnales affectus *fortiter* omnes / Caelibis et vitae *durum* luctamen inire, / Quo *victrix* hostis corruptelam suadentis / Iungi caelicolis meruisset in aethere sanctis" [endeavoring by the faithful preservation of holy virginity to spurn *resolutely* all carnal affections and to enter upon the *severe struggles* of a celibate life, so that, *victorious* over the blandishments of the persuasive enemy, she might merit to be joined to the blessed inhabitants of heaven above the stars].[45]

In addition, Hrotsvit changes Constantia in the second part of Ælfric's legend by projecting her leprosy and paganism onto male Roman figures of the state—onto the lustful son of the prefect Simpronius, Constantine's pagan general Gallicanus, and the aggressive Roman soldiers—in her first legend and first play, *Gallicanus I* and *II*. Although Hrotsvit in her first legend omits Constantia's petition to Agnes for aid for her leprosy and paganism, she does introduce the leprosy-like disease that afflicts the son of Simpronius, caused by the "arrows of his desire" [*spiculis . . . amoris*], and therefore impossible to cure by normal medicine.[46] This projection dissociates Constantia from sin and disease, particularly in *Gallicanus I*, and legitimizes her assumption of Agnes's apostolic role and mission through her own conversions to Christianity of her suitor Gallicanus and his daughters.

In the two-part construction of her play *Gallicanus*, given the emphasis on the resistance to marriage and masculine desire throughout, Hrotsvit may also have been guided by the invisible but feminizing presence of the Old English St. Agnes, virgin healer of virgins. Specifically, the theme of Agnes's healing of the madness of male pagans (legend 8) continues in *Gallicanus I* through the efforts of Constantia (legend 1). To Constantia, not to Agnes, all the other converts in *Gallicanus I* and *II*—Gallicanus, his daughters, and Terrentianus's son—are directly indebted for their newly found faith in Christianity. At the same time, Hrotsvit emphasizes the conversion of virgin Constantia, which does not appear in her own legend but only in *Gallicanus*.

Both the conversion and the apostolic mission of Constantia emphasize her agency in an environment in which Roman imperialism—as embodied by the emperor himself—governs decisions that intertwine state and family and impact on colonized Christians and female family members. For example, as a reward for the loyalty and obedience of the Roman general Gallicanus to his emperor, Constantine will present him with the hand of his convert daughter if she consents (a decision that appears to abrogate the emperor's promise to her that she may preserve her virginity for the love of God).[47] But the emperor's apparent imbroglio does not in reality matter, for under Constantia's influence Gallicanus forgoes the reward of her hand by choosing to avoid living in the same house as the women because of the danger of lust of the eyes. Convert Constantia then exchanges Gallicanus's daughters Attica and Artemia for her confessors John and Paul, who will heal Gallicanus through conversion to Christianity while she converts the girls.

At the same time, even in *Gallicanus I* Constantia acknowledges the aid of Agnes as dual healer—of the diseases of leprosy and of paganism—after Gallicanus sends his daughters to her. The two diseases are explicitly coupled by Constantia in a speech to Christ in which she attributes her healing from leprosy and the "leprosy" of madness to Agnes's specific mediation through her prayers: "Amator virginitatis / et inspirator castitatis, / Christe, qui me precibus martiris tuae Agnetis / *a lepra pariter corporis / et ab errore eripiens gentilitatis* / invitasti ad virgineum / tui genitricis thalamum, /...ut Gallicanum, qui tui in me amorem surripiendo conatur extinguere, post te trahendo ab" [You who love the virgin state, / And inspire the virtue of chastity, / O my Christ, who through the prayers / Of your martyr Agnes have snatched me / *From the leprosy of the body and the error of pagan ways,* / Who called me to the virginal halls of your mother, . . . / Deter Gallicanus from his unholy intention / To steal my love for you and quench it with his own].[48] Although the daughters, "servientes idolis" [slaves to idols], are quickly converted, pagan general Gallicanus takes longer.[49]

John and Paul (*Gallicanus I*) take over from Constantia (legend 1), who has taken over from St. Agnes (legend 8) as a type of Christ (or an anti-Vesta, if we understand the parallelism in their festival dates, as mentioned above). Indeed, the specific catalyst in Gallicanus's conversion is his instruction by his "household companions," the Christian saints Paul and John: "Mis familiares socii, Iohannes et Paulus, suaserunt mihi votum fecisse creatori" [The friends of my household, John and Paul, / Persuaded me to make a vow to the Creator].[50] In an echo of Constantine's conversion (*Gallicanus I*), Gallicanus similarly converts to Christianity when, in the middle of battle, like Constantine he realizes he and his troops will lose against the Scythians and witnesses them fleeing. Initially, Roman general Gallicanus obediently intends to offer sacrifices to the gods before he leaves for Thrace to battle with the Scythians.[51] Appropriately, he invokes Jupiter when he first sees the enemy host approaching: "O tribuni, pro Iuppiter!" [By Jupiter, men!].[52] Hence he is shocked at the spineless desire of his soldiers to surrender without a fight, assuming that he has the backing of the pagan gods—"Nolit hoc Apollo!" [Apollo will surely never permit such a thing to take place][53]—an ironic salute to Apollo, god of truth and healing in Roman religion. While surrender—a feminized retreat—makes the Roman soldiers seem less than manly (*vir.* virile), their paganism is equally debilitating, that is, effeminizing. Surrender signifies a strategic and metaphoric *remedium* for the soldiers' equally metaphoric wounding in battle and subsequent deaths: "Edapol faciendum: en, undique secus circumdamur, vulneramus, perimimur" ["By Pollux, sir!" cries the First Tribune, "We'd better do it . . . Our men are wounded, we are being slaughtered everywhere"].[54] These failures of masculine imperialism and paganism constitute the first step in the general's conversion to Christianity. When Gallicanus narrates the sequence of events to the emperor, he finally blames the gods: "Ego quidem nefanda sacrificia iteravi, / nec aderant, qui adiuvarent dii" [So

I renewed my criminal sacrifices / To gods who should have helped: / They did not come].[55] As a consequence of his conversion, Gallicanus wins the battle. During the crisis, he also witnesses the vision of a young Christ, armed as if for battle: "Apparuit mihi iuvenis procerae magnitudinis, crucem ferens in humeris, et praecepit, ut stricto mucrone illum sequerer" [There appeared to me then a young man of great height, / Bearing a cross on his shoulders; / He ordered to follow, with drawn sword, / Wherever he would lead].[56]

In the second part of *Gallicanus*, postconversion, the loyalty and obedience of Constantia's suitor, Gallicanus, and her spiritual advisers, Paul and John, are directed to God (rather than to the reactionary and idolatrous emperor Julian the Apostate), but again, still motivated by the invisible influence of Constantia and, behind her, Agnes. Agnes the Roman Christian virgin was, indeed, *constantia* personified when she became a healing physician for the idolatry of paganism and the leprous sores of the unchaste (legend 8) after the conversion of Constantia. The circularity in the history of Constantia in Hrotsvit is mirrored in the circularity of the relationship between Hrotsvit's last legend and first play in the manuscript. The circle, symbol of virginity, is also the symbol of eternity and godhead; Hrotsvit's genius is to manipulate the materials of the legends she inherited into a perfectly coherent whole.

In *Gallicanus II*, Julian the Apostate reverts to paganism twenty years later—which reversion, if Agnes had chosen the Temple of Vesta in legend 8, would have violated her spiritual virginity, paganism as a kind of insanity. The choice that Julian offers to Gallicanus duplicates Simpronius's offer to Agnes in both her legends, by Hrotsvit and by Ælfric: either sacrifice to the gods (pagan idolatry in displacement of Christian faith) or exile (in the case of Agnes, abandonment to the house of prostitutes). The more elaborately allegorical choice in *Gallicanus* correlates paganism and madness (as an antitype of Christian sanity) and leprosy and lechery (literal possession by the devil). For example, in *Gallicanus II*, when the imperial guards attempt to occupy the castles of Gallicanus, "tuaeque servituti usurpasse; / sed, si quis ex nostris pedem admovit, / *leprosus seu inerguminus est factus*" [whoever went inside them, / Putting as much as a foot within, / Was *at once affected by leprosy, / Or possessed by the devil himself*].[57] And when Julian later insists that John and Paul be compelled to sacrifice to Jupiter or be executed by the Roman soldier Terrentianus and they refuse, Terrentianus's son goes mad, or is possessed. Specifically, a Christian informs Terrentianus: "Stridet dentibus, sputa iacet, torquet insane lumina; nam plenus est daemonio" [{Your son} is gnashing his teeth, / He spits out, he rolls his eyes about, / In an insane manner. / He is obviously possessed by a devil].[58] After his confession the son of Terrentianus is redeemed through the saintly intercession of Paul and John: a Christian notes, "En filius tuus respicit / et per martirum suffragia *sanum* recepit" [Through the intercession of these martyrs / He is back *in good health* once again],[59] which results in the dual conversion and baptism of father, Terrentianus, and son.

One important additional substantiation for the connection between Old English legend and *Gallicanus II* exists in the surely intentional name "Terrentianus" of Hrotsvit's Roman soldier, healed of his madness through conversion to Christianity. To a real "Terentianus" Ælfric's Old English legend of Agnes, at least in the portion on Constantia, is attributed, "sumne hæðenne wer" [{some} heathen man] whose mission was to convince Paul and John to pray to a golden idol.[60] The name of Hrotsvit's character Terentianus is reminiscent of that of the Roman dramatist Terence, an allusion that reveals Hrotsvit's sense of humor in *Gallicanus II* in depicting the misogynistic classical playwright as a mad pagan boy who is converted to Christianity and made sane, at least indirectly, through feminine, not masculine, influence.[61] Also, in her preface to the dramas, Hrotsvit has admitted that she will convert the "turpia lasciviarum incesta feminarum" [shameless acts of licentious women] depicted in the plays by Terence into the praiseworthy virtue of virginity, just as, in *Gallicanus II*, the faith of Constantia converts Terrentianus's son. Thus, Hrotsvit herself as playwright becomes a type of St. Agnes, "converting" (the text of) Terence to Christianity, or in her own plays feminizing conversion in works by Ælfric's pagan "Terentianus." (The similarity of names also reinforces Hrotsvit's likely indebtedness to the Anglo-Saxon abbot.)

Hrotsvit adds even herself in this Terentian "divine comedy" as a type of Christlike Agnes and apostle Constantia in order to rewrite the Anglo-Saxon hagiography of Agnes. The Saxon playwright demonstrates by analogy how public masculine rulers of state should prudently follow the example set by the emperor's constant daughter and her doting convert father. She also constructs Roman pagan masculine belligerence as spiritual weakness in contrast to the spiritual strength of Christian feminine meekness. Conversely (and ironically), real *virtus* and *virilitas* come through the spiritual heroic battle accomplished by the Christian and virgin martyrs, especially the women and the peaceful men in Hrotsvit. A young but manly Christ appears to Gallicanus at the moment of petition to the Creator for help, "crucem ferens in humeris" [bearing a cross on his shoulders], but demanding that Gallicanus follow with a drawn sword, in imitation of the *miles Christianus*.[62] So with her own father's general, Constantia carries on the virile Christianizing mission of Agnes. Leprosy and paganism, as coupled diseases, are constructed as equivalent sins of masculinized spiritual weakness—lechery and pride. By erasing Constantia's disease, Hrotsvit in these plays and some of the other legends and epics, ingeniously empowers women and others similarly colonized to provide a source of spiritual—and physical—renewal, as a feminized foundation for the early Roman Church open to all virgins. Writing in Latin, she nevertheless provides a keystone for a literature that can truly be described, in the sense meant by Deleuze and Guattari, as significantly minor.

CHAPTER 3

MARIE DE FRANCE VERSUS KING ARTHUR: LANVAL'S GENDER INVERSION AS BRETON SUBVERSION

The twelfth century, with its panoply of Arthurian chroniclers and romance writers, established King Arthur of England as a preeminent founder of a Round Table renowned for its chivalry and idealized masculinity to advance the prestige of the Plantagenet connection with the British throne. Although Breton Geoffrey of Monmouth had finished his popular *Historia Regum Britanniae*, with its chivalric rendition of King Arthur and his reign, between 1135–37, only in 1155 did its French verse-translation—the *Roman de Brut* by the Norman-French Wace, in which the invention of the Round Table prominently figured—make Arthurian exploits accessible to others aside from the predominantly male clergy. The octosyllabic translation—notable for its emphasis on *courtoisie* as much as on *chevalerie*—was also written for Wace's royal patron, Henry II, who had married Eleanor of Aquitaine in 1152. Henry might thus see himself figured in the portrait of the generous and just Arthur, who because of his reputation draws knights to him from far-flung lands and creates for them a Round Table at which no one will be considered superior to another:

> N'oeit parler de chevalier
> Ki alques feïst a preisier,
> Ki de sa maisnee ne fust,
> Pur ço qu'il aveir le peüst;
> Si pur aveir server vulsist,
> Ja pur aveir ne s'en partist.
> Pur les nobles baruns qu'il out,

> Dunt chescuns mieldre ester quidout,
> Chescuns se teneit al meillur,
> Ne nulls n'en saveit le peiur,
> Fist Artur la Runde Table
> Dunt Bretun dient mainte fable.
> Illuec seeient li vassal
> Tuit chevalment e tuit egal;
> A la table egalment seeient
> E egalment servi esteient;
> Nul d'els ne se poeit vanter
> Qu'il seïst plus halt de sun per,
> Tuit esteient assis meain,
> Ne n'i aveit nul de forain.
> N'esteit pas tenuz pur curteis
> Escot ne Bretun ne Franceis,
> Normant, Angevin ne Flamenc
> Ne Burguinun ne Loherenc,
> De ki que il tenist sun feu,
> Des occident jesqu'a Muntgeu,
> Ki a la curt Artur n'alout
> E ki od lui ne sujurnout,
> E ki n'en aveit vesteüre
> E cunuissance e armeüre
> A la guise que cil teneient
> Ki en la curt Artur serveient.

[{Arthur} never heard of a knight who was in any way considered to be praiseworthy who would not belong to his household, provided that he could get him, and if such a one wanted reward for his service, he would never leave deprived of it. On account of his noble barons—each of whom felt he was superior, each considered himself the best, and no one could say who was the worst—Arthur had the Round Table made, about which the British tell many a tale. There sat the vassals, all equal, all leaders; they were placed equally round the table and equally served. None of them could boast he sat higher than his peer; all were seated near the place of honour, none far away. No one—whether Scot, Briton, Frenchman, Norman, Angevin, Fleming, Burgundian or Lorrainer—whoever he held his fief from, from the West as far as Muntgieu, was accounted courtly if he did not go to Arthur's court and stay with him and wear the livery, device and armour in the fashion of those who served at that court.][1]

However admirable the chivalric virtues of King Arthur, Wace's romance does not present his beautiful, courteous queen, Genuevre (Guinevere)—from a noble Roman family, but brought up by Cador, earl of Cornwall, whose mother had been Roman[2]—as positively as he does the king. Not only was this gracious woman unable to bear Arthur a child, but Wace notes that, later, after Arthur's nephew Modred takes her to his bed as queen when Arthur has left him in charge of the kingdom while he fights in Rome, "Membra lui de la vilainie / Que pur Modred s'esteit hunie, / Lu bon rei aveit vergundé / E sun nevou Modred amé; / Cuntre lei l'aveit espusee / Si en esteit mult avilee" [She remembered the wickedness she had done in tarnishing her honor for Modret's sake, shaming the good king and desiring the nephew. He had married her illicitly and she was badly degraded by it].[3] In guilt and shame Genuevre flees to the southern Welsh outpost of Caerleon to enter a convent as a nun. The lecherous actions of both Modred and Genuevre are anticipated by Cador's misogynistic speech after receipt of the letters from the emperor of Rome that chastised Arthur for disputing the demanded tribute. In it, Cador declaims against the idleness of British knights during peacetime: "Uisdive met hume en peresce, / Uisdive amenuse prüesce, / Uisdive esmuet les lecheries, / Uisdive esprent lé drueries" [Idleness brings indolence, idleness lessens prowess, idleness inflames lechery and idleness kindles love affairs].[4]

Such misogyny, if not xenophobia, characterizes other late-twelfth-century works, both vernacular and Latin. The vernacular Arthurian romance the *Chevalier de la Charrette* [Knight of the Cart] featured the first mention of the adulterous relationship between Guinevere and Lancelot, perhaps influenced by Wace's adultery between Modred and Genuevre. Left unfinished by Chrétien de Troyes in the late 1170s, the romance was dedicated to Countess Marie de Champagne, daughter of Eleanor of Aquitaine and King Louis VII of France, from whom its Celtic material about fairy abductions had been ostensibly obtained.[5] Guinevere, whose whimsical and narcissistic behavior is here fitted into the courtly love ethos that demands obeisance from the lover to the liege lady, might well represent an anti-exemplum in a mirror for princesses. Among many instances, most convincing is her unreasonable insistence that Lancelot has failed her because he hesitated a few moments before mounting the ignominious cart after his horse had died. Surprising fare for the author who claimed to have translated into French the "commandemanz d'Ovide" and "l'art d'amors," as his second romance, *Cligés*, attests, but possibly reflective of Chrétien's dissatisfaction with the subject matter that had been allegedly imposed on him by Countess Marie.[6]

Certainly a climate of clerical misogyny existed in the latter half of the twelfth century, to judge from the popular Latin epistle "Dissuasio

Valerii ad Rufinum philosophum, ne uxorem ducat" [Argument of Valerius to Rufinus the Philosopher against Taking a Wife] (ca. 1181–82) written by a scholar employed by Henry II, Walter Map (b. ca. 1130s–d. ca. 1210). In this letter that introduced Walter's commonplace-book magnum opus, *De nugis curialium*, "Valerius" accuses "Rufinus" of being "totus inflammaris" [completely inflamed] by passion and characterizes his friend's beloved as a three-headed monster, a chimera "venustetur facie leonis, olentis maculetur ventre capri, virulente armetur cauda vipere" [adorned with the face of a lion, besmirched with the belly of a stinking goat, armed with the tail of a poisonous viper].[7] The catalogue of negative examples that follows begins with Old Testament Eve, Bathsheba, and Solomon's women and continues with the pagan Deianira and Venus. Walter praises only those long-ago Roman wives who, like Lucretia, maintained their chastity until death and those goddesses such as Pallas Athena, who generally represents wisdom and study in the Middle Ages. During Map's lifetime this letter found a welcome reception from clerics such as Peter of Blois in the mid-1180s, no doubt in part because of a desire to maintain a celibate culture by highlighting the spiritual death associated with excessive sexual activity.[8]

Within such opprobrium directed against female sexuality, it comes as a surprise to find a female voice that attempts to retell an Arthurian story, and with it, to refigure in the vernacular the gendered roles of both her male and female protagonists. Although much about the Old French *Lai de Lanval* by Marie de France (fl. 1160–78) has puzzled its critics, of all the Breton *lais* in the High Middle Ages *Lanval* lays claim to the most enthusiastic reception. The *lai*, preserved in four manuscripts, was copied more frequently than any other.[9] It was also translated more frequently—into Old Norse in the thirteenth century and into Middle English in the early-fourteenth-century *Landevale*, adapted in Thomas Chestre's more masculinized and misogynistic version of *Launfal* in the last quarter of the fourteenth century and in the early-fifteenth-century Percy Folio *Lambewell*, with perhaps an intermediary early fourteenth-century version now lost.[10] Finally, it was also the most imitated Breton lay in the Middle Ages (noticeably in the Old French *Graelent, Guigemar, Guinhamor*, and the *Chastelaine de Vergi*).[11]

Lanval, the only Arthurian lay penned by Marie, deconstructs to their detriment the Arthurian court, the masculine practice of chivalry and courtly love, and the figures of both British King Arthur and his queen, an opposition that previous scholarship has only recently recognized, but without full consideration of the separate components involved, including its register as that of a minor literature. Scholars initially perceived the Arthurian backdrop merely as evidence that Marie was responding to the popularity of Wace's *Brut* or to the satire of Chrétien de Troyes in *Le Chevalier de la Charrette*, particularly to his weak Arthur and demanding, treacherous Guinevere.[12] More recent suggestions that Marie intended the "Arthuricity" of the lay to invoke an oppositional world have been voiced by Michèle Koubichkine and Edgard Sienaert.[13] David Chamberlain has suggested that Marie intended the obtuse Arthur as the inverse of the king for whom these lays were written, Henry Plantagenet.[14] By setting up the Arthurian kingdom as rude, hostile to foreigners, and dominated by incompetent rulers, Marie in this lay projects onto this culture a masculine identity, one underscored by feudal landholding and primogeniture. Sharon Kinoshita observes that the lack of female characters in this lay "challenges patriarchal practices precisely by taking to its logical extreme the courtly discourse meant to mystify the project of primogeniture."[15] The "real" world that Lanval rejects—as we see in this chapter—fetishizes Christianity (King Arthur's court held at Pentecost),[16] male (homosocial) bonding (the Order of the Round Table), class distinctions (the noble chevalier, along with the practice of chivalry), nationality (English), material wealth and landholding (vassalage and primogeniture), and male hegemony within gender relations (customary law and the medieval legal system).[17] Indeed, because of "women's limited room for maneuver in the medieval legal system," Katherine Kong suggests that Arthur must represent Guinevere in the baronial court.[18]

In this lay Marie also constructs a feminized and powerless male hero whose alien nature—he is from a foreign land, Brittany—matches his cultural inability to manage the chivalric and masculine duties of valor and loyalty to liege lord and the indoor and courtly virtues of courtesy and homage to a lady. Why Lanval fails so miserably in Arthur's British kingdom has not been adequately explained in the burgeoning criticism on *Lanval* and Marie, which verges, on the one hand, between discussions of its feminism as opposed to its gender balance and, on the other, between its new historical mirroring of late-twelfth-century law, politics, and social history as opposed to its Celticism.[19] Key to Lanval's failure is his image as an otiose chevalier who chooses to become horseless, his abandonment of his horse symbolizing his departure from social rank.[20] Shedding this signal attribute of chivalry allows Lanval to open the door to a fantasy world ruled by a fairy queen.[21] Whether the knight changes in the course of the lay is also a contested issue among critics: Koubichkine believes that he does, and that his quest is for existence from nonbeing; but Elizabeth Wilson Poe believes that he does not change, remaining the same from the beginning.[22] I believe the situation is more complex than has been previously understood, because of the protagonist's negative behavior at the beginning coupled with his increasing feminization and the fairy queen's masculinization. Some critics have read this regendering situation too literally and have dismissed the entire work for this reason: Katharina Wilson and Glenda McLeod argue that "for Marie, merely inverting usual patterns—feminizing Lanval and in many ways masculinizing the fairy—does not improve the tale or the relationships realized therein."[23]

The alteration in the hero is the emphasis in this chapter, for it points to Marie's subversion of Arthur: Lanval has to change, to diminish, because the English nation that he now inhabits does not allow him cultural space to exist as a marginalized knight. For a knight to dismount from his horse is tantamount to rejecting the ordinary world—or to converting to another world. At the end of the lay, Lanval will remount a horse, but not his: it will be as an ancillary and symbolic female on the palfrey behind the fairy queen. Thus Marie leaves blank in her text the names of the two most significant women in the lay, the fairy queen and Arthur's queen, to allow for gender slippage between men who act like women and women who act like men or who are part of a male-hegemonic social system. I argue in this chapter that foreign vassal Lanval as Other diminishes in the lay symbolically to knight, then to man alone and less than man, and, finally, to "woman" and then a woman silenced and "disappeared," or erased from this world. The lay feminizes this register for alterity within the antiknight's *aventure*—a quest more passive and psychological than active and chivalric, and one certainly more representative of marginalized female social and cultural position.

Male failure and female heroism in this lay reflect Marie's signature proto-feminism, which may explain why *Lanval* resembles exactly no other Arthurian romance except those adaptations that came after it, namely, those of Geoffrey Chaucer, Thomas Chestre, and even Heldris of Cornwall.[24] Acts of feminized fairy grace repeatedly rescue Marie's antihero, seemingly insubordinate and insolent to King Arthur and his queen, whose disloyalty to her own lord Lanval unmasks. Given her female voice, Marie's use of a male protagonist thereby offers a "radical challenge to the structure of feudal society through her canny manipulation of literary codes."[25] In contrast, Jacqueline Eccles sees in *Lanval* "a balanced challenge to feudal society, where male and female weaknesses, and strengths, are presented alongside each other in an effort to criticize an unjust society."[26] But if King Arthur is uncharitable, and Queen Guinevere, licentious, as they appear to be in the lay, then the feminized figure of Lanval is right to reject the symbolic order of the Arthurian world of Britain, with its chivalric values, for the Real—for his desire for a more virtuous, even noble condition of being in a faerie realm governed by a true queen, generous, loyal, and gracious.

From the gender inversions in the *lai*, I argue, proceed other cultural subversions. As Lanval is disfeudalized, dispossessed, unknighted, unclassed, unmanned, disgendered, feminized, and then silenced into complete alterity and nonbeing before his transportation—his *translatio*—to the Other World, Marie simultaneously narrates the divestiture of a masculine and specifically British feudal culture that conventionally and legally displaces female autonomy and voice. Guinevere is an alter ego for Lanval, as the fairy queen is an alter ego for King Arthur.

The Transgendering of the Male Hero in *Lanval*

Lanval begins as an antihero precisely because as a foreign vassal he is mistreated by Arthur and thereafter falls into a depression (line 34) over his inability to fulfill his feudal and chivalric roles. Certainly Lanval's lack of funding from the king—even though he is "de la meisne{e} le rei fu" [of the king's household] (line 29)—coupled with his prodigal ways ("Tut sun aveir ad despendu" [he had spent all his wealth], line 30) enhances his depression. But Marie also acknowledges his own alterity in this rough land: "*Hume estrange* descunseillez / Mut est dolent en autre terre, / Quant il ne seit u sucurs quere" [*a strange man*, without friends, / is very sad in another land, / when he doesn't know where to look for help] (lines 36–38, my emphasis). Without his role as a vassal, Lanval begins to lose his chivalric identity and becomes lazy, self-centered, and dreamy. He "s'est alez esbaneer" [goes off to amuse himself] (line 42), away from civilization and into isolation in nature. Symbolically, he dismounts from his *destrer* [warhorse, line 41], unsaddles it, and then abandons the very sign of his *chevalerie* [chivalry]—his *cheval* [horse]—who rolls in the meadow just as Lanval himself lies down as if to sleep (lines 42–48). After the two girls appear as representatives of the fairy queen, he is reduced to a mere man, no longer the figure of a knight, "de sun cheval ne tient nul plait" [giving no thought to his horse] (line 78), who remains behind grazing in the meadow. Lanval departs on his horse only because it is brought saddled to him by the girls after he and the fairy queen eat. Indeed, even at the end of the lay, once the fairy queen testifies on his behalf before the barons and the king, horseless Lanval leaves the kingdom for Avalon by leaping from the marble mounting block onto her ladies' horse, her palfrey, and rides away behind her (lines 633–40). In effect, here in the meadow he renounces the male gender role of king's son, vassal, and knight. With that, he also begins to relinquish the very rationality normally associated with the male in the Middle Ages—to become, in effect, female.[27]

In this chivalric world of England, the alien Lanval, a "stranger in a strange land," to adapt a concept from modern fantasist Robert Heinlein, takes on a marginalized and passive role conventionally marked as female. As a Breton knight in a kingdom in which Wales remains the site for political activity, Lanval encounters a world strange and distant because of its transgressive sexual, inheritance, and legal practices. Marie in "Yonec" and "Milun"—both of which take place in southern Wales—according to Kinoshita responds to the problems of Cambro-Norman society caused by decentralization and Welsh sexual transgressions, such as endogamy, concubinage, trial marriages, and the rights to inheritance by illegitimate children.[28] Elsewhere, Kinoshita, reading *Lanval* as a "male Cinderella story," compares *Lanval* with *Yonec*, with the protagonist in the passive role of the courtly lady, just as R. Howard Bloch remarks on the fairy queen's rescue of Lanval as "almost a parody of the damsel in distress rescued by the valiant knight."[29] So scholar William E. Burgwinkle, advancing a queer theory argument, has understood Guinevere's defamations of Lanval as pointing, not so much to reflections of his feminized role as an Other in a hostile court, but instead to his possible practice of sodomy and, therefore, his position as a queer Other.[30] But Lanval may also have functioned as an Other in a role as a younger son: socially and economically, according to the rule of primogeniture, both twelfth-century women and younger sons shared a dispossessed class and generation, according to R. Howard Bloch, although the lay does not explicitly indicate that Lanval is a younger son.[31]

Certainly without his horse and his chivalric role, Lanval takes on increasingly stereotypical female characteristics, beginning with a more courtly and passive posture as a beloved and diminishing into the embodiment of desire and emotionality. The beauty that marks him as feminized is what apparently attracts the fairy queen, who lies on a bed in her tent almost completely naked (she has on her shift and a carelessly strewn ermine cloak, but it is hot and her side, including her bosom, is exposed [lines 97–105]). Yet, clinging to his stereotypical male role as knight, Lanval first pledges himself to her to show that he will be, as she asks, "pruz e curteis" [brave and courtly] (line 113), the epitome of the knight both outdoors, performing valorously for his lord in the field, and indoors, behaving courteously with his lady. If the fairy queen will love him, this courtly lover swears, he will obey her—but then, rather desperately (and signaling his loss of manly reason), he adds, "Pur vus guerpirai tutes genz" [For you, I shall abandon everyone] (line 128), a serious renunciation of society, civilization, and his own family. This total commitment of self, body, and soul is rewarded equally fantastically with the promise of satisfaction of all his desires (lines 135–37), namely, for wealth and her body, as long as he keeps secret their relationship and love (lines 47–50). While secrecy represents a contingent condition in conventional courtly love because of the lady's marriage and her need to preserve her reputation socially and morally, there is no sign this lady is married or that Marie intends their relationship to be courtly.[32] In fact, the lovers meet out of doors and away from court. Their secrecy endows the love affair with a private, unreal quality, but one also curiously monogamous for a man's dream: the fairy says, "Nul hum fors vus ne me verra / Ne ma parole nen orra" [No man but you will see me / or hear my words] (lines 169–70). As the fairy queen warns him, if he tells anyone, he will never see her again. If he has pledged his love to fantasy, to dream and impracticality, it explains why he does not wish to leave and has to be told by his beloved to get up and leave (lines 159–60).

Although Lanval's vow of loyalty and secrecy to the fairy queen is tested twice—during the attempted seduction by Arthur's queen two weeks after Pentecost, on St. John's Eve (24 June), the summer solstice, or Midsummer Night's Eve, and during the trial itself, when Walwains and others press him to identify as his beloved, first, two magnificently dressed girls, and, then, his beloved herself—on neither occasion does he actually abrogate his agreement to keep secret his love. Lanval conceals the fairy queen's identity, but he does reveal to Arthur's queen that he loves someone more noble and virtuous than she. Both the attempted seduction by Arthur's queen and the trial by Arthur more fully reveal Guinevere's immorality and infidelity (and treachery) to the king and Arthur's poor judgment as king in siding with such a queen. The seduction and trial also reveal Lanval's refusal to betray his lover and his king, whatever his alleged failure in courtesy and courtly love to Guinevere and, therefore, his appropriate renunciation of this patriarchal world for that of faerie.

During the first testing of the protagonist, Lanval faces private accusations of homosexuality from Guinevere, not to say of rudeness and discourtesy, the antitheses of the indoor virtues of a knight. Arthur's queen, as if enchanted on Midsummer's Night Eve, mirrors the fairy queen's prior advances to Lanval and succumbs to his beauty. And, both echoing the promise of satisfaction by Lanval's queen and anticipating Bertilak's wife in the fourteenth-century *Sir Gawain and the Green Knight*, Guinevere aggressively offers herself entirely to Lanval: "Tute m'amur poëz aveir" [You may have all my love] (line 265). Although Lanval might have demurely refused, instead he rudely rejects and insults her: "Jeo n'ai cure de vus amer" [I have no desire to love you] (line 270). He also adduces his loyalty to King Arthur as the reason, in fact as only one of the reasons, he refuses her, after Guinevere's subsequent accusations of homosexuality intimate his almost total feminization by the court because of his avoidance of its ladies.

> "Lanval," fet ele, "bien le quit,
> Vuz n'amez gueres cel delit;
> Asez le m'ad hum dit sovent
> Que des femmes n'avez talent.
> Vallez avez bien afeitiez,
> Ensemble od eus vus deduiez.
> Vileins cuarz, mauveis failliz,
> Mut est mi sires maubailliz
> Que pres de lui vus ad suffert."
>
> ["Lanval," she said, "I am sure
> you don't care for such pleasure;
> people have often told me
> that you have no interest in women.
> You have fine-looking boys
> With whom you enjoy {or pleasure} yourself.
> Base coward, lousy cripple,
> my lord made a bad mistake
> when he let you stay with him."]
>
> (Lines 277–85)

Guinevere's charges against him also pinpoint his alleged cowardice ("Vileins cuars" [Base coward]) (line 283) and lack of valor ("mauveis failliz" [lousy cripple]) (line 283)—the very antitheses of the ideal knight. Further, Lanval's irrationality at this point leads him to boast spitefully, out of control, of a beloved who returns his love, "cele ke deit aver le pris / sur tutes celes que jeo sai" [one who should have the prize / over all the women I know] (lines 294–95). Compounding what Andreas Capellanus would describe as his courtly love violations—failure to maintain secrecy and the expression of courtesy to a lady—Lanval brags recklessly that his own beloved's poorest servant girl is superior to the queen in beauty, breeding, and virtue (lines 301–2). It is interesting, in this regard, that Walwains comes to Lanval's aid, even before Guinevere flirts with him. Gawain will figure in *Sir Gawain and the Green Knight* as a varlet who is similarly rude and discourteous toward the ladies, in his diatribe against women at the Green Chapel after failing in courage and shying away from the edge of the Green Knight's ax. English Gawain who kisses his host, Lord Bertilak, may veil similar same-sex proclivities like those attributed to Lanval.[33]

As antihero, unknighted and dispossessed, Lanval is then unmanned and further feminized when he protests Guinevere's accusation of homoeroticism and displays an insecurity or sense of inferiority about his masculinity, after which he sinks even further, into criminal status and social nonbeing. First, during a moment of hotheaded pique and irrationality more conventionally ascribed to women in the Middle Ages, he confesses to others the existence of his secret love: "Teu chose dist par maltalent / Dunt il se repenti sovent" [He says something out of spite / that he would often regret] (lines 289–90). While it is true Lanval does not reveal the fairy queen's identity or homeland, he does admit he loves and is loved by a beautiful woman who is also wealthy. Second, when the barons rule that he deserves a trial but must (as a foreign knight) post bond—*plegges* [pledges]—to ensure he does not flee before judgment (lines 389–92), the criminal charges laid by Guinevere and then Arthur divest Lanval of his position and stature in the kingdom and not just in the court. Walwains explains Lanval's otherness in his reasons for his support: he is a foreigner, "sul e esgaré" [alone and forlorn], and has neither relative nor friend (lines 398–99); Walwains recognizes his despair when he urges him to forgo his love for the lady and worries about his possible suicide (lines 408–9, 414). And the barons, who profess to be similarly distressed because of Lanval's very nobility, nevertheless stick to the law (as they see it: they create the law as they adjudicate) that he provide proof of his love, or else "tut sun servise pert del rei" [he will forfeit his service to the king] and must leave the court and country (line 459).

Does Lanval also fail the fairy queen? The proof of Lanval's love for her emerges from his willingness to embrace as a consequence shame, dishonor, and dispossession of goods in and exile from England (the abandonment of all his affiliations, *tutes genz* [line 128], as he has contractually sworn to her he would). Analogously, the veracity of his boast (and, therefore, his nature as truly noble) is proved by the legitimization of the fairy queen's unparalleled wealth and class and his transportation to the Other World. His beloved arrives to rescue him because Lanval repents of his infraction against her and remains loyal to his vow to her—even though he will face loss of property and dismissal from the king—through his silence in refusing to recognize as her servants either the two girls approaching the court in purple taffeta and riding palfreys (lines 472–75) or the girls in Phyrgian silks on Spanish mules (lines 510–12). In addition, even though Lanval completely abrogates his vow to the fairy queen when he sees her—"Ceo est m'amie! / Or m'en est gueres ki m'ocie, / Si ele n'ad merci de mei; / Kar gariz sui, quant jeo la vei" [That is my love! / Now I don't care if I am killed, / if only she forgives me, / for I am restored {*gariz*, "healed"}, now that I see her] (lines 597–600)—he also places himself totally at her mercy (and he ceases to speak after this line).

The fairy queen's appearance in court itself attests to the truth of Lanval's claims and, therefore, by extension, to the dishonesty, pettiness, and lack of true nobility of the English queen and king. Marie's jab at land-rich, cash-poor royalty signals a contemporary danger in financial management at the top levels of the kingdom. According to Marie, who trumps both Arthur's queen and Arthur with her gendered truths, the fairy queen is more beautiful than any woman in the world (line 550) but also richer than any man: "Riche atur ot al palefrei: / Suz ciel nen ad cunte ne rei / Ki tut [le] peüst eslegier / Sanz terre vendre u engagier" [The palfrey's trappings were rich: / under heaven there was no count or king / who could have afforded them all / without selling or mortgaging lands] (lines 555–58). In contrast to Arthur's knight and barons, the fairy queen, like a knight ready for the hunt, bears a sparrow hawk on her wrist and a greyhound by her side (lines 573–74); her dark purple cloak (lines 571–72) signals her royal birth and stature as a queen. A faithful and monogamous lover, Lanval wins release in the legal court because his fairy lady speaks on his behalf as a sovereign would for a liege[34] (or a man would for a woman), saying that "la reïne ad tort eü" [the queen was in the wrong] (line 620), that he never made a pass at her (line 621), and that, in fact, his boast can be validated by the fact of her presence and her nature, one both beautiful and noble. So the fairy queen, like a sovereign, demands of Arthur, "De la vantaunce kë il fist, / Si par me beot ester aquitez, / Par voz baruns seit delivrez!" [And for the boast that he made, / if he can be acquitted through me, / let him be set free by your barons!] (lines 622–24).

The ending of the lay tells us that the fairy queen conveys him to "Avalun"—"Ceo nus recuntent li Bretun, / En un isle que mut est beaus" [so the Bretons tell us, / to a very beautiful island] (lines 641–43). The word Marie uses for the fairy queen's abduction of Lanval is the same as that for rape or kidnapping, *raviz*, used in *Guigemar* when the hero is similarly conveyed on the mysterious unmanned ship to another world where the lady he will fall in love with finds him.[35] Although the reader never actually sees it in the lay, the fairy queen's realm is traditionally associated with Morgain,[36] matriarchal Celtic supernature, and the Other World to which Arthur is in some (mainly Welsh) texts ferried after the battle of Camlann. Marie's world of the fairy queen in *Lanval* celebrates a feminized immateriality through the following: magic and a noninstitutional supernatural (Guinevere's attempted seduction in an appropriately Celtic orchard—*vergier* [lines 223, 247]—at the summer solstice); female bonding (the fairy queen and her equally well-dressed representatives); classlessness (true nobility springing from inner virtue); permeable unmanned boundaries (the Other World being instantly accessible through fantasy and desire); spiritual wealth (faith, self-sacrifice, generosity, love); and female desire for and rule and rescue of the male (the fairy queen's selection of Lanval, her gifts to him, and her vindication of him as his sovereign at his trial).

Avalon is also an anagram for "Lanval"—"Lanvao"[37]— a signifier for the restoration or final attainment of the protagonist's identity, if the lay narrativizes his quest from nonbeing to existence, or, conversely, from ironic "existence" to nonbeing. In Marie's eyes, the unchivalric and effete alien Lanval wins this prize because of his ideal feminized qualities, both physical and spiritual, chiefly his beauty, loyalty, and gentleness: truly Other in masculine terms. The more unmanned he seems to become, even leaping onto the palfrey of his lady, the more manly, chivalrous, and regal his beautiful and heroic rescuer appears. Unlike Chrétien's Knight of the Cart, who in Queen Guinevere's eyes fails her by hesitating before climbing on the ignominious vehicle in order to pursue her, Lanval readily leaps into a secondary position literally and figuratively behind his beloved, on the horse a true chevalier would never ride, the palfrey. His leap of faith—to paraphrase Kierkegaard—commits him to Avalon, to himself, that is, a feminized culture of magical power, true nobility, and transcendent love, as he simultaneously renounces the patriarchal material culture of Arthur's court and its dependency on feudal oath, lineage, martial prowess, national identity, warfare, and landholding and wealth.

Most troubling, for Marie, Arthur's Britain is apparently a culture in which women, bought and distributed as wives, must seek sexual satisfaction in secrecy through adultery and political and social manipulation of subordinates. Appropriately, in Marie's Celtic Avalon, a site that may appear to exist only in the imagination, women rescue men heroically through peaceful means, as men love them gently and faithfully, even until disappearance and death.

The Other as Hero in the *Lais*: The Divestiture of a Masculine Feudal Culture

The culture to which Lanval ideally belongs is that of the Celtic Other World (the isle of Avalon, unidentified until the last few lines),[38] ruled by a true (fairy) queen,[39] his beloved rescuer, who assumes the roles of the romance hero, the Arthurian knight, and the sovereign. In this feminization of the Breton lay, Marie remains consistent in her approach throughout her collection of lays, in which female protagonists, despite the apparent masculine subjects, outshine in virtue and nobility the knights with whom they are connected.[40] Marie's women take the initiative throughout the *Lais* by exhibiting excellent judgment and wisdom, guiding and educating the suffering men, and establishing for themselves a subject position (or a world) that provides them greater autonomy. However the lay may differ from the romance, chief among those differences is the attention to what might be termed a medieval *écriture féminine*.[41] As *Lanval* will attest, the very nature of the lay as a short romance set in Brittany or somehow affiliated with Bretons or Briton émigrés and interwoven with the supernatural feminizes the genre of the Arthurian romance as brief rather than long; Breton rather than English; devoted to the celebration of gender issues and most especially twelfth-century feminism rather than chivalry or courtly love; and privileging feminized fairy magic rather than either a Christian and ecclesiastical supernatural or a Celticized mythological.

Marie promotes the female beginning with the first *lai* in the Harley collection—"MS H," the only manuscript in which all twelve *Lais* appear along with the prologue[42]—in which the unloving knight

Guigemar is wounded by the arrow that kills the antlered white hind and healed and rescued by a girl in a foreign land. Marie also promotes the female ending with the last lay, *Eliduc*, with which *Lanval* has been specifically compared in its restructuring of female power.[43] In *Eliduc*, even though the insensitive, married Eliduc allows his courtly love for the foreign king's daughter Guilliadun to supplant his conjugal relationship with the virtuous, faithful, and wise Guildeluec, daughter and only heir of the king of Exeter, Guildeluec through her subsequent behavior maps on to the *lai* a feminized form of hagiographic conversion and redemption. Indeed, wife Guildeluec is the hero of *Eliduc*: Marie tells us that, at first, this lay was titled *Eliduc*, but altered, apparently, to *Guildeluec and Guilliadun* (even though the title was not changed in the manuscript): "Mes ore est li nuns remüez, / Kar des dames est avenu" [but now the name has been changed, / for it happened to the women] (lines 24–25). Guildeluec not only heals and, like Christ, raises from the dead her rival, Guilliadun (lines 1059–62), but she also becomes a nun and founds a convent, with its own rule and order (lines 1142–44). Guildeluec thereby adapts this paradigm of conversion and renunciation for the other characters: Guilliadun joins her in the convent after her marriage to Eliduc (lines 1165–66), and Eliduc founds a church, sends his new wife to the old in that same convent, and becomes a monk (lines 1155–64). Guildeluec also replaces St. Benedict of Nursia as creator of the Benedictine rule with a convent of her own. A leader and educator of her own nation and of her sexually errant knight husband (rather than a knight errant—"one who wanders"), Guildeluec assumes a fantastic position as Christ manqué, head of a religious order and abbess extraordinaire. If Marie was, in fact, an abbess, possibly herself in exile in England from 1181 to 1215, and daughter of Geoffrey (Plantagenet) of Anjou— therefore, Henry II's half sister—at either Shaftesbury (the largest convent in medieval England), or at Reading, as some scholars have speculated,[44] she appropriately ends her collection with a triumphant alter ego in Guildeluec.

In each of these three lays, if we pinpoint the beginning, roughly the middle, and the end of Marie's Harley collection of twelve, a visit to the Other World spurs change in the psychological identity of the knight because of the impact on the hero of a foreign woman in a foreign land—the girl on the ship in *Guigemar*, the fairy queen in *Lanval*, and the courtly mistress in *Eliduc*. In many of these, as Michelle Freeman has noted, Marie's feminist "poetics of silence" depends upon "private codes" centered on symbolic objects.[45] In the first and last, but not the middle lay of *Lanval*, the concrete images bear a supernatural cast: in *Guigemar*, the androgynous hind, which the hero wounds with an arrow that also wounds him, and the mysterious captainless ship he enters; in *Eliduc*, the magical red flower that resuscitates the slain female weasel that also heals Guilliadun. Each image bears a feminized iconography—the white hind mothers a fawn but bears antlers; the ship has no head, no (male) captain, but autonomously and wisely guides itself to the appropriate port; the red flower suggests secular passion, but also, in its regenerative role, the Passion of Christ—and the female sex, in that its herbal nature and woodsy origin points to a form of notably feminized medicine in the Middle Ages.[46] In *Lanval*, for which no concrete image exists (unless it is the *destrier* at the beginning), the Celtic magic of the fairy queen similarly provides Lanval with the weapons to restore his reputation—wealth that he might dispense with largesse to his own men—and the truth about the queen's advances toward Lanval as validated by the fairy queen at just the appropriate legal moment, which vindicates him (or at least allows the fairy queen to take him away). In terms of Marie's "poetics of silence," however, feminized Lanval is, like most women in the feudal system and the law courts, silenced—an epitome of Lacanian lack. He cannot reveal that he is loved by the fairy queen, so that in the judicial proceeding his new sovereign "king"—the fairy queen—must speak on his behalf, as Arthur does for Guinevere.

The nature of the restoration in Marie's lay of *Lanval* differs from that in either her first or last lay: while the fairy queen is female and her magic is the agent of the restoration, what she practically accomplishes in the "actual" world of Arthurian romance is not magical but literal and legal. That the fairy queen is described as "a girl" makes her rescue all the more amazing. "La pulcele" [the girl] (line 93) transports Lanval from this alien world—a culture harsh because of its patriarchal hierarchy—into her own real world at Avalon to save him. Her entry *from* a fairy Other World *into* an actual kingdom ruled by a hostile Arthur saves Lanval socially from chivalric and courtly opprobrium and, literally and politically from death for treason and lies. Arthur's kingdom in Cardoel (Cardolle, or Carlisle, in Cumbria, in the rough north of England) is no idealized Camelot. Its court is headed by a promiscuous, selfish, manipulative queen who has cuckolded her husband many times within a feudal system that regards women as commodities. The masculine world of early-medieval England or Cornwall represents a culture dominated by competition, ambition, and envy among Arthur's knights of the Round Table and xenophobia and discrimination toward those who differ in class, race, and nationality. Like rescuer Lancelot in other Arthurian romances, the fairy queen saves a Guinevere-like Lanval not from burning but from charges of treason raised against him by Arthur's queen and, then, by Arthur. Ironically, the charges of treason are also those raised against foreigner Lancelot by Meleagaunt in Chrétien's *Le Chevalier de la Charrette* and by Aggravayne, Mordred, and then Sir Gawain, the sons of Morgawse, in Sir Thomas Malory's *Le Morte Darthur.*

King Arthur, "li pruze e li curtieis" [the brave and the courtly king] (line 6), is in reality neither valorous in battle and wise in decision making nor fair and equitable toward his people, both men and women, and foreigners—points Marie raises through disjunctive moments in the text. For example, Marie presents Arthur as sojourning—"surjurnot" (line 5)— in Cardoel because the Scots and Picts have successfully invaded and laid waste to Loengre (Logres) (lines 5–10). Why is Arthur not fighting the invaders? True, the court is held at Pentecost, a time when Arthur offers gifts to the knights of the Round Table: "N'ot tant de teus en tut le munde" [such a company had no equal in all the world] (line 16), Marie notes, tongue in cheek, although she may be referring here to number as much as to quality. But Arthur also provides his barons with "femmes et tere" [lands and wives], as if women were disposable possessions (line 17). In handing out these gifts, Arthur also deliberately ignores alien Lanval, the son of a Breton king (lines 4, 27) whose chief stigma appears to be his beauty, "sa beauté" (line 22). Further, as Arthur leads, so the other knights follow: despite Lanval's long service to the king (line 40), Arthur "ne l'en sovient, / Ne nul de[s] soens bien ne li tient" [forgot him, / and none of his men favored him either] (lines 19–20)—identical to Eliduc's initial predicament. Envy appears to be the chief attitude toward Lanval, with even those who feign friendliness secretly hoping for disaster to befall him (lines 23–26).

Indeed, the real legal issue in *Lanval* involves the king and queen's fear of cultural (national) and class difference within the court and kingdom. At the beginning of the lay, Arthur has no other reason to ignore a noble vassal like Lanval in the distribution of gifts—the only protagonist in the lays identified as vassal[47]—given the king's establishment of the Round Table as a means of lessening unequal treatment of knights. Clearly Marie assumes her auditors' knowledge of this purpose because of Wace's *Roman de Brut.* Later, when Guinevere charges Lanval with homosexuality and then lying and turns to the king for support, the issues appear to be Lanval's chivalric disloyalty, violations of courtly love and courtesy, and treason (the Count of Cornwall lists *felunie* and *mesfait*, "misdeed," in this case, *mesdire*, "misspeaking," or lying [lines 439–41]).[48] In reality, the king may not wish to empower a foreign knight, whatever his feudal allegiance, by distributing wealth to him and thereby weakening the treasury or the kingdom, a point driven home by the reiteration of Lanval's foreignness during the trial (his judges— the barons—describe him as a "franc humme d'autre païs" [noble man from another country] (line 429). Safer, perhaps, for the king to restrict distribution of wealth through the ties of primogeniture to nephews such as Walwains or barons with landholding stakes. Because the king believes his wife (or else wishes to believe a foreigner is guilty) when Guinevere reveals Lanval's perfidy, Arthur charges Lanval with shaming and disgracing him; interestingly, both charges lead to the accusation of treason—a threat to the crown. In addition, when Guinevere reports Lanval's supposed infraction to the king, she emphasizes the class differ- ence and gentility in his boast about the beloved's royal household: "De tele amie se vanta, / Que tant iert cuintre enoble e fiere / Que meuz valut *sa chamberere*, / *La plus povre que tant serveit*, / Que la reïne ne fes- eit" [he boasted of a love / who was so refined and noble and proud / that her chambermaid, *the poorest one who served her*, / was better than the queen] (lines 320–24; my emphasis). The king in his confrontation of Lanval then similarly identifies beauty as a signifier for the aristoc- racy: "Trop par est noble vostre amie, / *Quant plus est bele sa meschine* / E plus vaillanz que la reïne" [your love is much too noble / *if her maid is more beautiful*, / more worthy, than the queen] (lines 368–70; my emphasis).

True gentility transcends class and gender for Marie. What Lanval has actually boasted to the queen is more subtle and egalitarian: the equivalence of beauty, breeding, and virtue to true nobility, what Chaucer calls "gentilesse"[49]: anyone, "*Tute la plus povre meschine*, / Vaut meuz de vus, dame reïne, / De cors, de vis e de beauté, / D'enseignement e de bunté" [*the poorest girl of all*, / is better than you, my lady queen, / in body, face, and beauty, / in breeding and in goodness] (lines 299–302; my emphasis). Accordingly, Guinevere's lies, promiscuity and adultery, and her own insecurity about her social and economic status under- score the truth of Lanval's accusation—would a truly genteel queen have made advances toward another knight or worried she might be lesser in rank than another woman in a different kingdom?

The queen's legal recourse against Lanval depends upon a patriarchal system in which women have virtually no voice, except when queens are involved and sexual advances translate into treason against the king. As if

Lanval has gone too far in his protests, this powerless queen then approaches the king with the trumped-up charge that Lanval has tried to seduce her. Guinevere's private accusations against Lanval of homosexuality and then, publicly, of sexual assault parallel the charges laid against cross-dressing Silence by the similarly powerless queen who desires him/her in the Arthurian romance by Heldris of Cornwall, the *Roman de Silence*. In this etiological Arthurian romance, Queen Eufeme (behaving as Queen Guinevere has with Lanval) believes Silence, dressed as a man, may be homosexual for having rejected her sexual advances.[50] In fact, Silence has disguised herself because women cannot inherit. When Silence is proven right and the queen wrong, the king returns the rights of inheritance to all women. If Silence is a woman disguised as a man, then Lanval is a man who has concealed his femaleness. Just as Arthur shuts up Guinevere by taking her place as accuser, when the fairy queen appears, Lanval silences himself, becomes totally Other.

As an abbess—possibly the sister of Henry II and the daughter of Geoffrey of Anjou, or the daughter of William Manderill, Earl of Sussex, or of Waleran de Beaumont—Marie the outsider clearly sides with both the fantastic powerful fairy queen and the marginalized male protagonist in her Breton lay. While we know very little about Marie except her name and what she tells us in her prologues, she may have been an illegitimate daughter of an unidentified royal father. She reasonably projects her desire for royal stature onto the gracious fairy queen, who may also bear some affinity with another queen, Eleanor of Aquitaine (ca. 1124–1204), married to Henry Plantagenet, the Duke of Normandy.[51] More importantly, blunt, feminized Lanval also represents a persona for Marie, whose own power resides in her like ability to write truth—as she notes in her prologue—and thereby to reveal God's grace through the modest gifts bestowed on a mere woman.

Marie's ambitious program, as she tells us in her prologue, is to write down the lays she has heard, to preserve the adventures they record, rather than to translate Latin stories into *romaunz* [romance] (lines 28–38).[52] By this contrast she implies a preference for the short vernacular Breton lay rather than for the long Latin prose treatise intended for clerics. Setting up an antithesis between Latin and vernacular—the writings of the clergy and the orality of others, particularly women, for whom *lais* and vernacular romances were largely intended—Marie also juxtaposes the culture of Brittany with that of England by offering her lays to the "nobles reis" [noble king] (line 43), presumably Henry II of the house of Plantagenet (but possibly Henry's son, Henri au Cort Mantel).[53]

Through her program, Marie redefines the clerical claim to truth-telling. She feminizes her own project by privileging truth garnered from oral tradition as more egalitarian in its reach than glossation controlled by the schools. Note her admonition, as if directed to the cleric: "*Ki* de vice *se* volt defender / Estudïer deit e entendre / E grevos' ovre commencier: / Par [*ceo*] *se* puet plus esloignier / E de grant dolur delivrer" [*He* who would guard *himself* from vice / should study and understand / and begin a weighty work / by which *he* might keep vice at a distance, / and free *himself* from great sorrow] (Prologue, lines 23–27; my emphasis). Marie recalls "li philosophe" of old as having spent time studying in order to tease out meaning from convoluted passages (lines 17–22). By appropriating in her own lay the exegesis of Macrobian fable and allegory—which women or the nonclerical were generally untrained in unpacking—she simultaneously denigrates obscurity and secrecy as too private and inaccessible a mode of communication. For virtue, when disseminated to many, replenishes itself: "Quant uns granz biens est mult oïz, / Dunc a primes est il fluriz, / E quant loëz est de plusurs, / Dunc ad espandues ses flurs" [When a great good is widely heard of, / then, and only then, does it bloom, / and when that good is praised by many, / it has spread its blossoms] (lines 5–8). Marie means that reading aloud truthful, short vernacular works would enhance the moral fiber of their auditors, men especially, but also women, the literate and illiterate, aristocratic and clerical. The Bretons are gendered female in the prologue.

As a female author who tells the truth, Marie defends her own abrogation of the silence demanded by St. Paul of women in church and in preaching by taking a page, as it were, from Hrotsvit of Gandersheim, although Marie is neither in church nor is preaching. She claims that what gifts God has given an individual in the way of knowledge and articulation need also to be disseminated for this reason: she "ne s'en deit taisir ne celer, / Ainz se deit volunteers mustrer" [should not be silent or secretive, / but demonstrate it willingly] (lines 1–4). Conscious of the possibility of charges of pride (or asserting the modesty topos, as author and woman), she ends the prologue with her imperative: "Ne me tenez a *surquidie* / Si vos os faire icest present" [Do not think me *presumptuous* / if I dare present them to you {the king}] (lines 54–55; my emphasis).

Throughout the lays, in accord with Marie's initial privileging of truth over secrecy in the prologue, truth-telling triumphs over keeping things hidden, just as free will and choice triumph over the obligation and duty inherent in bondage, imprisonment, and legal contracts.

Le Fresne, for example, dramatizes the moral danger of the silence and disempowerment of women through the malicious nature of the wife's behind-the-scenes gossip. The slander that her friend gave birth to twins by lying with two men, one other than her husband, turns back on her when she herself gives birth to two daughters, but then secretly, out of shame, she abandons her second daughter to prevent similar rumors circulating about her. So also *Eliduc* dramatizes the ill consequences of the secret relationship of Eliduc with Guilliadun behind his wife's back and the secrecy of his marriage to Guildeluec behind his lover's back. In the case of *Lanval*, truth-telling ultimately rescues the foreign knight, despite his breaking of his vow to his beloved, as it exposes Guinevere's need for secrecy to advance her immoral desires (and subversion of her husband and kingdom) and to deploy her weapon of slander in order to manipulate others less powerful. And at the end of *Eliduc*, coming around full circle to Marie's statement of purpose in the prologue, she echoes herself when she reminds us that "li auntïen Bretun curteis / Firent le lai pur remembrer, / Que hum nel deüst pas oblïer" [the ancient courtly Bretons / composed the *lai*, to remember it, / so that no one would forget it] (lines 1181–84). So she has written it down for posterity, the "bele fin" [very good {beautiful} end] of the three characters, "la merci Deu, le veir devin" [thanks to God, the divine truth] (lines 1179–80). From God's mouth to Marie, who, as she notes at the beginning of *Guigemar*, "en sun tens pas ne s'oblie" [does not forget her responsibilities when her turn comes] in dealing with "bone mateire" [good material] (lines 1–4). Part of that responsibility has been to render her subject of the marginalized and colonized in the unique lays whose very form, by antithesis, demands recognition of its nature as a minor literature.

CHAPTER 4

MARGUERITE PORETE'S ANNIHILATION OF THE CHARACTER REASON IN HER FANTASY OF AN INVERTED CHURCH

Sometime between 1296 and 1306, the book *Le mirouer des simples ames anienties et qui seulement demourent en vouloir et desir d'amour* [The Mirror of Simple Annihilated Souls and Those Who Only Remain in Will and Desire of Love] by the beguine Marguerite Porete of Hainaut (b. 1250?–d. 1310) was burned in her presence by the bishop of Cambrai, Guy II, in her hometown of Valenciennes in northern France, southeast of Lille. She was simultaneously commanded to cease the dissemination of her ideas and the copying of her book. When she disobeyed the bishop's order, the archbishop of Paris in late 1308 imprisoned her. After a period of eighteen months, in March 1310 William Humbert of Paris, the Dominican inquisitor and confessor of the king, convened a clerical panel to interrogate her (she remained silent throughout these proceedings); these clerics recorded various charges that have not fully survived.[1] This commission of twenty-one canon lawyers, theological regents of the University of Paris, and her inquisitor condemned as heretical fifteen excerpted articles from her book on 31 May 1310. Porete was burned at the stake at the Place de Grève in Paris on 1 June 1310.

Whether correctly or not, Porete was later identified by an early chronicler as the first French "apostle" of the German sect of the Brethren of the Free Spirit (*Secta spiritus libertatis*) on the basis of her apparent antinomianism—the ignoring of moral law in one's actions—and autotheism—the indistinction after union with God between one's consciousness and God's. Indeed, Porete may have founded or influenced the heretical sect of the "Free Spirit," whose doctrines were summarized in the bull "Ad nostrum" issued in 1311 at the Council of Vienne.[2] However, the possession of the later trial documents by two royal ministers and confidantes of Philip the Fair—William of Nogaret and William of Plaisians, who played roles in the king's actions against the Templars—has suggested to modern scholars Robert E. Lerner and Paul Verdeyen that Porete's trial was connected less with the sect of the Brethren of the Free Spirit than with other political events of the day.[3] Lerner and John A. Arsenault also identify Porete's work as more orthodox in its mysticism than that of the Free Spirit movement.[4]

Whatever Porete's heresies, by her very being she reflected various cultural marginalizations: she was female, markedly slammed as a *pseudomulier* by the contemporary continuator of the chronicle of Nangis, Guillelmus de Nangiaco—apparently a monk from the royal Abbey of St. Denis who habitually expressed the crown's perspective.[5] Porete wrote in the vernacular; her work was also popular, extant in two Old French manuscripts, of which only one is currently accessible, and previously translated into four versions in Latin, two in Italian (of which thirty-six copies may have existed in the fifteenth century), three in Middle English, most likely by Carthusians.[6] Finally, she was described in the trial documents as a despised "beguine clergeresse."[7] In the later Middle Ages, beginning with the mendicants and the female equivalents, beguines, Poor Clares, and tertiaries, the itinerant women who begged, preached, and nurtured the poor and elderly provided a likely target for ecclesiastical prohibition and censure. The primary reason stemmed most assuredly from their lack of claustration or fixed abode (some beguines did live in communities, where they had to obtain permission to leave, or in their own houses)—their lack of control by the church or others in charge.[8] For such reasons, attacks leveled against another beguine, Mechthild of Magdeburg (ca. 1212–82), compelled her late in life to seek residence with nuns at the convent at Helfta near Eisleben in Saxony. Like Mechthild, unhomely Porete lifted her pen to inscribe a work of literature in a minor key.

To grasp why Porete appeared dangerous to the ecclesiastical authorities so far removed from humble beguine life, we need to understand the tenets of her doctrine of Simple Souls who have been Annihilated and their Holy Church the Great, conveyed by feminine personifications in a work that combines visionary allegory with autobiography. In this Holy Church the Great, being is not predicated on that faculty of reason so rarely attributed to women and yet so lauded by scholastic philosophy. Instead, Porete's ontology depends upon the Soul's quest for union with God through Love and Faith and an abdication of individual will to the divine, coupled with a dissociation from material life. Inverting the conventional ideal of human nature as governed by reason and will in the journey to God, Porete also inverts the actual church and court in her feminized fantasy of the Holy Church the Great, appropriating a concept of *seigneurie* for her "ladies of the house." Her radical literary subversion involves a complex revision of the church and society of her day into a feminized utopia.

Porete's Doctrine of the Simple Souls and Their Church

Noteworthy in regard to the issue of Porete's heresy, among the fifteen condemned articles from the *Mirror* are the two that position the Annihilated Soul in a state on earth where it does not need the Virtues, God's gifts,or consolation. In the first article, the Soul needs neither Virtues nor consolation because the Virtues obey the Soul, and in the fifteenth article, the Soul does not need God's gifts or consolation because the Soul directly confronts God himself. Two major theological implications arise from these suspect articles. First, as a consequence of the obedience of the Virtues to the Soul rather than the other way around, the *Mirror* repudiates the corporal presence of original sin and its manifestations, that is, bodily temptations, and, second, because the Soul can unite with God while on earth, it bypasses appeal to any sacerdotal (that is, male) intermediary such as a priest or confessor.

What do these two articles and their implications mean? Porete regarded Love as transformative in permitting the embodied Soul—the soul while on earth—union with God that is both "lasting and essential," according to Joanne Maquire Robinson.[9] How the Soul unites with God occurs, Porete believed, when she relinquishes her will to God and becomes nothing while being possessed by divine will—a state of being (*estat*) that Porete describes as "annihilated." Porete titles her allegorical work *The Mirror of Simple Annihilated Souls and Those Who Only Remain in Will and Desire of Love* to segregate a superior kind of soul from those "who only remain in will or desire of Love." Among the three classes are the Simple Souls, who are sad, that is, obedient to Jesus Christ—a type that Porete identifies as the souls of the Holy Church the Great, governed by Love. These Simple Souls can eventually join a second, more noble class, the Annihilated Souls, the end-point of the mystical journey. Third come those (apparently) complex (that is, not simple) Souls who are unfortunately Lost, that is, obedient to Reason and the Virtues, Faith, Hope, and Charity, and Holy Church the Little.

Through the concept of the Annihilated Soul, Porete attacks the institution of the actual church—what she calls Holy Church the Little—as governed by Reason and the Virtues and the concomitant sins of pride and other forms of pettiness and immorality; she also describes this lower church as Holy Church of Lost Souls. That Little Church is thereby inferior to and supported by Holy Church the Great. This greater Church—governed by divine Love, to which sad Souls and Annihilated Souls belong—does not involve any intermediaries during the Soul's journey to annihilation through six states, or estates (*estaz*, also known as beings, or *estres*).[10] That is, reflective of Porete's belief that the Soul is part of a community of Simples Ames (Simple Souls, or free souls) who should guide "Sainte Eglise la Grande" [Holy Church the Great], the Mirror does away with the usual priestly intermediary between the Soul and God as demanded by "Sainte Eglise la Petite" [Holy Church the Little] on earth. Porete, in addition to rejecting "mediary" clergy, omits the sacraments, mass, sermon, fasting, or prayers ("works"): "Ceste se saulve de foy sans oeuvres, car foy surmonte toute oeuvre, a tesmoing d'Amour mesmes" (Guarnieri, *Mirouer*, 40 [11.40–41]) [This one is saved by faith without works, because faith surpasses all work, as Love herself witnesses] (Babinsky, *Mirror*, 89). Nor does the Annihilated Soul look for God in penitence, the sacraments, thoughts, words, works, creatures on earth, creatures above, justice, mercy, glory of glory, divine understanding, divine love, or divine praise (Guarnieri, *Mirouer*, 242 [85.20–25]; Babinsky, *Mirror*, 160) and more or less excludes from the journey of the Soul as unnecessary an understanding of the scriptures and (as Ellen Babinsky notes in her preface, citing Caroline Walker Bynum) the "physicality of Christ"—fasting, prayers, and the sacraments (Babinsky, *Mirror*, 2).

Most important in the journey is the annihilation of the Soul, as preceded by the death of Reason and accompanied by the obedience of the Virtues to the Soul. Porete's *Mirror*, a prose dialogue interspersed with songs between Dame Amour (Lady Love) and La Raison (the Reason) about and with L'Ame (the Soul), emphasizes the resourcefulness of the Soul in its description of the six states of grace leading the embodied Soul on a journey to union with God (the seventh state occurs in paradise, after death). The other participants in this dialogue represent, according to Catharine Randall, "personifications of attributes or effects" of the main three: "While the subsequent person seems to devolve from the first, some *distance* is produced, but no real *difference* results. Instead, the secondarily produced *personae* add more precision to the previous concept."[11] The journey begins with an act of grace and ends with the Soul on earth becoming near-perfect, annihilated, in states five and six, when the individual stops encumbering it.[12] From the first state, the stripping away of sin and the adherence to God's commandments (that is, the New Testament commandments to love God with all her heart and her neighbor as herself), the Soul moves in state two to emulation of Christ's evangelical teachings, at state three sacrifices the performance of good works and relinquishes her will, and at state four attains true freedom and contemplation. Finally and most importantly, at state five the Soul removes herself from the will that must will only the Divine Will and becomes nothing, truly Annihilated; at state six, like the six-winged Seraphim, the Soul, although embodied, loves, understands, and praises only God. Annihilation represents the freedom to live in the world after having become Love and being served by the very Virtues, especially Humility, that the Soul herself previously served. As a journey it does not necessarily lead to the Other World or the afterlife, but state seven does involve the arrival of the Soul in paradise after death. In the course of this journey, three deaths are necessary: the death of sin (which makes the Soul die and, along with her, anything banned by God in the Law), through the life of grace; the death of nature, which gives life to the spirit; and the death of the spirit, which gives birth to the divine life (Guarnieri, *Mirouer*, 170 [59.3–7]; Babinsky, *Mirror*, 136).

The originality of Porete's work depends upon what Maria Lichtmann has termed a very antiauthoritarian, even postmodern, construction of "negative theology," which depends upon the idealization of the state of the Soul in state six of the seven states as unencumbered by the human will and, therefore, as annihilated, or made nothing, while on earth.[13] That is, literally it is a mysticism of denial, of nothingness. It is also unusual in positing the capability of human creatures (Porete's phrase) to give up, or possess, no will, in that, when in this sixth state, the divine Will lives in the Soul.[14] This "peace of charity in the annihilated life" (when one gives up one's will for Divine Will) has nine characteristics, all defined by relative clauses by analogy with the relation in scholastic logic between subject and accident: (1) A Soul; (2) who is saved by faith without works; (3) who is only in love; (4) who does nothing for God; (5) who leaves nothing to do for God; (6) to whom nothing can be taught; (7) from whom nothing can be taken; (8) nor given; (9) and who possesses no will (Guarnieri, *Mirouer*, 19–21 [5.6–14]; Babinsky, *Mirror*, 82–83). In fact, this life of the Soul is Nothing. The Annihilated Soul is neither lost nor sad but remains in the fifth state with her Lover (Loingprès, or FarNear, God in the Soul)—that is, without will, but filled with divine will—sometimes in the sixth, but ultimately is carried back to the fifth (in the fourth state, she still has individual will) (Guarnieri, *Mirouer*, 168 [58.12–23]; Babinsky, *Mirror*, 135).

The sixth state, of annihilation, represents a transcendence of the natural that the character and faculty of Reason cannot grasp: "Hee, pour Dieu, Amour, dit Raison, qu'est ce a dire, ce que vous dictes?" (Guarnieri, *Mirouer*, 26 [chap. 7, lines 6–7]) [Ah, for God's sake, Love, says Reason, what does this mean, what you have said?] (Babinsky, *Mirror*, 85). In this noble state the world of tribulation as we know it ceases to matter: "Ceste Ame, dit Amour, ne fait compte ne de honte ne honneur, de povreté, ne de richesse, d'aise ne de mesaise, d'amour ne hayne, d'enfer ne de paradis" (Guarnieri, *Mirouer*, 24 [7.3]) [This Soul, says Love, takes account of neither shame nor honor, of neither poverty nor wealth, of neither anxiety nor ease, of neither love nor hate, of neither hell nor of paradise] (Babinsky, *Mirror*, 84). In becoming nothing, the Soul has everything, "and so possesses nothing; she wills everything and she wills nothing; she knows all and she knows nothing" (Guarnieri, *Mirouer*, 26 [7.14–16]; Babinsky, *Mirror*, 85). To be "annihilated," Love adds in this chapter, is to be severed from external desires and "interior sentiments"—the Soul's will is dead. When the Soul has reached this certain state, she must no longer obey the Virtues because they have become perfected and instead serve her as mistress (Guarnieri, *Mirouer*, 30 [8.40–42]; Babinsky, *Mirror*, 86).

In this inversion of the actual "Little" historical church opposed to the imaginary and reconstructed "Great Church," Porete writes medieval fantasy, opening up a space for the subjectivity of marginalized women. The *Mirror*, with Porete's all-female cast of personifications that dramatizes female agency in the universe and the human soul, is a spiritual autobiography like that of thirteenth-century Angela of Foligno's *Memoriale*, fourteenth-century Catherine of Siena's *Dialogo* and Marguerite of Oingt's *Speculum*—but also like early-fifteenth-century works such as Julian of Norwich's *Revelations of Divine Love*,

Margery Kempe's *Boke*, Christine de Pizan's *Ladvision-Cristine*, and Marguerite of Navarre's *Miroir de l'âme pécheresse*. Among writings by women writers, scholars have compared Porete's *Mirror of Simple Souls* with the religious love poetry of beguine Hadewijch of Brabant and beguine Mechthild of Magdeburg's *The Flowing Light of the Godhead*, Carthusian Marguerite of Oingt's *Mirror*, and, later, Marguerite of Navarre's mystical work.[15]

Despite these similarities, some critics have rejected Porete as a feminist author, most recently Robinson: "This is not 'women's history' in any other way than it focuses on a writer who was a woman who lived a religious life outside the structure of monastic life; who was well educated and inclined toward mystical speculation; and who stirred up controversy with a stubbornness found only rarely among her contemporaries."[16] In this regard Robinson follows Amy M. Hollywood, a fellow student of Bernard McGinn, in her theoretical position on Porete in *The Soul as Virgin Wife*: Porete cannot be considered feminist or proto-feminist because (according to Hollywood) she rejects the essential feminization of the body. According to these scholars, Porete's allegorization of the limits of the historical church is important for its influence on a later male ecclesiastical and mystical tradition.[17] Specifically, religious scholars such as Edmund Colledge and J.C. Marler, McGinn, Hollywood, Lichtmann, Sells, and others have remarked on Porete's work as part of a female evangelical movement of beguines that affected male mystics such as the contemporary German Dominican Meister Johannes Eckhart (1260–1327?),[18] said to share a belief in the doctrines of the Free Spirit.

A chief difference between Porete's dialogic narrative and those of other women mystics in the Middle Ages is that it is not visionary (as Lichtmann suggests above), or not in the same way as theirs: the *Mirror* does not derive from dreams or voices that address the author; there is no "dark night of the soul" typical of most mystical treatises; it is not predicated upon a mystical ascent to and union with a divine Being that leaves the body behind; and it is focused less on the afterlife than on a return to life in this world (as described in stage six). Most importantly, Porete positions herself as a character in her narrative, as if she is *writing fiction* and not theology. As the character L'Ame, the Soul, Porete tells a story to the Trinity very late in her book about a *mendiant creature* (mendicant creature)—herself—who, in the course of writing this book, remains an encumbered soul because of her narcissism. The creature is *encombree d'elle mesmes* (encumbered with herself) because of her desire to help her neighbors through her soul. The mendicant has sought God *en creature* (in "creatureliness"), out of will rather than "ou fons du noyau de l'entendement de la purté de sa haulte pensee" [at the depth of the core of the intellect of the purity of her sublime thought] (Guarnieri, *Mirouer*, 266 [96.9], Babinsky, *Mirror*, 170). Because the Soul/Porete wants her neighbors to find God in her writings and thereby become perfect, she stays a beggar, "encumbered with herself" (meaning encumbered by her will). Porete describes herself so, as she also does in chapter 97 through the words of the Supreme Lady of Peace (Babinsky, *Mirror*, 171). At this late point in the narrative, when the Soul/Porete hears this criticism from the Supreme Lady, she finally confesses she was foolish: "Et non pour tant, dit ceste Ame qui escripsit ce livre, j'estoie aussi socte ou temps qu je le fis, mais ainçoys que Amour le fist pour moy et a ma requeste, <que> je mectoie en pris chose que l'en ne povoit faire ne penser ne dire, aussi comme feroit celuy qui vouldroit la mer en son oeil enclorre, et pourter le monde sur la pointe d'ung jonc, et enluminer le soleil d'ung fallot ou d'une torche" (Guarnieri, *Mirouer*, 270 [97.29–36]) [Yet even so, says *this Soul who wrote this book*, I was so foolish at the time when I wrote it; but Love did it for my sake and at my request, that I might undertake something which one could neither do, nor think, nor say, any more than someone could desire to enclose the sea in his eye, or carry the world on the end of a reed, or illumine the sun with a lantern or a torch] (Babinsky, *Mirror*, 171; my emphasis).

An autobiographical vision, *The Mirror of Simple Souls* also renders a fictional portrait of the mendicant as concealed by the personification L'Ame. Comparing the two types of writing, religious vision and dream vision, Barbara Newman in *God and the Goddesses: Vision, Poetry, and Belief in the Middle Ages* (2003) has remarked on links between the usual bifurcated genres of "authentic" visionary literature used so often by women mystics—as in Julian of Norwich's *Revelation of Divine Love*—and "fictional visions" by courtly and scholastic male poets, for example, Geoffrey Chaucer's *Legend of Good Women*. She reminds us that male mystic Henry Suso used allegory, parables, and imaginary dialogues to enhance the accessibility of his works.[19] However, Newman notes a signal difference between the female and male author: when a female author writes about female personifications or goddesses, she identifies with them, but when a male author uses such figures, "beneficent female guise" cloaks instead "patriarchal authority."[20] Female personifications—characters in this visionary debate—reflect the agency and authority of their female author, intent on creating a fictional vision that differs from the autobiographies of women mystics in the Middle Ages.

If we accept Newman's argument, we can assume that Porete both (1) identifies with her female personifications and (2) uses allegory and her imaginary dialogue as a means of clarifying the purpose of her work. But what do we do with her antagonistic figure, Reason, who is female but who is killed by Love before the Soul's annihilation? And how exactly is Porete's literary apparatus a means of clarifying her purpose? Do we see her masculinization of imagery as a subordination of the hegemonic patriarchy to some fantastic feminine? In Porete—and in other mystics, as is well known, for example, in the work of Hadewijch[21]—courtly love, chivalric, and magisterial idioms and images are used to masculinize the female soul's relation to a feminized God in the Soul, FarNear. And yet Catharine Randall has described Porete's purpose in this literary technique as "to illustrate, empower, and expand traditional theological positions," particularly (but incorrectly, I think), in regard to the Trinity, with Reason representing God; Love, the Son; and Faith, the Holy Spirit.[22]

Instead, Porete creates an original space for an individual woman to define herself through a new discourse on which this beguine's feminized theology depends, one that deflects the usual gender roles of women in French medieval religion, culture, and society and allows them to spiritually and metaphorically "cross-dress." When Robert D. Cottrell hints at an explanation of this female/male divide in Porete, he singles out discourse itself as a representation of patriarchal hegemony:

> [P]atriarchal discourse is the linguistic representation of a social order that guarantees masculine supremacy and dominance. By inserting the female self in the registers of subjectivity and power, Porete implicitly calls into question a social order in which the female is inscribed as what is seen and the male as the eye (I) that sees, the eye (I) that, from a position of preeminence, "commands" what falls within its gaze. . . . [B]y usurping the prerogatives of patriarchal discourse, by deviating from the "model," Porete in fact subverts the social order of which that discourse is a sign.[23]

However excellent Cottrell's explanation of Porete's deviation, he does not fully explain the tension between her subversion and patriarchal discourse at this time—or how she specifically inserts the female self in those registers of power given the *literary* character of her work.

In order to interrogate discourse in Porete as a social register, we must look at her positioning of the faculty of reason as a vehicle of transmission of social dominance. I would argue more specifically that the *Mirror*, which purports to be words of Dame Amour as she appears before Porete, in fact masks its author through L'Ame, and the clergy, through interrogator La Raison. Kathleen Garay notes that "in an age where scholastic learning was preeminent and reason and religion were inextricably intertwined, Marguerite's rejection of reason also implied a rejection of the powerful intellectual element of the thirteenth-century church."[24] But Garay does not develop this hint, nor does she examine the literary character of the work, specifically, its scholastic metaphors and its plane of correspondence between macrocosm and microcosm.

Porete is specifically repudiating a concept of acculturated and gendered reason—which according to Aristotle women lack—through her appropriation of magisterial images that pose Reason as a *puer* and her magister as Love teaching her in a Boethian-style debate. Further, whatever Reason is in the microcosm, the church and the nobility embody in the macrocosm. What is confusing about Porete is her literary difference from other medieval women writers in her complete inversion of the usual material and feudal associations found in the socioeconomic practice of courtly love. Porete's feminization of Reason as an embodiment of the scholastic faculty and her appropriation of the metaphor of a masculinized nobility for the Annihilated Soul celebrate inversion as subversion of the conventional. As Porete creates a new version of the microcosm in which the Virtues obey the Soul, so also in the macrocosm Holy Church the Little follows Holy Church the Great, and the Annihilated Soul—after the death of Reason—forms part of a new nobility. Reason represents not just the clergy, but the masculinized—gendered—discourse that women appropriate in their own writing that must "die." Key, then, to the spiritual vision of the *Mirror* is the annihilation of the Soul in stage six, after the dramatic and symbolic climax of Reason's "death" from Love in chapter 87, freeing the will to join with the divine will—the very hinge that links both the suspect and heretical articles one and fifteen.

The Subversion of the Culture of Scholasticism

A response to twelfth- and thirteenth-century scholasticism and its insistence on reason as characteristic of a humanity that appears to exclude the female, Porete's work, like other visions by both male and female mystics of the period, denigrates the epistemological limitations of reason and idealizes the wisdom of love as shared between God the Holy Spirit, the third person of the Trinity, and the Soul. Unlike other mystics, Porete adopts clerical and feudal metaphors to draw attention to her new "church" of feminized values as an inverted mirror of the traditional church, and she embeds them in a Boethian debate or *disputatio* drawn from the influential *De consolatione Philosophiae* (524 AD). In form, the *Mirror* is a prosimetrum, with Reason preferring prose and Love preferring poetry. Thus repudiating the methodologies and tools of the scholastic philosopher, Porete appropriates the form used by fifth-century Roman North African Martianus Capella, sixth-century North African grammarian Fulgentius, twelfth-century Bernardus Silvestris and Alan of Lille, and other medieval scholars—and then subverts it. But in genre, *The Mirror* is a dialogue, or debate, between Dame Amour (Love) and Raison (Reason) about and with Ame (the Soul), in particular, L'Ame Adneantie (the Annihilated Soul). It thus shares themes with Boethius's *Consolation of Philosophy*,[25] Petrarch's *Secretum meum*, and the medieval dramas of tenth-century Saxon canoness Hrotsvit of Gandersheim that present the faith and love of Christian martyrs in confrontation with imperial justice and law. In Porete's hands, the dialogue realizes the journey to Love without Boethius's despair and without a male narrator. Here Reason—in the position of the Boethian narrator—must learn from a Philosophy-like Love through questions and answers and eventually "die" (in chapter 87).

In genre Porete thus responds to the literary character of the Platonic fictions of the Orléanists and the Chartrians (or Parisians)—of Lille, too, given its proximity to her hometown, Valenciennes. Alan of Lille (d. 1202) probably trained at Paris. Both Guillaume de Lorris (ca. 1230–35) and Jean de Meun (ca. 1275), authors of *Le roman de la Rose*, were associated with the Orléans region, from whose schools so many humanistic scholars sprang; Jean de Meun likely left Orléans for Paris.[26] In regard to Jean's link with Orléans, it is interesting to note that one of the only two extant French manuscripts of Porete's *Mirouer* originally came from the convent of the Magdalenes in Orléans (Chantilly, Musée Condé XIV F26 [Catalog 157]; a third was lost on the way from Bourges to the Bibliothèque nationale).[27] Barbara Newman has recently acknowledged Porete's indebtedness to the title "Le Miroër as amorous" [The Mirror for Lovers]—as Jean and the God of Love rename Jean's continuation, especially for its promotion of Love and concomitant discreditation of Reason.[28] Newman notes that "the very form of Marguerite's text—a sprawling and, at first blush, shapeless allegorical dialogue—seems to be self-consciously modeled on the *Rose*."[29] The mirror image was used by Guillaume de Lorris and Jean de Meun in their two parts of the *Rose* to describe the Mirror of Narcissus in the garden of Deduit, the personification of desire, which reflects back to the viewer's gaze only half of the garden. The mirror was also used to figure forth the carbuncle of the Holy Trinity in the equivalent park of the Bon Pasteur (Good Shepherd, Christ), which contains the ideal images of everything in the universe.[30]

While I agree with Newman that Porete is reacting to the *Rose*, I suggest an alternate reason for Porete's title that makes hers ironic: the mirror, or *speculum*, as a medieval image of natural representation suggests the learned treatise or compendium of all knowledge. The image of the mirror, after all, was used most famously by Vincent of Beauvais (d. 1264) to name his Latin four-part encyclopedia of the wisdom of the world, *Speculum mundi* (*doctrinale, naturale, historiale, morale*). Further, if the mirror in the twelfth century often symbolized the equivalence between reason and order in nature and human nature,[31] Porete's mirror of "Simple Souls" instead reflects the governance of the spiritual world by divine Love and its correspondence in the human soul. In the prosimetrum *De planctu Naturae* [The Plaint of Nature], when Alan of Lille describes Nature as having "ad exemplarem mundanae machinae similitudinem hominis exemplavi naturam, vel turrim, ut in ea velut in *speculo* ipsius mundi conscripta Natura compareat" [formed the nature of man according to the exemplar and likeness of the structure of the universe so that in him, as in a *mirror* of the universe itself, Nature's lineaments might be there to see], his reason mirrors the heavens: "Rationis enim motus, ab ortu caelestium oriens, per occasum pertransiens terrenorum, caelestia considerando regyratur in caelum" [For the movement of reason, springing from a heavenly origin, escaping the destruction of things on earth, in its process of thought turns back again to the heavens].[32]

In her *Mirror* Porete inverts the image of man to suggest the greater wisdom of utterances by an apparently unschooled (and female) beguine. Thus, the *Rose*'s mirror of Narcissus might reflect back the gazer's self, but Porete's *Mirror*, like the mirror in the garden in the *Rose*, also reveals to her auditors (the work was read aloud) what Lichtmann calls "boldly gendered" inversions of the contemporary state of the church and society.[33] If the mirror also appears as belonging to the beautiful Oiseuse (Idleness) in the garden of Deduit in Guillaume's *Rose*—an image implicitly critical of the vain aristocratic woman with too much time on her hands[34]—one might also describe the mirror in Porete as has Lichtmann, as "an apparently apt symbol of woman's narcissism" that "becomes equally emblematic of her willingness to lose herself in a most radical otherness."[35] In this modern feminist sense, the *Mirouer* of Marguerite Porete and the *Speculum* of Marguerite d'Oingt (d. 1310) project *écriture féminine* as the other side of the mirror, that which represents female subjectivity.[36]

To a large extent, through the debates between Reason and Love, Porete reacts to and subverts a second and even more powerful literary and courtly love model, one in which Raison opposes the protagonist lover, Amant. Jean de Meun, in his continuation of the aristocratic dream vision left unfinished by Guillaume de Lorris, like Guillaume presents Raison as an antagonist to Amant's desirous quest for the Rose; however, Jean also dehumanizes woman into a silent and passive flowery image—the lady Rose—whose Bel Accueil (Fair Welcome) nevertheless encourages what appears to be a sexual assault by the triumphant Amant [Lover] at poem's end.[37] Further, the kind of love portrayed throughout the *Rose* equally appears to be carnal, without any spiritual or even courtly aspect (despite the Lover's initial encounter with the Rose in the garden of Deduit).

Where the two works differ is in their conception of true nobility, which (according to Robinson) is inborn in the *Mirror* for certain souls but in the *Rose* open to all (except merchants) on the basis of virtue.[38] Although critics who have examined Porete's courtly metaphors have generally not acknowledged this connection with the *Rose*, Kathleen Garay pushes further in the direction in which I point: "Appropriating the language and metaphors of a monarchy that was one of the most powerful in Europe, along with the familiar conceits of courtly love, Marguerite created nothing less than an alternative hierarchy."[39] Here, I argue, Porete also borrows and makes ironic the courtly love antagonism of Reason and the Lover in Jean's *Rose* and its implicit clerical misogyny.

Porete counters Jean's text with the trajectory of a love motivated by a spiritual desire for God and, therefore, signified by a true nobility—neither the (masculinized) nobility conveyed by birth and title nor that marked by wealth and material addition, but instead the (feminized) nobility that comes from annihilation, reduction, and marginalization.[40] Porete associates those of the lower servant class with Reason and Holy Church the Little and those of the true higher nobility with Love and Holy Church the Great. This classist feature has led Robinson to argue that Porete employs metaphors of lineage especially to clarify her doctrine of annihilation, although her concept of nobility does not relate to the typical medieval identification with birth (lineage), or even with virtue (deeds), which crops up in Dante, Hrotsvit of Gandersheim, Hildegard of Bingen, Hadewijch of Brabant, Bernard of Clairvaux, and Guillaume de Lorris and Jean de Meun.[41] Further, although Robinson perceives Porete's concept of nobility as an "explicitly *nongendered* classification of souls into noble and non-noble, a hierarchy based on a God-given inborn spiritual status,"[42] all the personifications in Porete's dialogue are female; Love and Reason, like the Soul and the Author (now that we know the author previously regarded as "anonymous" is Porete), are figured as obviously female (but the Beloved is imagined as "Ami," masculine). I argue in addition that the Annihilated Soul is symbolically gendered feminine in its very depletion and stripping away of qualities afforded by material aristocracy, which, after all, communicates its importance through patrimony and inheritance through the male.

And other feminized aspects exist in the *Mirror*. Porete writes in the vernacular instead of in Latin, she privileges the imaginative and fabulous over the logical and deductive,[43] and she begins with an *accessus* (statement of purpose in a Latin commentary)—actually a proem and a prologue—that is on the one hand poetic and figurative rather than prosaic and didactic and on the other fabulous and imaginative. Porete's proem clarifies her primary purpose: to illustrate—but not necessarily rationally or logically—the primacy of Love and Faith over the epistemological faculty of the cleric, Reason, his *entendement* [*intellectum*, intellect], no matter his *engins* [*ingenium*, invention and genius] (Guarnieri, *Mirouer*, 8 [proem, lines 9–10], Babinsky, *Mirror*, 79). In her proem, Porete criticizes (male) theologians, if not theology per se, along with clerks, for their arrogance; instead, her feminized Humility keeps the treasury of Knowledge and "mothers" the Virtues (Guarnieri, *Mirouer*, 8 [proem, lines 5, 7], Babinsky, *Mirror*, 79). While Faith is one of two major mentors of the Soul (Love being the other), Humility is also necessary for them to have any sway over Reason. Porete imagines the Soul as a feminized aristocratic household or castle run by ladies, her domestic well-being ensured by the nurturing qualities of Dame Amour (Love) and Foy (Faith), two "dames. . . .de la maison" (ladies of the house) (Guarnieri, *Mirouer*, 8 [proem, 14]; Babinsky, *Mirror*, 79) in charge of both quotidian and spiritual duties. Porete warns the clergy and scholars that they might not understand her work if they lack humility (Porete's warning suggests, perhaps, that this is a common flaw). In stanza 2, she notes:

> Theologiens ne aultres clers,
> Point n'en aurez l'entendement
> Tant aiez les engins clers
> Se n'y procedez humblement
> Et que Amour et Foy ensement
> Vous facent surmonter Raison,
> *Qui dames sont de la maison.*
> (Guarnieri, *Mirouer*, 8
> [proem, 8–14])

[Theologians and other clerks,
You will not have the intellect for it,
No matter how brilliant your abilities,
If you do not proceed humbly.
And may Love and Faith, together,
Cause you to rise above Reason,
{Since} *they are the ladies of the house.*]
(Babinsky, *Mirror*, 79,
my emphasis)

The privileging of those qualities accessible and available to all, whether male or female, and democratized in the sense that the educated and the uneducated have an equal access to them, is here set within a larger primary world frame that acknowledges the specific sins of the cleric as pride and arrogance. The masculinized act of feudal homage and submission in the third stanza becomes the model in the text for subordinate Reason's later posture as a humble servant to the "lord," identified as the dominant ladies Amour and Foy. Looking ahead to the thirteenth chapter, Porete informs her readers that there Reason will accept the gendered *seigneurie* [lordship] of Love and Faith over her and "humble herself" (Guarnieri, *Mirouer*, 8 [proem, lines 22–23], Babinsky, *Mirror*, 79): only through them can Reason live. There, Reason herself "tesmoigne" [witnesses] and "n'en a vergoigne" [has no shame about it], "que Amour et Foy la font vivre / Et d'elles point ne se delivre, / *Car sur elle ont seigneurie,* / Par quoy il fault qu'elle s'umilie" (Guarnieri, *Mirouer*, 8 [proem, lines 15–21]) [that Love and Faith make her live / And she does not free herself from them, / *For*

they have lordship over her, / Which is why she must humble herself]
(Babinsky, *Mirror*, 79, my emphasis). Feminine lordship is attained
through the domination of reason via Faith and Love, the figures of
language.

Marguerite appears to gloss and invert Hugh of St. Victor's
metaphor of the lower souls as domestics when she characterizes Love
and Faith in her proem as the "ladies of the house" whom a humbled
Reason must obey. Reason as the premier psychological faculty of
understanding pervades twelfth-century treatises and allegories, one
example of which, from an influential text about the nature of
medieval education, suggests imagery and interrelationships that
Porete will appropriate and subvert in her proem to the *Mirror*. Hugh
of St. Victor, in the *Didascalicon: De studio legendi* [On the Study of
Reading] (ca. late 1120s), celebrates the seven liberal arts in general;
extant in nearly a hundred manuscripts through the fifteenth century,
its canonical status within centers for learning (monastery and cathedral
school libraries) suggests its pivotal stature at the "dawn of the twelfth-
century renaissance...when centers of education had moved from the
predominantly rural monasteries to the cathedral schools of growing
cities and communes."[44] The Victorine analyzes the three faculties of
the soul as a hierarchy, with the vegetative soul (vivifying bodies) and
animal soul (sense perception) serving their superior, the rational soul.
The metaphor Hugh employs reminds us of Porete's quotidian and
castellary image of service within feudalism: "Sed vis animae tertia,
quae secum priores alendi ac sentiendi trahit, hisque velut *famulis atque
obedientibus* utitur, eadem tota in ratione est constituta, eaque vel in
rerum praesentium firmissima conclusione, vel *in absentium intelligentia,
vel in ignotarum inquisitione versatur*" [But the third power of the soul
appropriates the prior nutritional and sense-perceiving powers, using
them, so to speak, *as its domestics and servants*. It is rooted entirely in the
reason, and it exercises itself either in the most unfaltering grasp of
things present, or *in the understanding of things absent, or in the investigation of things unknown*].[45]

Closer to Porete's allegory, the *Anticlaudianus*, an allegorical epic by
Alan of Lille, features Reason in a more earthly and limited role as the
intellect that knows but does not always understand and Faith as a more
reliable guide for matters pertaining to the heavenly. Alan also portrays
Phronesis (Prudence) as an epic hero whose journey-quest on a chariot
constructed by the seven liberal arts is to ask God for a soul so that
Nature can construct what Alan typifies as a New Man, Novus Homo.

Interestingly, Phronesis accomplishes this task ultimately with the aid not of Reason but of Faith, who accompanies her only so far into the universe, at which point she is joined by Theology. When Phronesis is entranced by the light of heaven and Theology cannot cure her lethargy, Faith allows her to complete her task by giving her a mirror in which "omnia lucens / Quae mundus caelestis habet" [shines clear everything which the heavenly universe holds].[46] As close as Alan's work is in some ways to Porete's *Mirror*, celestial agency is not accorded to personifications of imagination or love.[47]

Porete consciously and explicitly valorizes the fabulous and poetic in Old French as a more appropriate vehicle to convey truth than the Latin treatises written by philosophers who teach at the University of Paris—which, of course, she cannot do. Therefore, she chooses a second proem to the *Mirror*, to centralize imagination, faith, and love. To proclaim her own literary subversion upfront, Porete inverts the proem used by three major medieval exegetes at the opening of their commentaries—the fable of Syrophanes of Egypt—that explains and rationalizes the creation of gods by men through the use of imagery, or idols. Her targets are the male scholars who wrote commentary, prosimetrum, visionary allegory, and *satura*, for example, the *De diis gentium et illorum allegoriis* of the Third Vatican Mythographer (most likely, Albericus of London) (ca. 1177), the *De planctu Naturae* of Alan of Lille, and the vernacular long poem and dream vision of the *Rose* of de Lorris and de Meun (1240–77).[48] All three clerics had used pagan gods to establish the nature of fabulous narrative (*narratio fabulosa*) as dependent on the stories of the gods to veil the truths of nature. Albericus of London (and before him Fulgentius the grammarian and the ninth-century Second Vatican Mythographer) had written an extremely influential mythographic handbook to explain the allegories of the major planetary deities; he and his predecessor mythographers had also penned an etiological *accessus*, or prologue, about the fable of Syrophanes to justify the use of pagan gods and other idolatrous images.

In Fulgentius, the Third Vatican Mythographer, and John Ridewall, the fable involves a father, Syrophanes, who, mourning the loss of his son, makes an image of him as consolation; the image becomes an idol when both he and his servants out of fear or grief turn to it as if it were real.[49] About such a *species*, or image, influential sixth-century grammarian Fulgentius, at the beginning of *Mitologiae*, has the goddess of epic poetry, Calliope, note its character as an apparition, clearly an error born of ignorance and a symptom of irrationality.[50] The twelfth-century Third Vatican Mythographer, Albericus of London, also known as "Alexander" (possibly Alexander Neckam, author of a commentary on the first two books of Martianus Capella), in the prooemium to *De diis gentium* [On the Gentile Gods] stresses the father's loss of his posterity, his very *virilitas* and his future, when he compensates by constructing the idol, or image, the *similitudo* or *simulacrum*, of his son; the Third Vatican Mythographer accordingly structures his handbook through a genealogy beginning with Saturn and Rhea and progressing generation by generation down to the heroes Bacchus, Hercules, and Perseus.[51] His book, often called *Liber ymaginum deorum* [Book of the Likenesses of the Gods], analyzes these figures for their allegorical meanings, but, like Fulgentius, the Third Vatican Mythographer stresses the father's fear and sadness as the motivation to idolatry, which John Ridewall, in his use of the same fable (of Cirophanes the Lacedomonian), will later define as a movement toward sin.

An alternate view, one proclaimed by Porete, is that the reality of this image making is not the construction of a false God; it is the immanence of God's love in humanity and also the likenesses of God through words that humans create to recall Him to the present. For Porete, her equivalent of Syrophanes exemplifies the truth of love and its images—and therefore functions antithetically to that reason so celebrated by clergy as a natural faculty. Porete's "Exemplum" describes a king's daughter who falls in love with the idea of the nobility of King Alexander (Alexander the Great),[52] whom she has never met, and attempts to console herself by creating an image of him as she imagines him. This allows her to dream of the king—to fantasize. Like the earlier male mythographers, Porete describes the ancients' etiology of idolatry out of sadness and longing, but with a signal gender difference. Her fiction—*exemple*—involves a female protagonist, rather than a male grieving father, and a romantic infatuation expressed not by a male courtly lover but by the female beloved, with an allowance both for the existence of female subjectivity and the importance of the faculty of imagination. There is no dead son but instead a distant lover; it is geographical separation and not death that causes the image making.

Porete iconoclastically invokes the fable of Syrophanes to make, and then break, an explicit connection with scholastic exegesis, clerical obeisance to rationality, and patrilineal nobility. Note Porete's inversions of this masculinized tribute to genealogy and male lineage, on the one

hand, and figuration and exegesis, on the other. In chapter 1 (the prologue), Porete's Love relays an exemplum of love in the world as a "parallel to divine love" (Babinsky, *Mirror*, 80): "Et quant elle vit que ceste
amour loingtaigne, qui luy estoit si prouchaine ou dedans d'elle, estoit si
loing dehors, elle se pensa que elle conforteroit sa masaise par *ymaginacion
d'aucune figure* de son amy dont elle estoit souvent au cueur navree"
(Guarnieri, *Mirouer*, 12 [chap.1, lines 25–28]) [When she saw that this
faraway love, who was so close within her, was so far outside of her,
she thought to herself that she would comfort her melancholy by
imagining some figure of her love, by whom she was continually
wounded in heart] (Babinsky, *Mirror*, 80, my emphasis). Most importantly,
Porete celebrates the Aristotelian faculty of imagination, or the capacity
to imagine someone or something outside oneself as inside. The fiction
of the figure is itself truth.

For Porete it is indeed the imagination—not reason, the faculty
celebrated by Alan of Lille throughout *De planctu Naturae* as the sign of
human nature—that allows humans to begin the process of annihilation
of the will, to unite with God. So also *ymaginatio* in Aristotle's *De anima
et de potencies eius* transforms the image (*similitudo, ymago,* or *fantasma*) into
the thing itself, even if absent: "Ymaginatio vero convertit se super
similitudinem rei (que similitude dicitur ydolum vel fantasma) tanquam
super rem; et recepit eam a sensu communi et servat eam etiam in absen-
cia rei" [Imagination in truth transforms itself into the likeness of a thing
(and this is called *ydolum*, idol, or *fantasma*, phantasm), just as if into the
thing; and receives it from a common understanding and preserves it,
even in the absence of the thing].[53] Porete informs us in the gloss on the
exemplum that immediately follows that Ame (Soul)—the very soul of
the woman who had this book written (herself)—identifies the noble
king as God and her book, "qui represente en aucuns usages l'amour de
lui mesmes" [which makes present in some fashion His love itself], as His
image, even though she does not reside in a strange land far from His
friends (Guarnieri, *Mirouer*, 12 [1.39–40]; Babinsky, *Mirror*, 80–81). In the
person of the Author, Porete tells us directly that "Amour l'est de lui pour
nous" [Love is from Him for us], and apparently without sin, "car Amour
peut tout faire sans a nully meffaire" [for Love can do everything without
any misdeed] (Guarnieri, *Mirouer*, 14 [1.46–48] Babinsky, *Mirror*, 81).

Porete's FarNear, by definition, is that which is far away but appears
near. Accordingly, Reason in her *Mirror of Simple Souls* cannot understand FarNear, that is, God within the Soul, or anything beyond the
boundaries of rationality, in contradiction to Hugh's claim above. The

affective mood of love (as we learn from the beginning exemplum of King Alexander)[54] coupled with the imagination, or the Intellect of the Soul (what Porete calls *engin* [*ingenium*]), and understanding, as the Height of the Soul (*cognissance*), motors the Soul into the seven states of being during Porete's allegorical journey.[55] Where Reason as a student of Love appears to be dense, ineducable and incorrigible,[56] Love in Porete soars, again, in contrast to Hugh's role for the suggestive glimpses of the imagination. Hugh declares that the third power of the soul—the rational—

> ...non solum sensus imaginationesque perfectas et non inconditas capit, sed etiam pleno actu intelligentiae, quod imaginatio suggessit, explicat atque confirmat. Itaque, ut dictum est, huic divinae naturae non ea tantum in cognitione sufficiunt, quae subiecta sensibus comprehendit, verum etiam ex sensibilibus imaginatione concepta, et absentibus rebus nomina indere potest, et quod intelligentiae ratione comprehendit, vocabulorum quoque positionibus aperit.

> [...not only takes in sense impressions and images which are perfect and well founded, but, by a complete act of the understanding, it explains and confirms what imagination has only suggested. And, as has been said, this divine nature is not content with the knowledge of those things alone which it perceives spread before its senses, but, in addition, it is able to provide even for things removed from it names which imagination has conceived from the sensible world, and it makes known, by arrangements of words, what it has grasped by reason of its understanding.][57]

Where Porete substitutes the faculty of imagination for reason, Hugh substitutes the faculty of reason for imagination.

We have not yet examined in detail the rigidity and lack of educability in Porete's Reason, which is dramatically central to her narrative and epistemologically central to her theology. In this dialogue, Reason (unlike persona Boethius and Hugh of St. Victor's faculty in the passage just cited) cannot grasp love or the imagination. By Reason Porete means the agent of Church the Little, the clergy, and Scripture, who functions as a suspicious inquisitor of Love and the Soul. By Love, Porete means both God and the Holy Spirit that succors the Soul in her spiritual and intellectual journey to the joys of annihilation, or a form of dematerialization very modern in its description.

The Death of Clerical Reason

Reason as cloaked in the fiction of the magister and cleric, the university and the church, manifests a stultifying literalness, ridigity, and rudeness throughout the dialogue, whether she speaks with Love or the Soul. Only gradually does Reason's obtuseness dawn upon the Soul, at which point she is annihilated. Given the literalness of Reason, Porete structures the debate in the *Mirror* by necessity as a *disputatio*, with questions and answers, but the very being of Reason itself frustrates Love, which demands a logic based on faith.

Briefly let us indicate examples of Reason's rigidity and her incapability of understanding the contradictions of Love and Faith. In chapter 11 alone, nine times Reason responds to Love's statements with almost exactly the same words, "Hee, pour Dieu,...qu'est ce a dire?" (Guarnieri, *Mirouer*, 40 [11.30, 43–44, 53, 64, etc.]) [For God's sake!...what can that mean?] (Babinsky, *Mirror*, 89–92). Love is the magister educating Reason, but it is Reason whose determined, even arrogant, obtuseness demands further elaboration, so unlike the respectful question and answer format of medieval educational colloquies or even Boethius's *Consolation of Philosophy*. By these reiterations Porete illustrates that reason is limited in understanding both faith and love, following the Augustinian dictum "credo ut intelligam." Of course the character Reason's density and interminable questions also allow Porete to define in greater detail what she means by the concept and character of "Love." When Reason validly and logically questions the ninth point made by Love in chapter 11—that the unencumbered Soul has no will, Love answers with a series of causal relationships beyond logic:

> "Car toute ce que ceste Ame veult en consentement, c'est ce que Dieu vieult qu'elle vueille, et ce veult elle pour la voulenté de Dieu acomplir, non mie pour la sienne voulenté; et elle ne peut ce vouloir d'elle, mais c'est le vouloir de Dieu qui le vieult en elle; par quoy il appert que ceste Ame n'a point de voulenté, sans la volunté de Dieu, qui luy fait vouloir tout ce qu'elle doit vouloir." (Guarnieri, *Mirouer*, 48 [11.161–67])

> [Because all that this Soul wills in consent is what God wills that she will, and this she wills in order to accomplish the will of God, no longer for the sake of her own will. And she cannot will this by herself, but it is the will of God which wills it in her. Which is why it appears that this Soul has no will without the will of God, who makes her will all that she ought to will]. (Babinsky, *Mirror*, 92)

The Soul eventually realizes Reason's deficiency after an excursus by Love in what Porete rather ironically terms *fine amour*, given its usual association with courtly love, here presented more closely to the Song of Songs paradigm. Initially, Love explains to Reason that it is through divine grace that the Soul possesses God, which means all things, or nothing, because the gift of divine grace appears as nothing to the Soul in comparison to what she loves in God: "Ceste Ame a tout et si n'a nient, elle scet tout et si ne scet nient" (Guarnieri, *Mirouer*, 60 [13.92]) [this Soul possesses all and so possesses nothing, she knows all and so knows nothing] (Babinsky, *Mirror*, 96). The courtly metaphor surfaces at one point in the exchange a little later, when the Soul declares that "rien ne me fault, puisque *mon amy* a assez en luy de *sa droicte noblesse* sans commancement, et aura sans fin" (Guarnieri, 106 [32.7–8]) [nothing is lacking to me since *my Lover* possesses in Himself sufficiency of His *righteous nobility* without beginning, and will have it without end] (Babinsky, 113; my emphasis). The Soul employs the metaphor to suggest that whatever God has is more hers than what she possesses, or what she has "en possession de luy mesmes" [in possession of Him] (Guarnieri, *Mirouer*, 106 [32.12]; Babinsky, *Mirror*, 113).[58]

To this assertion, Reason replies, "Prouvez ce" [Prove it], a task the Soul takes up easily through an apparent logical (but in reality, ironic) syllogism in relation to God's goodness and understanding and her love. What the Soul loves in God but does not understand is a hundred thousand times better than the gifts from Him or what she understands in her intellect. Thus, that which she loves in God but does not understand is more hers than what she has and understands, making the greater part of her love a greater part of her treasure, and Him more hers (Guarnieri, *Mirouer*, 106 [32.14–25]; Babinsky, *Mirror*, 113). The syllogism is actually predicated on the part and the whole—the part being her lack of understanding and the whole being God's perfect understanding—which is, ironically, hers through her love (the part receiving the whole, or becoming part of the whole). Eventually the Soul herself tires of Reason's stupidity: when Reason once more demands "Prove it," the Soul replies, "Hee, Raison. . .comme vous estes ennuyeuse, et que ceulx ont de mal et de paine, qui vivent de vostre conseil!" (Guarnieri, *Mirouer*, 114 [35.25–27]) [Ah, Reason. . .how tedious you are, and those have pain and suffering who live in your counsel!] (Babinsky, *Mirror*, 116). The Soul also tells Reason to be quiet "avant de vous mesler de moy" (Guarnieri, *Mirouer*, 116 [35.39–40]) [before you tangle with me further] (Babinsky, *Mirror*, 116). And, therefore, Reason, seeing Love guiding the Soul, gives up contradiction and debate with her and promises obedience.

The need for Reason's demise is triggered by the Soul's recognition of Reason's true nature as both rude and petty. After the Soul has united with God, she sees Reason clearly: "O tres petite gent et rude et mal convenable" (Guarnieri, *Mirouer*, 192 [68.9–10]) [O very small person, rude and poorly behaved] (Babinsky, *Mirror*, 143). The insensitive, dense Reason replies, "A qui parlez vous?" And the Soul, finally overcome by Reason's slow-wittedness and the need to speak in a language not her own in order to be understood, tells her in a great outburst the truth about the person to whom she is speaking:

> A tous ceulx. . .qui de vostre conseil vivent, qui sont si bestes et si asnes que il m'esconvient pour la rudesse d'eulx celer et non parler mon langage, ad ce qu'ilz ne prengnent mort en l'estre de vie, la ou je suis en paix, sans de la me mouvoir. Je di. . .qu'il m'esconvient pour leur rudesse taire et celer mon langage, lequel j'ay aprins es secrez de la court secrete du doulx pays, ouquell pays, courtoisie est loy, et amour mesure, et bonté pasture. (Guarnieri, *Mirouer*, 192 [chap. 68, lines 12–19])

> [To all thosee. . .who live by your counsel, who are such beasts and donkeys that on account of their rudeness I must hide from them and not speak my language to those who prefer death to the being of life where I am in peace without moving myself. I say. . .that on account of their rudeness I must be silent and hide my language, which I learned in the secrets at the secret court of the sweet country, in which country courtesy is law, and Love moderates, and Goodness is the nourishment.] (Babinsky, *Mirror*, 143)

By chapter 84, when the Unencumbered Soul finds sovereignty, L'Ame Esbahie de Nient Penser (the Astonished Soul in Pondering Nothing) relinquishes Reason and her limitations and accepts her death. Because Astonished Soul in Pondering Nothing believes that God has guarded her so that the disciples of Reason do not provide counsel to her, in addition to which she is no longer interested in listening to their doctrines (even donkeys, she notes, would be unable to perform work of interest to the disciples, for the little minds of those who obey Reason cannot understand anything of great value) (Guarnieri, *Mirouer*, 240 [84.33–34]; Babinsky, *Mirror*, 159), she allows Reason to die at a mysterious moment. But it is Reason herself who swoons that "I have no more life," according to Marguerite, killed by the Soul with Love (Guarnieri, *Mirouer*, 246 [87.2–13]; Babinsky, *Mirror*, 163).

Reason dies because she is incapable of understanding the Soul's identification with Love, or God, and, therefore, her eternal being. The Soul declares, "Mais je suis. . .et suis et seray tousjours sans faillir, car Amour n'a commencement ne fin de comprennement, et je ne suis, fors que Amour" (Guarnieri, *Mirouer*, 246 [84.34–36]) [But I was, ...and I am, and I will be always without lack, for Love has no beginning, no end, and no limit, and I am nothing except Love] (Babinsky, *Mirror*, 162). Once Reason dies, Love asks the questions that Reason might have, wanting to know "qui est mere d'elle," who "mothered" Reason, and those Virtues "d'elle germaines," of Reason's generation, and "se elles sont meres," whom they "mothered" (Guarnieri, *Mirouer*, 248 [88.5–7]; Babinsky, *Mirror*, 163). The answers that Love supplies clarify the female genealogy of this "family": the Virtues mother holiness, but Humility mothers the Virtues. In celebration, the Soul sings a song about this maternal genealogy: Divine majesty has mothered Humility, as she herself is "daughter" of Deity (Guarnieri, *Mirouer*, 248 [chap. 88]; Babinsky, *Mirror*, 164).

Once the significance of this key gendered event of Reason's death in the allegorical narrative and its fabulous embellishment are emphasized, it becomes clear how society and the church might be changed, as if created anew, with a fresh nobility, heritage, and genealogy to rule and a Holy Church the Great to lead and inspire. All depends on recognizing that it is arrogant and obtuse Reason who should be condemned, not the Soul while it is embodied in the flesh—a feminized concept that Porete shares with the fifteenth-century Julian of Norwich. The extent of Reason's limitation and Love's transcendence of all limits emerges from Porete's scholastic trope that dramatizes the former as puer/puella and the latter as true magister. Theologically, through her rejection of Reason and her apotheosis of Love as the Holy Spirit, Porete responds to the scholastic and ecclesiastical milieu of her day. And she does so through the deployment of the literary and the ironic.

Tropes of Inversion in Education and Class

Porete's Annihilated Soul rejects the hierarchical, epistemological, and scholastic trappings of the institution of the church, as symbolized by Reason; so also Holy Church the Great rejects the material trappings of the aristocracy: castle and manor, court and courtly behavior, and nobility of lineage, as symbolized by the practice of what Porete calls Fine Amour. Annihilated Soul's rejection is signaled by inversions of actual social and ecclesiastical practice in both symbolizations. We examine these two microcosmic and macrocosmic allegories one at a time.

The interesting gendered role-reversal—of the Soul instructing Reason—is highlighted as a scholastic inversion of the usual relation between magister and pupil at a time in her journey when the Soul is unencumbered. Scholastic (reading, writing) metaphors surface occasionally to describe the school of Love, especially after the Soul's preliminary tutelage by Reason and the Virtues and her switch to "lessons" from the Holy Spirit and Love. The annihilated life (of the Unencumbered Soul) does not depend on a magisterial or sacerdotal intermediary: "elle ne quiert pas la science divine entre les *maistres* de ce siecle, mais en vrayement despriser le monde et elle mesmes" (Guarnieri, Mirouer, 20 [chap. 5, lines 21–23], my emphasis) [she does not seek divine knowledge among the *masters* of this age, but in truly despising the world and herself] (Babinsky, Mirror, 83). In Porete's "university" of the Unencumbered Soul, Love educates with her special glosses on an aristocracy of Souls. Love tells Reason, for example, that what has given the Soul the most joy is leaving behind Reason and the works of the Virtues in the school where lessons are conducted with closed mouth and written on the parchment of the Soul: "Car quant ceste Ame fut en amour *enmantellee*, que elle print *leçon a vostre escole* par desirer des oeuvres des Vertuz. Or est elle maintenant si entree et seurmontée en *divine leçon*, que elle commence a lire la ou vous prenez vostre fin; mais ceste *leçon* n'est mie mise *en escript* de main d'omme, mais c'est du Saint Esperit, qui *escript ceste leçon* merveilleusement, et l'Ame est *parchemin precieusement*; la est tenue *la divine escole*, a bouche close, que sens humain ne peut mectre en parole" (Guarnieri, *Mirouer*, 188, 190 [66.11–19]) [For as long as this Soul was *cloaked* {like a school boy?} in love, she took *lessons in your school* through desire of the works of the Virtues. Now she has entered upon and is so surpassing in *divine learning* that she begins to *read* where you take your end. But this *lesson* is not placed in *writing* by human hand, but by the Holy Spirit, who *writes this lesson* in a marvelous way, and the Soul is the *precious parchment*. The *divine school* is held with the mouth closed, which the human mind cannot express in words] (Babinsky, *Mirror*, 142; my emphasis). When Reason asks the Soul who guides her, the Soul replies, God alone, "about whom the *teaching* [la doctrine] is not written, neither by the works of exemplars [pars oeuvres d'exemples] or by teachings of men [pars doctrine de hommes], for His gift cannot be given form" (Guarnieri, *Mirouer*, 194 [69.23–25]; Babinsky, *Mirror*, 144; my emphasis).

Ironically, Reason at one point seeks clarification of "ce motz couvers" [the hidden meanings] mentioned by the character Fine Amour (Fine Love)—ironically, because the exegetes in the universities have been trained to gloss hidden meanings, and here the inversion is that Reason must beg the Soul to explain those of Fine Amour (Guarnieri, *Mirouer*, chap. 53, Babinsky, *Mirror*, 131). The Soul, in exasperation, laments that Reason would not understand even if someone should tell her; all of her queries instead "ont honny <et> gasté. . .ce livre. . .et vos demandes l'ont fait long pour les responces dont vous avez besoing, pour vous et pour ceulx que vous avez nourriz, qui vont le cours du lymaçon. Vous l'avez ouvert a ceulx de vostre mesgnee qui vont le cours du lymaçon" (Guarnieri, *Mirouer*, 156 [53.11–15]) [have dishonored and ruined this book. . . .But your questions have made it long because of the answers you need, both for yourself and for those whom you nourish who move along at a snail's pace. You have revealed this book to those in your domain who move along at a snail's pace] (Babinsky, *Mirror*, 131). When the Soul calls those who believe in Reason cattle and donkeys, namely, because of their insistence on the priority of human institutions and writings, she explains: "Telz gens. . .que je appelle asnes, quierent Dieu es creatures, es monstiers par aourer, en paradis creez, en paroles d'ommes, et es escriptures. . . .Il semble aux novices que telx gens, qui ainsi le quierent par montaignes et par vallees, tiennent que Dieu soit subgect a ses sacramens et a ses oeuvres" (Guarnieri, *Mirouer*, 194, 196 [69.35–37, 41–43]) [Such folk. . .,whom I call donkeys, seek God in creatures, in monasteries for prayer, in a created paradise, in words of men and in the Scriptures. . . .It seems to the novices that such folk, who seek Him on the mountains and in the valleys, insist that God be subject to their sacraments and their works] (Babinsky, *Mirror*, 144). When Reason asks the Soul where she finds God, the Soul replies that she finds Him everywhere—indistinctly and imprecisely, "La" [There] (Guarnieri, *Mirouer*, 196 [69.53]; Babinsky, *Mirror*, 145).

Another invocation of scholastic logical terminology occurs through the metaphor of the gloss, or Love's own hermeneutical explanations of scriptural figures. When Reason—assuming the name of the Soul should be grand and important—asks why Love has called her by such a "small" name, Love replies that it is because of Reason's rudeness that she has used the Soul's surname many times: "Et pource que on entend *la glose par surnom*, nous nous en somez aidez et encore ferons; mais son droit nom est *parfaictement noble*. Elle a nom 'pure,' 'celestielle,' et 'espouse de paix' " (Guarnieri, *Mirouer*, 206 [74.6–9]) [And because one understands the *gloss by means of a category*, we will be helped by it, and so let us proceed—but {Soul's} right name is *perfectly noble*. She has the name "pure," "celestial," and "spouse of peace"] (Babinsky, *Mirror*, 148; my emphasis). As does any homilist or glossator, Love also compares the Soul to scriptural figural antecedents—to peaceful Mary rather than her sister Martha, who is troubled by "ses empeschemens"

(Guarnieri, *Mirouer*, 208 [74.19]) [her impediments] (Babinsky, *Mirror*, 149). Love chastises the recalcitrant students Encumbered Soul and Reason to heed the gloss at the moment that Reason asks when one in need—the Encumbered Soil—will be aided, if not at the time of need: "[E]ntendez, dit Amour, *la glose* de ce livre" (Guarnieri, *Mirouer*, 216 [77.45]) [give attention, says Love, to the *gloss* on this book] (Babinsky, *Mirror*, 151; my emphasis). When Love needed the Encumbered Soul, that is, commanded the Encumbered Soul, unfortunately, both Reason and the Soul refused her request.

Porete's symbol of her book as wisdom and her pedagogical imagery continue during the phase when the Soul becomes unencumbered by the will. When Love transforms the Soul, Love commands the "auditeurs de ce livre" to "Entendez *la glose*" [grasp the *gloss*] (the "sense," the "meaning"; an imperative repeated several times in this section of the dialogue) because "le grain y est, qui l'espouse nourrist" [the kernel is there which nourishes the bride {i.e., the Soul}] (Guarnieri, *Mirouer*, 234 [82.33–34]; Babinsky, *Mirror*, 158; my emphasis). A reference to the long-standing image of the nut as a useless outer shell of fiction combined with the important inner meat of truth—derived from Augustine in *De doctrina christiana* and repeated later by Julian of Norwich—the "savory" kernel, because it is nourishing, signifies "Il est de luy en luy pour elle ce mesmes" [Himself in her for her sake this same One], a state in which the Soul loses her name but acquires "sovereignty" (Guarnieri, *Mirouer*, 238, 234 [84.26; 82.30–31]; Babinsky, *Mirror*, 159, 158).[59]

Porete also uses the "book" as an image of authority and authorship, signifying a reference as if to the Bible or any other magisterial source. When the Annihilated Soul, teaching resurrected Reason close to the end of Porete's vision, tells her she has done everything, she means "des le temps. . .que Amour me ouvrit son livre" (Guarnieri, *Mirouer*, 278 [101.18–19]) [since the time. . .that Love opened her book to me] (Babinsky, *Mirror*, 174). A book imbued with love by Love, it is magical: when Love opened it, the Soul "scet tout, et si a tout, et si est toute oeuvre de parfection en elle emplie par l'ouverture de ce livre" (Guarnieri, *Mirouer*, 278 [101.20–21]) [knew all things, and so possesses all things, and so every work of perfection is fulfilled in her through the opening of this book] (Babinsky, *Mirror*, 174). Porete also describes light emanating from the opening of the book, and righteousness—that which has given what is hers back to her and shown her what she is not—as "*enscript* en my le milieu de *livre*" (Guarnieri, *Mirouer*, 278

[101.25–27, 30]) [*written* in the marrow of the *book* of life] (Babinsky, *Mirror*, 174–75; my emphasis). The book is at once divine and human, like the Annihilated Soul.

The second macrocosmic inversion, of class, Porete employs also to show that in the Holy Church the Great the Soul does not serve the Virtues or Reason (a point hammered repeatedly through the denigration of Reason first by Love and then by the Soul). Reason taught the Soul to obey the Virtues until death; those who obey the Virtues through mortification of the body in charity work and belief in death by martyrdom, through prayers, and through enhancing good will are happy but lost: "called kings [*roys*], but they are in a country where everyone is one-eyed [*bourgne*]. But without fail, those who have two eyes consider them to be servants [*sers*]" (Guarnieri, *Mirouer*, 160 [chap. 55, lines 20–22]; Babinsky, *Mirror*, 132; my emphasis). After the Soul has learned so much from the Virtues (*Vertuz*), she then has within her the "maistresse des Vertuz" (mistress of the Virtues), Divine Amour (Divine Love), who entirely transforms her (Guarnieri, *Mirouer*, 80 [chap. 21, line 35]; Babinsky, *Mirror*, 104).

Through such metaphors Porete establishes a spiritual nobility for her Annihilated Souls (a nobility in no way predestined) and suggests grace from God without the church's mediation (a most dangerous transgression). Like no other definition of nobility in the Middle Ages—a point argued in Robinson's recent book—Porete's concept of nobility is, however, neither arrogant, elitist, or expressive of "hauteur," as some critics who have read the metaphors associated with it as literal have indicated.[60] Indeed, such superior spirituality evolves from the abandonment of desire and human will and from absolute humility. In the country of God the Father and the Trinity, where the Soul lives after departing from Reason, nobility is the metaphorical class of the Annihilated Soul (Guarnieri, *Mirouer*, 190 [67]; Babinsky, *Mirror*, 143). Porete nowhere states that nobility is equivalent to literal lineage, class, or wealth but, instead, it depends upon the metaphor for this state of spiritual evolution as "nobility." Strictly speaking, nobility signifies superior spirituality that depends, ironically, on absolute nothingness, emptiness, complete abandonment of all material concerns. This nobility, like that of the Intellect of the Annihilated Soul, is a true nobility of spirit untied to anything Dante or Chaucer would recognize because it reflects only inspiration by divine Love: when the Soul is opened by "l'aprouchement de son oeuvre" [the approach of His work], which is noble, she becomes annihilated (Guarnieri, *Mirouer*, 172 [59.16]; Babinsky, *Mirror*, 136).

The Mirror of Simple Souls, despite its bridal imagery, is a philosophical and theological treatise illustrating the freeing of the Soul from Reason and Will rather than a mystical treatise tracing the union of God and the female self.[61] The latter appears more usually to reflect *Bräutmystik*, or "bridal" mysticism, dependent on the erotic language of the Song of Songs as a celebration of the union of God and creature as different beings.[62] This freeing is couched in a class metaphor that subsumes the bridal relationship of Soul with Love: the Soul acknowledges that "*la noblesse de la courtoysie* de mon espoux ne me daigneroit plus lesser en vostre *servaige*, ne en celluy d'aultruy; car aussi il es convient que *l'espoux* afranchisse *l'espouse*, laquelle il a prinse de sa voulenté*" (Guarnieri, *Mirouer*, 116 [36.4–11]) [*the nobility of the courtesy* of my *Spouse* would not deign any longer to leave me in {Reason's} service, nor in that of any other. For it is necessary that the *Bridegroom* should free the *bride* whom He has taken by His Will] (Babinsky, *Mirror*, 117; my emphasis).

Porete is fond of using feudal and chivalric metaphors to differentiate the Annihilated from the Lost and Sad Souls. For example, Annihilated Souls are addressed through a feudal metaphor as "tres noble gent" [you most noble ones] and "amye chere" [dear love] and "heritiere" [heir apparent] to God the Father's "royaulme" [realm] (Guarnieri, *Mirouer*, 174 [60.14–15]; Babinsky, *Mirror*, 137). According to the Personne de Dieu de Père, the Unencumbered Soul is the heir apparent because she knows the Son's secrets through Love from the Holy Spirit (Guarnieri, *Mirouer*, 150 [50.21]; Babinsky, *Mirror*, 128). Love demands, "Or entendez par *noblesse l'entendement* de la *glose*" (Guarnieri, *Mirouer*, 224 [79.42]) [Now grasp the *gloss* through *nobility of intellect*] (Babinsky, *Mirror*, 154; my emphasis). If the Unencumbered Soul is aristocratic and noble, suggestive of divine Love, then the weakness and rudeness of peasantry— linked with the encumbered, lost Souls—are characteristic of selfishness and willfulness: "Fut il oncques foible, dit Amour, ne encombré de luy mesmes?" (Guarnieri, *Mirouer*, 224 [79.45–46]) [Would one ever be weak, says Love, who was not encumbered with himself?] (Babinsky, *Mirror*, 154).

The nature of the "sovereignty" attained by the Unencumbered Soul is summed up through the appropriation of gendered social class as a metaphor for spiritual status. Four aspects befit a "noble homme, ains qu'il puisse estre gentilz homs appellé et ainsi est il a l'entendement espirituel" (Guarnieri, *Mirouer*, 232 [82.5–6]) [noble person before he might be called a gentleman and thus of a spiritual intellect] (Babinsky,

Mirror, 157). These are, first, the Soul's complete lack of reproach; second, her lack of will; third, her complete inferiority and simultaneous superior belovedness by the One; and, fourth, the goodness of God's will, in which her will inheres (Guarnieri, *Mirouer*, 232 [82]; Babinsky, *Mirror*, 157). The Annihilated Soul is "franche et plus franche et tres franche" [free, yet more free, yet very free], as determined by her license to respond, or not to respond, to any other being if he "n'est de *son lignage*" [is not of *her lineage*] (Guarnieri, *Mirouer*, 240 [85.3–5]; Babinsky, *Mirror*, 160; my emphasis).

The class analogy Porete employs as a metaphor for *estres* depends upon social difference between knight and peasant, as demonstrated by chivalry, gentility, and appropriate decorum: "ung gentilhomme ne daigneroit respondre a ung vilain, se il l'appelloit ou requeroit de champ de bataille" (Guarnieri, *Mirouer*, 240, 242 [85.8–10]) [a gentleman would not deign to respond to a peasant, even if such a one would call him or attack him in a battlefield] (Babinsky, *Mirror*, 160). Therefore, the Soul does not need to respond to her enemies. The kind of nobility the Soul increasingly manifests comes through in prosperity, adversity, and all places "quelx qu'ilz soient" (Guarnieri, *Mirouer*, 242 [85.19]) [whatever they might be] (Babinsky, *Mirror*, 160). The Ame Franche (Unencumbered Soul) in the description of the first estate uses language that describes her as a brave knight who desires to search for God: "Or ne se esmaye nul de venir au plus hault; non fera, se il a le cueur gentil, et par dedans plain de noble courage; mais petit cueur n'ose grant chose entreprendre, ne hault monter par deffaulte d'amour. Telz gens sont si couars" (Guarnieri, *Mirouer*, 318 [118.19–21]) [Now no one should be afraid to come higher. And one will not be afraid if he has a gentle heart and is full of noble courage. But a petty heart dares not to undertake a great thing or to climb high, because of a lack of love. Such folk are so cowardly] (Babinsky, *Mirror*, 189).

Porete occasionally also employs a castle metaphor, invoking a whole context of the court and courtly behavior to invert it as an ideal. She will speak of the courtesy of the Soul and the antithetical rudeness of Reason (linked usually with clergy), or she will identify the Soul as a courtly lover wooing the Beloved, the Holy Spirit. Porete even calls the form of higher love that the Soul experiences Fine Amour, the exact name for courtly love in the secular romances. But in Porete it is the class allegory of Fine Amour that she instantiates: note Love's egalitarian socioeconomic response to Reason in chapter 13: "telles Ames, lesquelles *Fine Amour* demaine, ont aussi cher honte comme honneur, et honneur comme honte, et pouvreté comme richisse, et richesse comme pouvreté. . .et petit estat comme grant, et grant estat comme petit, pour elles ne pour leurs personnes" (Guarnieri, *Mirouer*, 58 [13.57–65], my emphasis) [such Souls, whom *Fine Love* governs, possess as equally dear, shame as honor, and honor as shame; poverty as wealth, and wealth as poverty; . . .and in small estate as in great, and great estate as small: [this] for themselves and for their station in life] (Babinsky, *Mirror*, 95, my emphasis).

In both instances of symbolic inversion, microcosmic and macrocosmic, Porete depends on irony of tone to convey her implicit meaning. When Love praises the Annihilated Soul, Love describes her as a "tres bien nee" [very highborn one] and a "precieuse marguerite" [precious pearl] (a pun on Porete's first name): "bien soiez vous entree ou seul *franc manoir*, ouquel nul ne entre se il n'est de vostre *lygnage*, sans *bastardise*" (Guarnieri, *Mirouer*, 152 [52.1, 2–5]) [it is well that you have entered the only *noble manor*, where no one enters if he is not your *lineage* and without *bastardy*] (Babinsky, *Mirror*, 129; my emphasis). Obviously the Soul is none of these things, nor is her new residence anything as exceptional as a noble manor. In contrast, according to the Unencumbered Soul, a view echoed by Desire, those who have passed just the first state and are dead to mortal sin are "petis en terre et tres petis en ciel, et *mal courtoisement* se sauvent" (Guarnieri, *Mirouer*, 180 [62.18–19]) [little on earth and very little in heaven and are saved in an *uncourtly* way] (Babinsky, *Mirror*, 139, 140; my emphasis). The little souls are then described by the Soul and Love as "villains" [peasants], who are "tellement pour eulx" [exceedingly selfish] because of their rudeness, a "grant villanie" [great crudity]; they are like merchants whom the world calls *villains* [crude] (Guarnieri, *Mirouer*, 182 [63.4, 8–9]; Babinsky, *Mirror*, 140). A "gentilz hons" [gentleman], say the Soul and Love, "does not know how to mingle in the marketplace or how to be selfish" (Guarnieri, *Mirouer*, 182 [63.10–11]; Babinsky, 140). For this reason the little souls are kept out of the "court" of Lady Love as if they are peasants who cannot join "la court d'ung gentil homme" [a gentleman's court] or the "court de roy" [king's court] without proper "lignage" (Guarnieri, *Mirouer*, 182 [63.12–15, 18–20]; Babinsky, *Mirror*, 140). In a direct but ironic echo of the assault and rape scene in the *Rose*, Love comforts Reason by telling her that once the Soul has arrived at the death of the life of the spirit and led the divine life, Reason, along with Modesty and Fear, will serve as "garde de sa porte" [guardians of the gate] so that any enemy of Love who attacks her lodging will be dispelled (Guarnieri, *Mirouer*, 186 [65.20]; Babinsky, *Mirror*, 141). The underlying and implicit analogy to the *Rose* offers a stronghold recognizably feminized.

Conclusion: The Value of Being Nothing

If we now return to the two articles singled out for theological condemnation by Porete's commission—the Annihilated Soul while on earth requiring neither the Virtues nor God's gifts because the Virtues obey the Soul and because the Soul relies on its own resources to confront God—we recall the implications that seem to be so heretical, namely, the repudiation of the corporal presence of original sin and the possibility of unification of the Soul with God while on earth without sacerdotal intermediary. Porete clearly demonstrates through magisterial and class metaphors that the true church on earth is her Holy Church the Great, not the literal Holy Church the Little, and that the individual Soul will find a true home through the former rather than the latter by rejecting the agency of Reason and the clerical apparatus of that Holy Church the Little. In this last section, Porete imagines as a consequence of her soul's journey to annihilation a means also of stripping the soul of original sin not far removed from the state of grace that exists after the administration of the sacraments.

Late in Porete's work, the Unencumbered Soul presents two fantastic petitions. The force of both the petitions presents Porete's Soul as being able to strip away original sin in a theology that begins before the Fall of Adam and Eve. The Soul's first petition is to see herself in the state in which she existed at the moment God made the Creation (Guarnieri, Mirourer, 290 [107.2–7]; Babinsky, *Mirror*, 179). (As Babinsky's note clarifies, "This refers to the virtual existence of the soul as the nothing from which all things were made at creation."[63]) Second, the Unencumbered Soul wants to see how her free will is faring—to see if she has "a Dieu mesmes sa voulenté tollue, en ung seul moment de consentement de peché" (Guarnieri, *Mirourer*, 290, 292 [107.10–11]) [removed her will from God Himself in one sole moment of consent to sin] (Babinsky, *Mirror*, 179).

Porete, through her doctrine of the Annihilated Soul and having annihilated Reason, participates in a newly developing, feminized theological and literary tradition that rejects the doctrine of original sin as demeaning to women. Porete recasts the so-called Fall of humankind through Eve and the first Disobedience through the annihilation of original sin, which creates the possibility of a fresh start for a female soul whose will has been given over to God.[64] Although Eve is not mentioned anywhere in *The Mirror*, Porete begins the Soul's journey to perfection at the point in the first state that her Soul is touched by grace in "the land of life," having been "removed from sin." The removal of sin from humanity opens the door to human—and female—divinity.

This most radical of all of Marguerite Porete's concepts concerns the divinity of humanity as expressed through the Trinity.[65] Her argument consists of a series of equations: God the Father joins human nature to the Son, God the Son joins human nature to the person of God Himself, and God the Holy Spirit joins human nature to God the Son. Then comes the spiritual syllogism: if God has a single divine nature, if the Son has three natures—divine, corporeal, and spiritual—and if the Trinity in one person has both the One (God the Father) and also, as the Trinity, the three (human) natures, then God shares in humanity, as human nature must share in divinity (Guarnieri, *Mirouer*, 60, 62 [chap. 14]; Babinsky, *Mirror*, 96). Further, says Porete, through Love, "Je suis Dieu. . .car Amour est Dieu, et Dieu est amour, et ceste Ame est Dieu par condicion d'amour, et je suis Dieu par nature divine, et ceste Ame l'est par droicture d'amour" (Guarnieri, *Mirouer*, 82 [21.44–47]) [I am God. . .for Love is God and God is Love, and this Soul is God by the condition of Love. I am God by divine nature and this Soul is God by righteousness of Love] (Babinsky, *Mirror*, 104).

In addition, Porete clarifies the stainlessness of the Encumbered Soul (who cannot release her will) through the example of Mary Magdalene, the repentant sinner, who was dishonored only by those who condemned her in the desert when she was "sourprinse, prinse, et emprense" (Guarnieri, *Mirouer*, 210 [76.11]) [overtaken, captured, and filled] (Babinsky, *Mirror*, 150). In this regard, it is interesting to note that the only manuscript now accessible—one of only two extant French manuscripts of *Mirouer*—was owned by a chapter of the Magdalenes in Orléans.[66] Considered by the beguines to be Mary, the sister of Martha, Magdalene for Porete attained a level of spiritual nobility that cannot be taken from her because—according to Jesus—she has "chosen the better part" (Luke 10:38–42).[67] But Mary and Martha also serve to type the contrast between the Encumbered and the Unencumbered Souls: Reason admires Magdalene when she seeks Jesus Christ through desire of will; after Love overtakes and annihilates her in the desert, she lives by divine life (Guarnieri, *Mirouer*, 260 [93.5–11]; Babinsky, *Mirror*, 168). Similar to this parable about Magdalene is Porete's story about a "mendicant creature" told by the Soul to the Trinity (Guarnieri, *Mirouer*, 266 [96]; Babinsky, *Mirror*, 170–71), discussed above. Further, the Annihilated Soul is able to give up her will, which relieves her of sinfulness: she "plante si nuement sa voulenté, que elle ne peut pecher, se elle ne se desplante. Elle n'a de quoy pecher, car sans voulenté nul ne peut pecher. Or elle n'a garde de pecher, se elle lesse sa voulenté la ou elle este plantee, c'est en celluy qui la luy avoit donnee de sa bonté franchement" (Guarnieri, *Mirouer*, 252 [89.4–10]) [plants her will so nakedly that she cannot sin if she does not uproot herself. She has nothing to sin with, for without a will no one can sin. Now she is kept from sin if she leaves her will there where it is planted, that is, in the One who has given it to her freely from His goodness] (Babinsky, *Mirror*, 165).

Porete's concept of the divinity of humanity, radical because it cleanses the human soul from all sin and willfulness, knocks against the idea that the flesh contaminates because of original sin and that the soul's struggle with its innate sinfulness cannot end except with death. Because the will is created free, it must be continuously exercised to forestall the advent of sin; if it is abandoned (which is humanly impossible to do until death), one assumes that it cannot be considered free. Free will is a condition of human existence. But for Porete, God "luy donna sa bonté, dont il la fist dame. Ce fut Franche Voulenté, qu'il ne peut de luy ravoir sans le plaisir de l'Ame" (Guarnieri, *Mirouer*, 258 [91.17–18]) [gave {the Soul} His goodness by which He made her a *lady*. {This goodness} was Free Will, which He cannot take from her without the pleasure of the Soul] (Babinsky, *Mirror*, 167; my emphasis). Apparently, the part of God in humanity is free will, which the Soul can at the sixth and most noble state bestow upon Him once more, divesting herself of that "goodness" (the way it was before God made her a lady) (Guarnieri, *Mirouer*, 258 [91]; Babinsky, *Mirror*, 167). One apparently chooses the possibility of sinfulness or its annihilation in annihilation: "Tous ce mucent encore donc par le peché de Adam, fors ceulx qui sont adnientiz: ceulx cy n'ont que mucer" (Guarnieri, *Mirouer*, 264 [94.31–33]) [All still hide by the sin of Adam, except those who are annihilated: those have nothing to hide] (Babinsky, *Mirror*, 169). Robinson explains that, for Porete, human souls that come from nothing still carry the mark of the Trinity inside; from this, noble souls can return through Love to "embodied 'nothingness.' "[68]

By stripping away all the external encumbrances—the cultural apparatus of religion, education, and class—that interfere with the soul's progress to God, Porete clarifies the value of becoming nothing. What remains behind is a kind of purity, achieved more conventionally through baptism or absolution, that allows the soul to begin anew, cleared of original sin, which, after all, stemmed from our first parents' pride in the Garden of Eden, a pride that, throughout human history, has stigmatized most institutions. The mark of the Trinity on the human soul signifies the love that will permit it to move forward internally and spiritually. What seems clear in this concept, of course, is the lack of necessity for any external intermediaries, such as priests, to achieve the kind of purity of annihilation that Porete envisages. Unfortunately for Porete, she lived two centuries before her time, but as we see in the conclusion, her views on original sin are echoed in the visionary theology of anchorite Julian of Norwich, suggesting the possible construction of a tradition of female writing in a minor key.

CHAPTER 5

UNHOMELY MARGERY KEMPE AND
ST. CATHERINE OF SIENA: "COMUNYCACYON"
AND "CONUERSACION" AS HOMILY

The singular Margery Kempe (born around 1373, but flourishing in the early 1420s and alive in 1438), the daughter of John Brunham, mayor of King's Lynn, married John Kempe and mothered fourteen children, after which she took a vow of chastity and traveled throughout England and to holy sites in Europe and the Mediterranean to obtain indulgences for her sins. Margery's very acts of apparent craziness in her own lifetime that marked her as eccentric, excessively attention-attracting, and antisocial project a form of resistance to marginalization because of her gender difference, although as acts of holy subversion they have been misunderstood by her peers and her critics. The most frequently cited aberrations include Margery Kempe's loud sobbing and tears in church,[1] her excited, unlettered speech,[2] her passions and (thinly veiled) erotic ecstasies,[3] her wearing of white clothes,[4] her refusal to eat meat, and her criticisms of her fellow pilgrims on trips to the holy land for their lack of spirituality and lax observance of religious practices. Behaviors suggestive of personality problems today, they understandably drew the ire of others in the fifteenth century. Her contemporaries accused her of heresy and witchcraft; early and even some modern scholars have diagnosed her as hysterical and mad.[5] Very recently Mary Hardiman Farley has identified Kempe's eccentricity as evidence of a psychosis known as Histrionic Personality Disorder, even though Farley admits that her "career is compatible with a model of feminist self-assertion and social change without romanticizing her behavior or postulating an unrealistic degree of personality strength and conscious control."[6] Further, Margery's hearing of melodies and other queer observances has led Richard Lawes to suggest an "endogenous psychological or neurological aetiology" for them, diagnosing her as having perhaps a temporal lobe epilepsy.[7]

This history of interpretation, coupled with the vexed form in which Margery's *Boke* exists—inscribed by at least two clerics, one of whom understood English poorly[8]—has diverted attention from the ways in which she represents a marginalized figure who also used her alterity through language and contributed to the establishment of a minor literature in the sense in which Deleuze and Guattari have defined it. Hope Emily Allen herself, no doubt reflecting patriarchal registers of her own day, pointed in this direction by describing Margery as a "minor mystic" who was "petty, neurotic, vain, illiterate, physically and nervously overstrained," but, nevertheless, interesting as a character[9]—and unhomely, in the sense intended by Homi Bhabha, in her attempts to traverse her own difference away from home.

The problem in understanding Margery is twofold, as critics have implicitly realized. First, her body is her first and most important "book" (we think of her tearing of hair and rending of skin early on after the priest refuses to hear her confession during her postpartum depression), but unfortunately, at least according to scholar Denis Renevey, the people who witness her performance "fail to perceive the diverse message encoded within," and she herself is "unable to provide a commentary with which to accompany this particular text."[10] Second, when Margery uses exempla to communicate a point to her audience, the exempla invariably reflect back on her—as a "preacher," she appears to gloss herself as her own text,[11] which can suggest the remanifestation of her own narcissism.

In defense of Margery Kempe, recent criticism has centered on the issue of identity and female authorship (given the vexing problem of clerical and scribal written authority and the accuracy of the transmission of oral and/or vernacular texts as constructed by an allegedly illiterate woman), but usually always within a feminist context.[12] Most significant here is Lynn Staley's powerful argument that Kempe artistically manipulated her persona "Margery" in the way that Geoffrey Chaucer manipulated his alter ego "Geffrey" in his works.[13] In addition, Margery's outrageous behavior has intimated to some critics the possibility of parallels with or influence by (or upon) female literary characters, most particularly, Mary Magdalene in the mystery plays and saints' lives and Chaucer's Wife of Bath.[14] Other scholars have ignored her behavior but implicitly justified Kempe by drawing parallels between her text and those belonging to a written, masculinized literary tradition: specif-ically, Franciscan meditations[15]; male mystics Walter Hilton and Richard Rolle[16]; Bede and Chaucer[17]; and William Thorpe and John Rogers.[18]

However inherently misogynistic such diagnoses of psychological aberration may appear, they lead us back into the fruitful area of exam-ining Kempe's eccentricity as a form of spirituality, which has only begun to be examined.[19] Scholars have not fully recognized the bizarre behavior of paradigmatic women from the thirteenth and fourteenth centuries as a form of gendered spiritual "unhomeliness," or holy alter-ity. Critical refusal to honor Kempe's eccentricity as gendered contin-ues, even though Margery has been studied in relation to other religious women—for example, Marie of Oignies, Christina Mirabilis, and Elizabeth of Spalbeck[20]; the king's daughter of Hungary[21]; Julian of Norwich and St. Birgitta of Sweden[22]; Angela of Foligno[23]; the beguines of Belgium and the Dominican nuns of Germany, including Mechthild of Magdeburg[24]; Joan of Arc[25]; and Margaret Paston.[26]

Unhoused beguines and other women like them who wandered at will clearly represented a danger to medieval society in the twelfth–fourteenth centuries—if not for licentiousness or heresy, according to the church, then for demoniac possession—and were often shunned or feared for their alterity. Marguerite Porete, as we have seen, provides one extreme example of how such beguines were viewed by the church in the fact of her burning for heresy because of her book *The Mirror of Simple Souls*. In her eccentricity Kempe most closely resembles that model for many beguines, Christina Mirabilis, or Christina the Astonishing of St. Trond (1150–1224), whose paradig-matic spiritual life was relayed, as support for the beguines, by the dis-ciple of Jacques de Vitry, Thomas de Cantimpré, in 1232. Such behavior included Christina's perching in trees or on the tops of houses, which began when her supposedly dead body began to rise "like a bird" from the coffin to the church rafters.[27] The married beguine Blessed Angela da Foligno (1249–1309) also wandered and exhibited extremely odd behavior (by any standard of social expectation); extremely odd was her wishing her husband, mother, and children dead so that she could devote herself more fully to God and being happy when, indeed, they died, as well as screeching and shouting while in the church of St. Francis in Assisi.[28] Both women's actions led their very families, friends, and men-toring confessors and scribes to regard them initially as possessed by demons and, in Christina's case, to shackle her in chains.[29] That this eccentric behavior—what Barbara Newman in certain cases terms demoniacal behavior—could be interpreted both as a sign of possession and spiritual dis-ease and also as a sign of holiness and sanctity helps to explain the ambiguity of alterity in the Middle Ages.[30]

Indeed, wandering St. Catherine of Siena (d. 1380), whose behavior was, like that of Christina, Angela, and Margery, equally odd—she levitated, cut her hair, wore men's clothes, and rebelled against her mother—also traveled widely, preached in cities, and counseled the pope. But for this, Catherine was not publicly stigmatized; in fact, after death she was eventually canonized. The difference in the interpretation of the lives of these three women, Christina, Catherine, and Margery, rests upon the relationship between the woman and her scribe, given that an authorizing confessor and/or mentor relays the first two lives but clerical scribes without such a sacerdotal role the third. Where, for example, Thomas is confident that Christina's sitting in a tree, howling, perching on fence palings, or forming herself into a ball exemplifies her very spirituality—that is, she is not like us; she is transcendently different—Margery, like her scribes, is initially perplexed by her own typical aberrant and female behavior, generally without authoritative answers from any institution, both at the beginning and the end (although mentors appear as she journeys), and guided only by the inner voice of Jesus, who tells her this is her rightful path.[31] As Margery learns to trust that inner voice, her very resistance to those in the outside world and to the (male) members of the Church who insist on chastising and condemning her grows.

In this respect, evolving as she does from eccentricity to spiritual empowerment through words, Margery more closely resembles St. Catherine of Siena. Catherine of Siena's life, or *legenda*—a work written shortly after her death by her confessor and scribe Raymond of Capua (Raimundus de Vineis, de Capua)—was translated into Middle English in the fifteenth century and later printed by William Caxton.[32] It consists of three parts, books with abstracts at the head of each chapter addressed to "Daughter, *filia*," that is, "she who should learn by this example." In the first book, which begins with Catherine's birth and early childhood (twelve chapters), she clearly exhibits antisocial and deviant behavior in an attempt to escape her class and gender. But in the second and most important book of the three, it continues with what the prologue describes as her "*conuersacion* from tyme of her despousacion to our lord" until she dies (twelve chapters; my emphasis). Here, she begins speaking, instead of fleeing, and uses "conuersacion" as a means to bridge those social and gender fissures as a form of resistance within a highly politicized ecclesiastical context. The third book (six chapters) concerns her dying and her miracles after death.

Like the first two parts of Catherine's legend, Margery Kempe's *Book* specifically mirrors the important stages of Catherine's life but, in addition, in both stages also memorializes Margery's alterity that invited cruel slanders as the cross she had to bear to test her spirituality. As Christ tells Margery, "I suffyr many schrewyd wordys, for I have oftyntymes seyd to the that I schuld be newe crucifyed in the be schrewyd wordys, for thu schalt non otherwyse ben slayn than be schrewyd wordys sufferyng" (Staley, *The Book of Margery Kempe*, 90 [chap. 34]). And, like Catherine's, Margery's own "comunycacyon" and "conversacion" equally provide the means for her to span the gap between her eccentricities and others' frequently gendered slanders in order to demonstrate in an unhomely way her ability as an orator. Initially in her preaching career, when she and her husband returned to London, "many worthy men desyred to heryn hir *dalyawns* and hir *comunycacyon*, for hir *communycacion* was so mech in the lofe of God that the herars wer oftyntyme steryd therthorw to wepn ryt sadly" (Staley, *Book*, 49 [16]; my emphasis). As far as Kempe is concerned, several critics have noted without making the connection with the slanders she has suffered the importance of both *comunycacyon* and *dalyawns* [dalliance] as her "good words." Karma Lochrie sees *comunycacyon* in terms of popular debates of Kempe's day and even Lollard arguments supporting women's right to preach.[33] Wendy Harding interprets *comunycacyon* as flirtation, *dalyawns*, even sexual intercourse, so that Margery's ministry "represents a return of much that is repressed in orthodox and authoritarian clerical practices."[34]

Margery transforms herself into a skillful preacher through her strategic manipulation of what she calls "conversacion." The connection between the cruel words of others and the "conversacion" she uses to subvert them rests on specific meanings of the term in her day, which suggest a means of being part of a group or place, a community, as defined by links among or between two things, places, groups, people, or ideas. Both "conversacion" and "dalyawns" surface many times in the narratives of both women's lives, as we see, to echo meanings current in 1340 and later. The word "conversacion," from Old French "conversation," or "conversacion," according to the *Oxford English Dictionary (OED)*, indicates a "frequent abode, intercourse,"[35] suggesting departures from home: Margery, like Catherine, was a frequently displaced person. The first denotation in the fourteenth century is "the action of living or having one's being *in* a place or *among* persons," for example, from Hampole's *Psalter* 18.1 (1340): "Haly men þat has þaire conuersacioun in heuen." *Conversacion* can also connote "of one's spiritual being," as in the *Ayenbite of Inwit*, 241 (1340), " 'Oure conuersacioun,' he zayþ, 'is ine heuene.' " Second, "conversacion" can also signify "the action of consorting or having one's dealings with others; living together; commerce, intercourse, society, intimacy," as exemplified by this line from Hampole's *Prose Treatise* 2.5 (1340): "And an other tym he lefte þe conuersacion of alle worldly men. . .and went into disserte vpon the hilles." Third, *conversacion* can refer archaically to behavior, the "manner of conducting oneself in the world or in society"—getting us back to the issue of Margery's behavior, as in *Psalter* 2.12 (1340): "Haldis goed lyf & fayre conuersacioun." In all these examples of *conversacion*, the action is not sexual at all or even definitely social but instead, spiritual. Similarly, "dalliance," "daliance," or "dalyawns," despite the modern sexual connotations (which were also rendered in the fourteenth and fifteenth centuries, as "sport," or "flirtation," as well as "triflying with"), in the *OED* lists its first (now obsolete) meaning as "talk," whether light or serious. Oskar Bokenham's *Seyntys* (1447), line 162, provides a spiritual example in Martha, sister of Mary: "Marthe first met hym [Christ]. . . .And hadde with hym a long dalyaunce."

In addition, whether it is the act of communicating, the information communicated, or Holy Communion, in all cases "communication," like "conversation" and "dalliance," implies a bridge between two bodies, agents, or groups—a bonding, and outside the usual "abode," site of identification. "Comunycacyon," a word that appears frequently in the *Book of Margery Kempe*, according to the *OED* has as its earliest (rare) meaning the act of imparting information, as when John Wycliffe, in his version of the Bible, in 2 Corinthians 9.13 (1382) declares, "Glorifiynge God. . .in symplenesse of comynycacioun into hem and into alle." Although there are few additional citations listed behind the concrete denotation of number 3, listing a line from Caxton (1490) as an example of "that which is communicated," there is one rare denotation of communication as reference to Holy Communion, appearing in *Women Saints* 131 (ca. 1310): "If the communication of Our Lords bodie was there celebrated."

In this chapter I will first compare Margery and Catherine for their eccentric behaviors as a sign of their gender difference and, therefore, of their testing by Christ—alterity as a measure of their very holiness—and then, in the second and third parts, I will compare their similar respective use of "conversacion" and "dalyawns" to resist the colonization created by their social (class, gender, and individual) differences in the community as they ventured outside their spaces—houses, cities, regions, nations. Through these subversions, as I hope to prove, both Margery and Catherine create an unhomely space for themselves and for their spirituality, despite the Pauline prohibitions against women preaching in church, interpreting Scripture, and teaching. Indeed, unauthorized "preaching," although she used no rhetoric from preaching manuals, was what brought Margery to the attention of the archbishop.[36] "Conversacion" and "comunycacyon" become the type of mediation that both women use as a bridge to reach others, but also to mitigate their own alterity by attainment of spiritual community and bonding and thereby subvert patriarchal structures of home, society, and church. In this sense, both Margery and Catherine were types of Christina the Astonishing, their lives parallel in relation to their transformation of the cross of their alterity into a powerful rhetorical weapon. Both Margery and Catherine were disruptive, unruly beings, Catherine, even in her youth and young womanhood.

Catherine and Margery the Astonishing

Although I do not believe it was necessary for Kempe to have read the works of Catherine of Siena, either her legend or the dialogue, it is likely that Kempe may have known of them or heard them read aloud. Catherine's legend, which existed both in Latin and Middle English, may have had greater currency and more literary influence overall in England than her important mystical work, the *Dialogo della divina provvidenza* [Dialogue of Divine Providence], written in Italian in 1378, about her visionary conversations with Christ. The *Legenda major*, by Raymond of Capua, was begun in 1384 and completed in 1395, then expanded in the *Libellus de supplemento* by Tommaso Antonio Caffarini of Siena, who used the notes of Catherine's first confessor, Tommaso della Fonten. Caffarini also eventually compressed her life, in the *Legenda minor*. But there were also memorials about her life, one from Cristofano di Galgano Guidini of Siena in 1390.[37] Based on fifteenth-century manuscripts by Raymond of Capua, the Middle English translation of her influential Latin legend was eventually published by Wynken de Worde, in 1493(?) from Caxton's plates (his mark appears at the end of the book), entitled *Here beginneth the lyf of Saynt Katherin of senis the Blessed Virgin; The revelacions of Saynt Elysabeth the Kynges doughter of hungarye*.[38] A somewhat shortened form of the original Latin, Wynken de Worde/W. Caxton's Middle English *The lyf of saint Katherin of Senis* is nevertheless closely based on Raymond of Capua's original Latin, according to the prologue: "This legende compyled a worthypfull clerke, fryer Reymond, of the ordre of saynt domynik, doctor of deuynyte and confessour of this holy virgin." The translator acknowledges its source on the first folio of the de Worde/Caxton edition as an "epistle": "Katheryne of Sene of þe whiche Epystle in sentence here foloweth parte translated in to englysche." Possibly the Middle English translation was completed by Thomas Gascoigne, chancellor of Oxford, who wrote the Latin *Life of St. Birgitta* and translated it into English for the sisters and monks at Syon Abbey.[39]

In addition, the influence of Catherine's own writings spread throughout Europe, including England, chiefly what she called her "Libro," or *Dialogo*, dictated to her scribes in her own Tuscan dialect before November of 1378, when she was summoned to Rome, and then translated into Latin and Middle English. The Middle English version, known as the *Orcherd of Syon*, was most likely based on a Latin translation of the Italian *Dialogue* by one of Catherine's disciples and early witnesses, Cristofano di Galgano Guidini, from a fifteenth-century English manuscript now at University of Edinburgh, MS 87, *Liber Divine Doctrine S. Catherine Senensis*.[40] But there also existed three earlier-fifteenth-century manuscripts of the *Orcherd*: British Library Harley 3432, St. John's College, Cambridge, 75, and Pierpont Morgan Library 162.[41] The original text was most likely brought to England either through the Dominicans, with whom Catherine was affiliated, or the Carthusians at Sheen or Mountgrace Priory outside York. (Oxford Bodleian Library Laud 154, fol. 7v, lists the *Revelations*—as the *Dialogue* was also known—of St. Catherine along with those of St. Matildis and St. Elizabeth of Schönau as books owned by Witham Charterhouse by the mid-fifteenth century.)[42] There may have been other means of transmittal, for example, through Adam Easton, from Rome.

St. Catherine's impact in England and, later, Scotland[43] was no doubt bolstered by the use of her writings to foster and nourish the members of the convent belonging to the newly founded house of St. Bridget (Birgitta in Swedish) of Sweden (ca.1302–23 July 1373) at Syon Abbey, belonging to the Rule of St. Savior (an adaptation of the Augustinian Rule). Bridget's convent was begun in 1414 in Twickenham, and completed in 1415, seven months after her canonization; its foundation stone was actually laid by Henry V, a supporter of St. Bridget throughout his life, on 22 February 1415.[44] Located opposite the Carthusian abbey at Sheen, Jesus of Bethlehem (founded in the same year by Henry V), Syon

Abbey was moved to Isleworth (across from Kew Gardens, in Richmond) in 1431, where it remained until the Dissolution in 1539.[45] Of the six monastic houses founded between 1360 and 1540 in England, that of St. Bridget and St. Saviour was the most important; Syon Abbey came to be a site of pilgrimage for which penitents earned what was known as the "Pardon of Syon."[46] According to the charter, there were to be sixty nuns, one of whom would be abbess, thirteen priests, four deacons, and eight lay brethern.[47]

Margery is known to have visited Syon Abbey. In 1434 in London, after crossing the Holy Roman Empire, Margery visited the Brigittine convent (perhaps, Anthony Goodman suggests, because she had never visited St. Bridget's tomb and shrine at Vadstena at the convent St. Bridget had founded in Sweden).[48] As Goodman notes, "The cult of St. Bridget received royal patronage in England in the early years of Lancastrian rule, in part coincidentally with the course of Margery's conversion."[49] Kempe's mentors facilitated the assimilation of this new Brigittine cult with the English devotional traditions of pseudo-Bonaventure and manuals in the vernacular.[50] That they may have regarded Kempe's unhomeliness in the same light as they did Bridget's is attested by the fact that *The Book of Margery Kempe*, which exists in a unique mid-fifteenth century manuscript (British Library Additional 61823) likely copied from the original, was initially owned, according to an inscription in a late-fifteenth-century hand, by the Carthusian house of Mount Grace Priory in Yorkshire, North Riding, and annotated, most likely, by a monk from this house.[51]

Although Margery may not have recourse to the actual Latin or vernacular manuscripts of either work by or about Catherine, certainly Syon Abbey was a hub of translation and copying activity throughout its life, both in relation to the writings of its founding saint, which furthered her cult in England, but also in relation to the writings of others, often intended for the Brigittine sisters.[52] One example, known to Margery and written for the "lady abbesse, of the worshypfull Monastery of Syon," was *The Myroure of Oure Ladye*, which presents a particularization of the divine services for Syon Abbey, a translation of the "Hours" in use, and the "Masses for the Virgin."[53] In addition, the Middle English translation of St. Catherine's major work, the *Orcherd of Syon*, whose publication by Wynken de Worde was paid for by Sir Richard Sutton, Steward of Syon from 1513 and founder of Brasenose College at Oxford, in 1519, is addressed by scribe "Dane Iamys" (whose identity is not known) to the reverend mother and sisters at Syon.[54] The image of the vineyard, which explains the title adopted by de Worde from the Explicit of Harleian MS 3432, is probably borrowed from the writings of St. Bridget.[55] A Gospel image found both in Matthew 20: 1–16, the parable of the workers in the vineyard that was also used by the *Pearl*-Poet, and in John 15: 5–6, "I am the vine, you are the branches," becomes a metaphor for the Church in St. Birgitta's *Regula Salvatoris* as the vine becomes Christ's extension of himself into new spiritual directions, that is, her new order.[56] So important was this image to the Brigittines that there were orchards at both Vadstena and at Syon Abbey intended for the sisters' edification, the latter even now extant in vestigial form in the gardens at Sion House at Richmond and in the grapevine tended within a greenhouse at the abbey now situated in Devon. Given this context, the Bishop-hermit Alfonso Jaén appropriately entitled two works taken from Bridget's *Revelations* as *viridiarium*, or "plantation of trees, pleasure garden."[57]

In her legend, initially Catherine's alterity takes the form of class and gender difference, the latter of which she attempts to expunge through curiously antisocial and aberrant behavior. Her lowly social class, as determined by that of her father as a wool-cloth dyer, in the *Lyf* merges with that of her lowly gendered role in service to God, and it is remarked upon both by Raymond and the translator:

> Ferthermore ye shall vnderstonde þat Jacob vsed the crafte of makyng of colours wherwyth wolle and wollen clothes ben dyed: This crafte used both he and his sonys: In that contree they ben called dyers. Wherefore full wonderfully god ordeyned that a dyers doughter shol be made the spouse of the Emperour of heuen; as ye shall see by goddes grace after in this boke.[58]

This humbleness of class will project into the symbol of the bridge in her *Dialogue* as a conscious joining of two differences, attendant to her purpose as a communicator between men and women and with God.

Of the two fourteenth-century women, Catherine most conspicuously manifests antisocial behavior as a child facing puberty in a large commoner family, with Margery's antisociality visible only after childbirth. In both instances, however, it is the gendering of their experiences that gives away the signification of their social aberration. As a child, Catherine consciously attempted to flee from, conceal, or deny the sexuality of the female "spouse," whether of the Emperor of heaven or of an earthly man. She demanded to be called Eufrosyne, after the cross-dressing saint who dressed as a man, although she also fled from the sight and conversation of men. One of Catherine's first miracles as a girl—when she flew through the air without her feet touching the grass—occurred "whanne she wolde flee a-waye oute of companye, and specyally from the syghte of companye of men."[59] Catherine, conscious that her gender would prove an obstacle if she attempted to enter the order of St. Dominic to aid men's souls, felt a desire that grew explicitly from the fact of her gender difference: "From that tyme forward there wext a grete desyre in hyr sowle to go vnto that ordre, that she myght profyte mannes sowle wyth other brethern of that ordre. But by-cause she sawe a grete obstacle in that she was a woman."[60] Like Eufrosyne, Catherine imagines she will wear the habit of a man and enter a monastery in some "ferre contree":

> Therfore she thought to folowe Saynt Eufrosyen—as men cleypd hir in childhode wonderfully as for a pronostycacion, that ryght as saynt Eufrosyen feyned hyr a man and went in to a monastery of monkes, in the same manere thys mayde is purposed to feyne hyr a man and go in to ferre contree, where she was not knowe, and take the abyte of the ordre of frere prechours: where she myght helpe sowles and saue them from peryffhyng.[61]

Although Catherine did not in fact achieve this aim, she did cut off her hair and wear both a "coyf" and a "kerchyf," acts that her distressed mother punished by the withdrawal of her room and, therefore, of her privacy, accompanied by the demand that she openly serve the entire house.[62] Rebellious Catherine then vowed never to leave the house again and made a "pryue chaumbre" for herself in her own soul with the help of the Holy Ghost.[63] After St. Dominic appeared to her in a vision, she adopted the habit and received a mystical ring from God to signify her wedding.[64]

Margery's sanctity—unlike that of Catherine, or of Christina Mirabilis, which begins when she awakens from the dead—sparks during a postpartum depression after an insensitive priest fails to listen to her confession of some unclarified (sexual) sin that she wished to have absolved; it strengthens when she arrives at a new state of being, in chapter 11.[65] Unlike the holy life of Christina, Margery's spiritual adventures—including her interactions with monks and other clergy, her pilgrimages to holy sites, her conversations with archbishops, vicars, and holy men—commence only after the clergy have "died" to her, when they have failed her spiritual needs, and when, on her own, she has shed acculturated antifeminism like a cloak. From the bewildered, eccentric rebel at the beginning, Margery develops into a skillful, confident rhetor whose quickness and intellectual faculties convince her opponents of her legitimacy despite her eccentricity.

It is alterity itself that draws the blame and mistrust of others and improves Margery's spiritually. Her particular trial as a holy woman was to be tested in her love for Christ by the odium and slander of others who did not believe her sanctity and who constantly reproved her. According to the important prologue in her *Book*, Christ's testing occurred because of her laxity in following him, which was then disciplined by the adversities he heaps upon her when he "turnyd helth into sekenesse, prosperyté into adversyté, worshep into repref, and love into hatered" (Staley, *Book*, 17). Ironically, this adversity sharpens her spiritual steel and enhances her growth into a preacher. Repeatedly we are told that she sobs out of contrition for her sins, but she is also suspected of manipulation by "sum men" who "seyden sche mygth wepen whan sche wold and slawndered the werk of God" (Staley, *Book*, 18). It is as if she transforms into sacrifices to God the very postlapsarian gifts of God to women—according to Chaucer's Wife of Bath, tears, spinning, and deceit, but they continue to be identified by others as associated with deceit and the sin of Eve, because of whose downfall women were assigned the skill of spinning to make clothing to cover their nakedness. But to Margery, her very suffering over these reprovals for God's love reassures her:

> Sche was so usyd to be slawndred and repreved, to be cheden and rebuked of the world for grace and vertu wyth whech sche was indued thorw the strength of the Holy Gost that it was to her in a maner of solas and comfort whan sche sufferyd any dysese for the lofe of God and for the grace that God wrowht in hyr. For evyr the mor *slawnder* and *repref* that sche sufferyd, the mor sche increysd in grace and in devocyon of holy medytacyon of hy contemplacyon and of wonderful spechys and *dalyawns* whech owr Lord spak and dalyid to hyr sowle, techyng hyr how sche schuld be despysed for hys lofe, how sche schuld han pacyens, settyng all hyr trost, alle hyr lofe, and alle hyr affeccyon in hym only. (Staley, *Book*, 18; my emphasis)

It is as if the very trace of difference exposed by female being magnifies to make incredible Margery's apparent love of and grace from God; she takes on (almost like a female Christ) a gendered suffering, in that women are socialized to want to please others. The greater her spirituality, the greater her reproof, blame, and social ostracism, which are followed by her eventual arrest and accusation of heresy. She symbolizes and suffers from female alterity. Like the female demoniac, however, Margery is often accused of being possessed, even though supportive clerics and anchorites frequently believe her "mevyinggys" come from the Holy Ghost (Staley, *Book*, 19). It is their urging and support that prompt her to have the book written down, even though this happens twenty years after she had experienced her revelations. Yet the very fear of being associated with her prevents the priest who would have copied the first, Germanized, version into a more legible script from doing so for more than four more years: "Than was ther so evel spekyng of this creatur and of hir wepyng, that the prest durst not for cowardyse speke wyth her but seldom, ne not wold wryten as he had behestyd unto the forseyd creatur" (Staley, *Book*, 19). The very use of the word "creatur" in this context implies her dehumanization, as a being created, without redeeming spirit or grace or even intelligence, although the epithet also echoes Margaret Porete's "mendiant creature" (herself) confessed at the end of *The Mirror of Simple Souls*. It is no accident that, in Margery's prologue, her priest begins writing on the day after that feast, in 1436, of Mary Magdalene—a sinner, but in particular the type of redeemed female sinner Christ most claims as his own (Staley, *Book*, 38). A woman who sins is doubly different—ontologically an agent of original sin but, simultaneously, refallen into fleshliness, as it were. Margery is not the only wandering, unhomely woman who resembles Mary Magdalene: beguine Marie of d'Oignies (d. 1213), who similarly married at fourteen and lived chastely, like Margery, was also afflicted with the embarrassment of weeping, according to her vita, as was St. Elizabeth of Hungary.[66]

Concerning the narrative trajectory in the *Book* proper, Margery's vow of chastity within marriage marks the end of the first stage of her transformation, from a highly gendered, materialistic, sinful wife to a more spiritual "creatur"—in this sense, the epithet denoting the change of being from gendered lack of humanity and intelligence into a more spiritual genderlessness, a transhumanization. The sequence of transformation early in book 1 is layed out by the various sins chapter by chapter. That is, Margery's sins begin with gendered occasions—postpartum psychosis (according to Clarissa W. Atkinson),[67] in chapter 1—but then move to more ordinary sins, including the sins of avarice and envy of the possessions of others, as demonstrated by fashionable clothes, brewing, and a horse-mill, in chapter 2; the sin of lechery, as demonstrated by having sex with her husband, which she resists, although he ignores her wishes, in chapter 3, and the temptation of an affair on St. Margaret's Eve, to which she succumbs, disastrously, in chapter 4; and the sin of gluttony, arising from Christ's demand that she sacrifice for him by not eating meat, in chapter 5, which she is compelled to forgo because of her husband's insistence that she join him in the sin as company for him. Her infraction, which is encouraged by Christ as a means of compromise with her husband, symbolizes the larger challenge to Margery that Christ will throw down to her as if a gauntlet: "I schal give the an hayr [hair-shirt] in thin hert. . . .Thow schalt ben etyn and knawyn of the pepul of the world as any raton knawyth the stokfysch" (Staley, *Book*, 31 [chap. 5]; Windeatt, *Book*, 51). If Margery's failures to succeed are more physical in their nature, they lead in the later portion of the *Book* inexorably, in the medieval allegorical and homiletic fashion, to greater sins, of wrath and pride, as mounted in the accusations against her of eccentricity and, eventually, heresy.

What Christ does throughout, however, is strip Margery of her socialized and pleasing femaleness, those material and physical attributes that ground misogyny, and of the female characteristics that suggest malleability and softness. He replaces them with a spiritual feminized grace to counter her physical sinfulness: for example, Margery envisions the pregnant St. Anne, St. Elizabeth, and the Virgin Mary, each of whom she serves as a handmaiden and midwife, because Christ has asked his "dowtyr" to "thynke on my modyr, for sche is cause of alle the grace that thow hast" (Staley, *Book*, 32–34 [chaps. 6–7]; here, p. 32). Thereafter, during Easter week, because of her continuing pleas to Christ for help, Margery's husband cannot enjoy her carnally (chap. 9); she subsequently negotiates with her husband to forgo sexual relations in exchange for payment of his debts and eating meat with him on Friday (chap. 11).

Most interestingly, Margery's *Book*, after the first part, gives greatest weight to her interactions away from home, to her "comunycacyons" and "dalyawnses" in the middle part, as will both the Latin and Middle English versions of Catherine's life, to her "conuersacions" in the second of three books. In the following section, we first examine conversation in Catherine's legend and *Dialogue* as a means of subverting the colonization imposed by gender, class, and church, and then return to Margery's unhomely "comunycacyons."

Catherine of Siena's "Conuersacion":
Bridge across Difference

In the second part of the *Lyf*, Catherine is specifically instructed by God to forget her gender (her "kynde") in attempting "conuersacion" with both women and men and to continue her spiritual activities despite the slanders of others about the inappropriateness of her actions:

> Ferthermore thyn herte shall be soo gretely kyndelyd of helthe of soules, that
> thou shalt forgete in maner thy owne *kynde* and chaunge al thy fyrst
> *conuersacyon*: ffor thou shalt not eshewe and shun the company of men and
> wommen as thou were wonte to do, but rather for theyr soule-helthe thou
> shalt put the to all maner of laboure to thy power and myght. Of thys maner
> of lyving many one shold be sclaundred, and so, of many thou shalt be
> ageyn-sayd that the thoughtes of theyr hertys may be knowen by theyr
> wordes.[68]

The modern English translation clearly mentions "sex": "You will
forget your sex and change your present way of life; you will not avoid
the company of men and women as you do now, but for the salvation
of their souls will take upon yourself every kind of labour. Many people
will be scandalized by the things you do and oppose you."[69] God insists,
not on her preaching, but on Catherine's *conuersacion* with others—a talent that she shares with Margery—despite the alienation both Catherine
and Margery will experience by their very social and gender difference.
Catherine's change in mission begins early in the second part. The rubric
for the beginning of chapter 2 in the second part of Catherine's legend
stresses God's emphasis on her conversation with men as a tool he
wished her to use: "Here begynneth the second partye, in the whiche is
shewed the *conuersacion* of this holy mayde with men, and how the gyftes
whiche she hadde receyued off oure lorde pryuely enclosed wythin herself, were openly shewed to the worlde. And first, how oure lorde bad
her that she sholde be *conuersaunt* amonges men."[70]

   The conversation, communication, and dalliance of Catherine
begin, as do Margery's, in modest ways, but they end with her ability
to transverse both class and gender in communicating with the pope
and other church officials. Catherine, poor like Chaucer's Griselda,
linked to a father named Jacob (Janicula is the name of Griselda's father
in Chaucer), achieves her power much as does Griselda—through her
speech and words.[71] Indeed, one story in Boccaccio's *Decameron*, that of
poor but virtuous Griselda, is said to have been influenced by this
power in Catherine's life.[72] While Catherine's canonization in 1461
resulted in an increase in convents dedicated to her throughout Europe
and renewed interest in writings by and about her, nevertheless, earlier
still, her power as what Noffke terms a "mystical activist"[73] must have
affected others, including writers in the fourteenth century such as
Boccaccio, Petrarch, and even Chaucer. Petrarch translated this vernacular
story into Latin, and Chaucer used the anonymous French translations

of Petrarch in constructing her story in the Middle English of the "Clerk's Tale." Chaucer may have learned of her importance as mediator between the Florentines and the pope (or of the existence of these Italian stories of Griselda based on her life) during his visits to Avignon and Florence in the 1370s. Just as Griselda remains entirely obedient to her tyrannical master, lord, and husband, Walter, even though her speeches become more and more powerful and stronger, so also did Catherine obey the pope and the church, acting as a bridge between the commoners and the aristocracy. In addition to these literary echoes of Catherine's life, the fame of the Dominican tertiary who traveled so widely (for which the Sienese women in particular criticized her) and wielded so much influence with the pope must have circulated in Italy and elsewhere even before the written testimonials.[74]

While there is not space to examine overall the significance of Margery's *Book* (both life and credo) and St. Catherine's *Dialogue*—theologically speaking her most important work—my purpose in using Catherine of Siena's alterity is to gloss Margery's spiritual autobiography through Catherine's own visionary book in which she speaks directly about the symbolic power of dialogue—conversation—in resisting colonization because of class and gender difference. For, I argue, St. Catherine functions as the paradigm to which Margery aspires throughout her *Book*.

Indeed, the power of Catherine's gendered "conversation" reached as high as the pope himself, suggesting a spiritual intercourse few women in the Middle Ages ever attained in this world. In the third, most political, book of her legend, after Pope Urban VI was elected, on 9 April 1378, the significance of Catherine's gender difference and homeliness is highlighted. This pope had asked Catherine to come to Rome because he had known her earlier, at Avignon, when he was archbishop of Acerenza, and thus held a high opinion of her.[75] When she refused, listing gender as a reason ("many of this Cyte of Sene and also of our owne susters by-cause of min goyng aboute hider and thyder ben sklandred therby and seyn that it is not semely to a Rely(gi)ous mayde for to go aboute"),[76] Urban put his request in writing and she went. In Rome she spoke to cardinals about the Great Schism that resulted when Clement VII was set up in 1378 in Avignon (only on 26 July 1424, at the Council of Constance when Martin V was elected pope, was peace restored), after which Pope Urban again situated her speech within a gendered context: "This woman hath shamed vus all: she sholde rather be aferd than we, by-cause she is a woman; yet in that we be aferde, she is not aferde, but conforted vs wyth her good counseyls."[77] Between a woman and a man, a wool-dyer's daughter and a pope, conversation serves as a means of advancing wisdom and linking two diverse entities through a common purpose, whether social ease or civil and ecclesiastical harmony. For Catherine, if we pause for a moment to look at her own words in the *Dialogue* on the subject, Christ was her bridge between difference among classes and between genders, and her homilies—words—reflect the symbolic purpose of Christ as the Word.

The bridge that dominates chapters 26–87 of Catherine's *Dialogue*, drawn perhaps from Gregory the Great, but as powerful as any other "apocalyptic" symbol in the works of the late Middle Ages, including *Piers the Plowman*, is the most important image in both her original text and the Middle English translation, despite the translator's flowery frame.[78] Sensitive to those who are below, other, behind, beneath, Catherine subverts gentrification of Christ when she imagines the body of Christ as a lowly bridge between humanity and his divinity through which the soul can attain salvation: "We se wel þat þere is maad a brigge of þis body of Crist for þe oonheed of dyuyn nature with oure nature of manheed."[79] Specifically, by Christ's body is meant the sacraments, especially baptism, confession, and Holy Communion. Christ is also a living bridge, a way of teaching, held together by the Trinity— God the Father's power, the son's wisdom, and the Holy Spirit's mercy. To be human is to be lowly, a laborer, or a servant, as was Christ: "this liif and domynacioun was take to 3ou of þe doctryn and þat glorious brigge of my dere sone. Whanne 3e weren seruantis of þe feend, my sone took 3ou out of þat seruage [*servitute*]. þat seruage schulde be take fro 3ou, I ordeynede my sone a seruant; and putte to hym obedience, þat þe inobedience of Adam schulde be putt out; and þat pryde schulde be confounded."[80] That we work for our salvation but that it is the quality of the work and not its quantity that matters is used in a similar allegorical context, in relation to the labor in the vineyard, from the Gospel of Matthew, most profoundly in the fourteenth-century *Pearl*.

In particular, both in the original and, even more emphatically, in the Middle English translation of the *Dialogue*, Christ and Christ's body become a metaphor for the empowerment of the Commons as depicted in the trades. The fact and figure of laboring—toil for the Christian worker—in the Middle English selection of words becomes more complex, to reflect the more multicultural background of the English whose words so often were loaned from French and the class differences those words reflect.[81] There will be no distinctions between social classes in the universal body of Christ. These tillers have been given a "swerd scharp on boþe sydis" (that is, love of virtues and hatred of sins) to "reende up þe þornes of deedly synnes" and to "plaunte þe hizenes of virtues." The tillers, who seem to be the individual souls, then merge with the body of Christ to become the church, as manifested in the bread and wine of the Eucharist—the harvest of their toil: "For oþirwyse ʒe schulen not resceyue þe fruyt of þe blood of þe tilyers [*lavoratori*], which I haue sett and ordeyned in holy chirche, of þe which tilyeris I haue seid to þee tofore þat þei voidid awey deedly synnes."[82] Only when they have uprooted [*tollevano*] sin from the *vyne ʒerd* of their souls will they be allowed the "holy blood in þe sacramentis ordeyned in holy chirche." For, of course, it is God himself who is the "tilyer" who has planted the vine of his son "in þe ground of ʒoure humanyte, þat ʒe whiche ben þe braunchis ioyned wiþe þe vyne mowe rynge forþ fruyt." God thus advises the workers to "do ʒe as my seruauntis" [*i servi miei*] and be "ioyned togyderis in þis sooþfast and verry vine" of the Church.[83]

Thus, the humbleness of Christ's common origin, like Catherine's, is enhanced through trades' images in the *Dialogue*—baking, the hammering of the smith, the constructing of a bridge, the making of cloth. The images continue to shift, but not in a haphazard way—from the bridge between human and divine, lowest of classes and perfection, Catherine turns to baking bread, which in its rising suggests change, metamorphosis, and Christlike movement. Her baking images suggest the baker's kneading of the daily bread and by analogy the Host, the Eucharist: "Wiþ þe humanyte he was knytt verily and couplid."[84] Catherine also makes of the cross an anvil, "a goostly anveeld, whereon þe sone of mankynde sculde be forgid, so þat man sculde be waische and clensid fro euerlastynge deepe, and þat he schulde be cloþid wiþ þe durable liif by a synguler grace"; again, Christ's body was made an anvil, a metaphor for the lower class from which Catherine comes.[85] In the Latin of Cristofano di Galgano Guidini, "forged" is *fabricaretur*, related to *fabrica*, an art, trade, profession of *fabri* [smiths], also a workshop or smithy; *fabricatio* denotes a making, framing, construction with skill; the fabricator is an artificer, with all of these images suggesting skilled labor, the workman, and the building of a literal bridge. The construction of walls for the bridge is a practical, earthy necessity for Catherine: because of these walls travelers will not be hindered by rain.[86] Catherine speaks also of the humble but necessary mortar that will bind the stones of the wall. Christ, both the builder and the bridge, is also the mortar holding the stones in place: "He made up þe wal of stoones, and medlid [mortared] it with chalk, and foorgide and foormede it vp wiþ his precious blood; þat is to seye, the blood is medlid with þe chalk and strenkþe of þe godheed and with þe greet fier of charyte."[87] Christ is also the foundation, as the roof of the bridge is mercy, and the Holy Church provides the bread of life and blood. In addition to the spiritual structural images of bread, bridge, and anvil, the body is yet another structure, one on which to place clothes (clothing must have been uppermost in Catherine's mind, given her awareness of her father's trade as a dyer).

The image that Catherine uses in one of the many passages in the *Dialogue*, however, is more feminized than it is class-constructed, in that it depends on clothing imagery as a reflection of the body—in the words of the Virgin Mary—in the relation between works and the soul.

> And whanne þe blessid soulis resceyuen þe fruyt of my sones blood, which sone is clepid þe trewe holy lomb, also þe blessid soulis seen þanne alle þe peynes whiche þei suffreden in þe world ordeyned for *þe ornamentis of her bodies* [*ornamentis in corporibus*], *as a raye of gold is put op a clooþ* [*pitti aurarium*]. & þat is not þoru þe vertu of þe bodi, but oonli þoru þe plenteuouse blis of þe soule, which representeþ to his body þe fruyt of hise traueilis, bycause þat þe body was asocyed to þe soule & to þe excercises of vertues. Also þe body schal be knowe outward. And riȝt as a myrrour representeþ & schewiþ þe face of a man, riȝt so þe fruyt of hise laburs schal be presentid and schewid in hys body.[88]

The soul imprints on the body, as if the body were a bridge between the heavenly and the earthly; it can be said to labor, in a resurrection of the class metaphor—the despised body becomes a text for artificing, adorning, like *pitti* (a label, a patch, something placed on a bottle or cloth or clothing)—which in this case, *pitti aurarium*, probably refers to gold-embossed cloth. In this sense Christ bridges what Dante posed as the symbolic tension between Dominican and Franciscan, for he is both truth and love.

The foregrounding of class and especially the Commons in Catherine's text provides a rich source of figuration for theological concepts difficult to convey plainly. Catherine's desire for a unified and harmonious society whose classes serve each other without demanding hegemony is both a utopian vision and apt metaphor for the unity of the Church. So God, close to the end of the *Orcherd*, suggests that different craftsmen need each other to complete their work as do religious the seculars, seculars the religious:

> O þis pou seest by ensaumple þat a werkman or a crafti man gooþ for to lerne sum þing of þe tilier, & þe tilier of þe crafti man, so þat oon nediþ to

ben enfoormyd of anoþir. For oon cannot do þat anoþir can do. In þe same maner a clerk & a religyous man neden seculeris, & seculeris religious. For þat oon wiþout þat oþir can noþing do; þus of alle oþir. Myȝte I not ȝeue to euerych al þat is needful to him?[89]

The book, Catherine's book, like Christ's body, becomes the equivalent of the Eucharist, a bridge between earth and heaven, and Christ's body becomes a means for the lowly to achieve the heights—for the commoner to become king. Christ *is* the "lowly earth" of humanity: "Whanne he had reisid hymsilf up, as whanne he was turmentid in þe cros, ȝit þe diuyn nature voidide hym not fro þe lownes of ȝoure humanyte."[90] In de Worde's edition the book is called "þe boke of diuine doctrine," its authority coming from God himself to "þe intellecte of þe glorious virgyn, Seint Katerine of Seene, of þe Ordre of Seint Dominike," and "endited in her moder tunge."[91]

The bridge metaphor and concept are useful in explaining the translator's description of the genre of the work both at the beginning and at the end as *dyalogys* and *reuelacyons* (a genre also used by St. Bridget and Julian of Norwich) that bridge the divine and human.[92] Like Christ, Catherine herself was a bridge between the human and divine, women and men, the lowest social class and the highest ecclesiastical position; like St. Dominic stamping out heresy, in her use of Sienese dialect she bridged the gap between the humble vernacular and the learned Latin of the pontiff.

Catherine's ability with words, which served her so well with the pope and the Florentines and which she used so powerfully in her many letters and in the *Dialogue* itself, she apparently acquired from her father, James, or Jacob Benincasa, a simple but virtuous man who her *legenda* tells us "myght neuer suffre in his presence a man to curse hym wronge ne to speke of hym harme in noo wyse; In soo moche that he blamed his wyf Lapa wyth softe wordes."[93] That this softness of speech appeared feminine—or more than feminine—is suggested by the standard of virtuous speech toward which his *meyny*, the women who taught in his school, had to aspire and by his daughter Bonaventura's insistence that her own husband reform his speech: "Also this good mannys softenes in speche was soo virtuous, that alle his meyny, namely wymmen damsels, taught in his scole myght not speke ne here noo worde that were not semely or dyshoneste."[94]

Only in the second part of her *Life*, on the "conversacion of this holy mayde and vyrgyn wyth men," as the prologue describes it, was

Catherine graced with the ability to use words with men, powerfully, in the service of the Lord; in the first part she had been graced like clerical men with the ability to read. Raymond acknowledges, "Now is this a merueylous thynge: She hadde not soo soone endeth her prayer but that she coulde rede lyuely her psalms, as redely as she hadde ben ony kunnyng clerke."[95] Again, this specific demand placed upon her by God and the grace of skillful words was also explicitly gendered by Catherine herself, who was conscious that women's words meant little in this world: "Thou knowest well, lord, that men setten lytyll store by womens wordes, speke þe neuer so vertyuously, as it were not semely, ne lyuest thou that wymmen sholde be more conuersaunt amonges men."[96]

Catherine's acknowledgment in her life of the homeliness and inefficacy of women's words anticipates the very charge leveled against St. Bridget of Sweden's vernacular language as rude and defective during the latter's canonization proceedings. Cardinal Adam Easton defended St. Bridget by noting that nuns and women are deficient in intellectual understanding and incapable of grasping the subtleties of the law of God: "Moniales seu mulieres satis imbecillas intellectu et rudes ad capiendum subtilia legis dei."[97] God reminds Catherine, as if in reply, that He transcends gender difference—that in Him difference is not possible: "Am I not he the whiche hathe made mankynde bothe man and woman and the shappe of euery eyther; and where that I wyl enspyre myn grace, al is one to me both man and woman."[98] Having said that, God adds His awareness that in this world and in His Church gender differences do apply. His idea is to use Catherine particularly as a gendered if spiritual educational tool, to teach proud men who cannot accept the efficacy of women's words: "I shall sende to theym freel wymmen endewed graciously wyth myn dyuyne vertu, in to confusyon and shame of theyr foly that been soo proude."[99]

That St. Catherine's mission would have irritated ecclesiastical men, in particular, is demonstrated, once again, by Easton's defense of St. Bridget for establishing women's authority over men in her rule. Against the charge that Christ forbade women to teach, or to speak in church, among other prohibitions, and that therefore St. Bridget was not permitted to speak in church, Easton responds that this is not true because, at the time Christ declared to her the Rule and wished it to be made known through her, both men and women were bound to the said Rule in the church or monasteries to be serving perpetually ("Non apparet verisimile quod christus ore proprie dictavit regulam et eam voluerit publicari per mulierem quam apostolus in ecclesia loqui non permittit et tam viros quam mulieres illius ecclesie sive monasterii ad dictam regulam servandam perpetuo obligari"). Easton also argues that women can teach others privately, even if not publicly in church, because St. Paul never forbade them to speak in church, just not to teach publicly.[100]

How God accomplishes his gendered goal occurs in Catherine's political and spiritual role in healing the Great Schism, chiefly through her prophecies during the rebellion of Italian cities against Pope Gregory XI (1375); her desire for daily Communion and Pope Gregory's special dispensation of a priest and portable altar to her; and her work for Pope Gregory as ambassador to Florence, which had rebelled against the Church (she went in December of 1377 and stayed till July 1378, refusing to leave until Urban VI was elected on 9 April 1378, because Pope Gregory had died on 27 March 1377), after which peace was established.[101] In the same year, 1378, she completed her *Book of the Dialogue with Divine Providence* and Barduccio, Stefano de Maconi, and Neri di Landoccio transcribed it.[102] Later Catherine was summoned to Rome by Pope Urban VI, and in 1380 she died, at the age of thirty-three.

Margery, first conversing with Christ, then with men in ecclesiastical situations, eventually develops her voice into a powerful instrument whose words—"comunycacyons" and "dalyawnses"— transform the sinfulness of her auditors and create through her as mediator a sympathetic bond between them and God, leading to conversion.[103] In this regard we are interested in the chapters from her "life" that deal with Christ and her husband through her arrest and charge as a Lollard (around chapters 46–54)—an early middle of her book, in which she evolves as a preacher.

Margery's "Comunycacyon" and "Dalyawns" as a Preacher

Margery learns to subvert her own alterity to achieve power within her community and to "converse" with clerics at the lower ranks and, ever increasingly, like Catherine of Siena, with more powerful ecclesiasts, including archbishops, if not the pope. Given her various social liabilities—her gender difference, her weeping, and so forth—Christ tells her that she would not be able to bear the scorn and spite of others without his grace: "It wer unpossibyl to the to suffyr the scornys and despytes that thow schalt have ne were only my grace supportyng the"

(Staley, *Book*, 42 [chap. 13]). Aside from God's support and an increasingly important role as preacher, Margery's conversion, according to Peter Dorsey, also gives her the freedom to resist her husband's advances and travel around the country and Europe and the Middle East.[104] Christ also informs her that He is in effect ventriloquizing her at his will—"I am an hyd God in the"—and that God bestows upon her tears and "swych *dalyawns*" [spiritual conversing] as he so decides (Staley, *Book*, 43 [14]; my emphasis).

The beginning of Margery's ecclesiastical "conversations" occurs after the Midsummer Night's Eve bargain she strikes with her husband and God about the trading of sex for meat and company with John Kempe on Friday (along with her payment of his debts)—presumably when she is free to begin her career as a "preacher." Although there is not space for an exhaustive treatment, I point out three types of "conversation" or "communication" with ecclesiasts and church officials, the first of which represents a Communion as if between sinner and priest as agent of God, with the end result of the spiritual advancement of the male cleric through Margery and despite her alterity in every instance. Indeed, the very source of annoyance in each case, ironically, proves to be the means of her communication with Christ and the agency for the ecclesiast's betterment and even salvation.

The first type of Margery's unhomely *dalyawns* as spiritual conversion occurs at a "place of monks" where she sits at mealtime next to the abbot and a monk who "despysed hir and set hir at nowt" begins to change his mind about her because of the "good wordys" she says—and because of "hir *dalyawns*" (Staley, *Book*, 39 [12]; my emphasis): "And thorw hir *dalyawns* hys affeccyon gan gretly enclyne to hirward and gan to have gret savour in hir wordys." Margery's weeping for the monk's sins while he is in Mass induces Christ to convince her that she must save him by relaying those truths about him and his sinfulness, so repugnant to say aloud that she prefers out of shame not to do so—for his sins are those deadly ones of lechery, pride (despair), and avarice (keeping of worldly things). Christ deliberately puts her in the position of being disliked for communicating such truths, but He also designates her as the vehicle of the monk's salvation. This depends upon the monk's following Margery's counsel as if she were a priest, relinquishing his sins (and his office outside the cloister—perhaps outriding), and confessing his sins. Thereafter the monk follows her advice and is later appointed a subprior, for which he was grateful to her ever after. Both her words and her counsel represent a kind of symbolic Communion, or Host, because they are divine wisdom incarnate and because they are ferried to the monk through a noisy woman whose tears, no matter how annoying, are shed on his account. Through gender difference, we might say, the monk finds God.

A second type of "dalyawns" and "comunyng" as between equals takes place away from home with a vicar and an anchoress in chapters 17 and 18; in both cases there are mutual respect and support for Margery despite the slanders against her and the oddness of the tale she relays about herself. The conversation in the first instance is with the vicar of St. Stephen's Church in Norwich (chap. 17), who initially finds it impossible to believe any woman could have enough to say for one or two hours about the love of God, but after hearing her conversation finds himself so moved that he thereafter supports her when she is attacked by enemies and even when she is brought before the bishop to respond to charges laid against her by "the steryng of envyows pepyl" (Staley, *Book*, 52 [chap. 17]). What she tells him that first afternoon involves her tale of conversion, her revelation of the celestial melodies she hears (and a resultant swooning fall), and the "dalyawns" she has with all three persons of the Trinity that is so exquisite that she falls down, sobbing and crying and wrestling with her body. But she also reveals that "mech pepyl slawndryd hir, not levyng it was the werke of God but that sum evyl spyrit vexid hir in hir body er ellys that sche had sum bodyly sekeneses" (Staley, *Book*, 51 [chap. 17]). The vicar's staunch belief in her story enables him to live seven years longer.

A similar positive experience of this second type, as if between ecclesiastical equals, occurs between Margery during her visit to anchoress Dame Julian of Norwich (chap. 18).[105] Further, *The Mirror of Simple Souls* by Marguerite Porete, as we have seen previously, was translated into Middle English from the Old French and then into Latin from the Middle English by Richard Methley, a Mount Grace mystic who had ecstasies like Margery's; he also annotated Porete's work at the priory.[106] Perhaps because of their unifying conversation, Margery stresses the bond of homeliness—*comunyng*—between Julian and herself, initiated when Julian declares that God wishes her to be Margery's "fosterer": "Mych was the holy *dalyawns* that the ankres and this creatur haddyn be *comownyng* in the lofe of owyr Lord Jhesu Crist many days that thei were togedyr" (Staley, *Book*, 54 [chap. 18]; my emphasis).

The third type of conversation involves a high-ranking church official's antagonistic interrogation of Margery as a Lollard or heretic during her trip to York. Initially, this interrogation appears to result in her failure, but it actually ends in her vindication, release, and even victory. Charged with preaching by the archbishop of York, Margery, brought into his chapel, claims that she uses instead only "comunycacyon and good wordys" that are her own and can be considered a form of female (or self-authorized) speech. This example of "communication" surfaces in her own parable of the priest-as-bear, told as a "tale" in response to the accusation of her preaching. She denies to the archbishop that she is a Lollard and argues that he will not be able to prove she is one. After demonstrating her knowledge of the Articles of Faith to the archbishop and his clerics, she is told by the archbishop that he has heard she is a wicked woman; she responds that she has heard that he is a wicked man and should amend his ways if he wishes to enter heaven. When he retorts, "Why, thow, what sey men of me," she replies, "Other *men*, syr, can telle yow wel anow" (Staley, *Book*, 125 [chap. 52]; my emphasis). She is then admonished by a cleric, "Pes, thu speke of thiself and late hym ben" (Staley, *Book*, 125 [chap. 52]).

In short, she is *told* to speak about herself. She does so by immediately resisting all demands made by the archbishop, among them, to swear she will leave the diocese. Instead, she wants to say goodbye to her friends and asks to stay for a couple of days; she also needs to see her confessor in nearby Bridlington. She is also told to swear not to teach people while there or "chalengyn the pepil" (call them to account), but she refuses to swear, declaring that God does not forbid speaking about God. She also cites the Scripture—Luke 11: 27–8—to prove that women in particular have been authorized to speak of God. It is this citation that triggers the Pauline injunction by a "gret clerke" that "no woman schulde prechyn" and her subsequent response that "I preche not, ser, I come in no pulpytt. I use but comunycacyon and good wordys" (Staley, *Book*, 126 [chap. 52]).

Margery provides two literal examples of "comunycacyon and good wordys" to identify and authorize speaking in her own voice, one from the Gospel text of Luke and the other from her fable about the priest and the bear (labeled by the examining Church doctor as one of the "werst talys of prestys that evyr I herde") (Staley, *Book*, 126 [chap. 52]). In the former, a woman who has heard the Lord preach "cam beforn hym wyth a lowde voys and seyd, 'Blyssed be the wombe that the bar and the tetys that gaf the sowkyn.' Than owr Lord seyd agen to hir, 'Forsothe so ar thei blissed that heryn the word of God and kepyn it'" (Staley, *Book*, 126 [chap. 52]). Although this Gospel text may be interpreted as criticism of the woman who honored Christ's mother rather than Christ,[107] according to Margery, from this account "me thynkyth that the gospel gevyth me leve to spekyn of God" (Staley, *Book*, 126 [chap. 52]). Margery defines her role as a listener as a complement to that of the preacher: "I preche not, ser, I come in no pulpytt" (Staley, *Book*, 126 [chap. 52]). In this passive and auditory role, this representative of the preacher's congregation is presumed willing to receive grace to amend faults. Just so, Christ has responded to the woman in the Gospel by acknowledging the blessedness of the auditors of the Word of God who follow it, as does auditor Margery when she speaks of God.

The two roles are here gender-distinct: if preaching is masculine, whatever is subsumed under not-preaching must be feminine. The feminized complement to preaching or to the masculine word/Word is identified first with the origin of the Word, or the feminine maternal as fruitful source, and identified in Margery's paraphrase of the Gospel text as such by the female respondent to Christ when she blessed the womb and breasts of Jesus's mother Mary. This feminine correlative to Christ also responds to the Word in an active and verbal form of articulation that can be described as a blessing, good words, conversation: "*Blyssed* be the wombe" (my emphasis). The blessing normally conferred by the priest, or the Word Himself, is here translated into the utterance of the female respondent who has listened and who speaks, refusing to remain silent in this dialogue.[108]

Therefore, when Margery is accused in this same transaction of preaching—the masculine activity forbidden to women by Paul—she then replies, rightly, that she uses "comunycacyon and good wordys," but not within any context where priests sermonize, that is, the pulpit. Under this rubric come "tale-telling," fiction, parables, and, in this case, her fable about a priest in the wood who witnesses a bear eating flowers from a beautiful pear tree and then defecating them (chap. 52). The priest (according to Margery) must learn from a palmer that he may be identified as the pear tree who administers the sacraments (the fruit of everlasting life) and as the bear who defecates, that is, when he performs his sacerdotal role without devotion and lives life viciously.

What does she mean by fabulizing the priest as pear tree/defecating bear? The role reversals continue: instead of the (male) preacher chastising his feminized but errant Christian congregation, or audience, the (female) tale-teller chastises her (male) preacher/priest. Here the doctor's role as auditor has been clearly identified as female, passive, whereas her role is clearly the conversational role of tale-telling, gossip; the female tale-teller (= liar) takes up the masculine role of the preacher. The origins of the Word—Mary, the Bible, the Church, Ecclesia—are holy, blessed, like the feminized pear tree, but he-who-should-speak, the priest, is speechless and troubled by what he sees (= the vision of himself). Instead of childbirth and lactation (= Mary's role) there is the faithless administering of the sacraments and their defecation (the masculine fantasy, or appropriation, of the feminine role of childbirth). Mostly, in the female pilgrim (palmer's?)'s accusation, it is the saying of Mass that is described as heedless babbling (speech without content), unlike Margery's tale of misconduct (which is full of content). That she has truly stepped into the role of Christ's mother/auditor-respondent is clear from the cleric's response to her tale, which resembles that of the troubled priest in her story: the clerk says to the archbishop, who has just admired the story as a "good tale," "This tale smytyth me to the hert" (Staley, *Book*, 128 [chap. 52]). Margery then (pilgrimlike) identifies the reason for his pain: she tells him of a cleric in her town who warns, "Yyf any man be evyl plesyd wyth my prechyng, note hym wel, for he is gylty" (Staley, *Book*, 128 [chap. 52]). The troubled cleric takes the place of the feminized auditor, and Margery appropriates the role of the priest when she says to the clerk, "And ryth so, ser, . . . far ye be me, God forgeve it yow" (Staley, *Book*, 128 [chap. 52]), after which, like any sinful member of the (feminized) congregation, the cleric begs her forgiveness and asks her to pray for him.

Ultimately the words of conversation and communication of St. Catherine of Siena and Margery Kempe transform collectively, within their narratives, into books, which have continued to manifest their alterity even today as a means of preaching their subject positions as the colonized. By using Catherine's own words in the *Dialogue* as a gloss on Margery's *Book*, we can perhaps understand better what Margery's life was intended to accomplish within that paradigm: a dialogue about alterity between a colonized woman and her auditors, in Margery's case, two priests. Such a strategy serves to emphasize the double nature of Margery's life in her *Book*, as both marginalized Other and as wielder of homely words, and thereby clarify both these women's political agendas as mediators and facilitators for the commoners who belong to the church.

Margery, whose good words and communications served the effect of resisting colonization and drawing attention to the empowerment of the Other, through her *Book* manages in bits and pieces of her own voice to relay less of a philosophical or theological perspective than exactly what she is heralded for, "dalyawns" and "comunycacyons." A symbol of that bridge between Self and Other, humble soul and loving God, her "comunycacyons" act to lessen intolerance, misunderstanding, and destruction of difference, whether personal, gender, or class in nature. Through her book, through her conversations, and through herself, Margery ultimately becomes that symbol, allowing Christ to be crucified once more through the malice and defamation—evil words—of others, but triumphing through a "resurrection" that has allowed her very alterity to continue to live on today as part of a minor literature of resistance and subversion through the dialogues and conversations of her students and scholars.

CHAPTER 6

CONCLUSION: TOWARD A MINOR
LITERATURE: JULIAN OF NORWICH'S
ANNIHILATION OF ORIGINAL SIN

M edieval women writers, as described in the previous chapters, created their own minor literature through dissonance within the larger literatures we call "medieval," that is, those essentially written by male clerics and court poets. Their various discursive strategies, whether of feminized encoding, gender inversion, fantasization, or legitimation of difference, have demonstrated a consistent overlay of methodology and purpose in constructing their minor literature. Together, as case studies, these essays may suggest the beginnings of a feminized literary tradition complementary and functioning as counterpoint to canonical medieval literature.

In most cases—whether early in the Middle Ages, in the tenth to the twelfth centuries, or late, in the fourteenth and fifteenth centuries— some intracultural or postcolonial connection also exists through which the European woman writer mediates or against which she resists. For Saxon Hrotsvit the connection exists in those Anglo-Saxon books that deal with Roman and Mediterranean saints—here, most likely Ælfric's lives of St. Agnes—brought to Saxony through royal marriages that foster inspiration for one of her key dramas. For French Heloise, as other studies have made clear, it is her Breton lover and husband, Abelard, whose irritating and distressing story of his calamities she counters and ameliorates through her own letters of instruction to him.[1] Marie de France, believed to have served as abbess at Reading or Shaftesbury, creates an alternate Celtic and feminized fantasy world in her Breton lay to set against the realism of a crude court and the Round Table of an

English king, Arthur, prejudiced against foreign knights, and his promiscuous and deceitful queen, Guinevere.

The writings of later medieval European women often appear to have had some influence on England and English women writers. Subversive Flemish beguine Marguerite Porete constructs a fantastic feminized theology in which a female soul and body are privileged over the usual abstract and disembodied soul favored by the church and its relationship with God. Porete's mysticism anticipates the maternal theology of the English anchorite Julian of Norwich a hundred years later. Significant copies of the autobiographies of Marguerite Porete, Julian of Norwich, and Margery Kempe were all made at the Mount Grace Charterhouse in north Yorkshire. In Italy, St. Catherine of Siena both feminizes and democratizes her Christ in her *Dialogue* through her vision of him as a mediating and literal bridge between man and God. It is no accident that this work and her *legenda* are copied at Syon Abbey, outside London, and translated into English after the Peasants' Revolt of 1381, with her *Lyf* later published by Wynken de Worde from William Caxton's plates. A convent establishing Catherine's rule also sprang up in Edinburgh, Scotland, in the fifteenth century.

In addition, in other studies, scholars have recognized Franco-Italian Christine de Pizan's connection with England in the similarity of her *Livre de la Cité des Dames* to Geoffrey Chaucer's unfinished *Legend of Good Women* and in the fact of the translation of several of her works into English, including the *Epistre Othea* (brought back by Sir John Falstaff from France) and the *Livre de la Cité des Dames*.[2] Perhaps through the Earl of Salisbury—Jean de Montfort—who had fallen in love with her, or through her son, who had served as page in his court, copies of English poems made their way into France, just as her French poems did in fact enter England.

Finally, two other women writers—Margery Kempe of King's Lynn and Julian of Norwich—lived north of London, and Margery, Julian, and Marguerite Porete inscribed manuscripts that surfaced in some form in the north, at Mount Grace Priory; other female writers or patrons authored or authorized manuscripts of poems held at the library at Longleat house in Derbyshire.[3] What Kempe and these authors share, whether they or their personae and subjects come from the middle class or aristocracy, is their resistance to a society and a church that seek to control and repress their female voices and their individuality as women.

That they have created a minor literature through their discursive strategies is attested by one further example, relating to the influence of

Marguerite Porete on subsequent writers, in particular, Julian of Norwich, who echoes her position on original sin and who seems also to echo the views of Hildegard of Bingen. Whatever intertextuality and intraculturality between the work of medieval women and those of other male and female writers, I would like to end this study by indicating how Porete's particular theological innovation—not heresy—in regard to original sin and the embodied Soul can be glossed by a literary and theological tradition of subversion belonging to both one earlier and one later woman—chiefly, Hildegard of Bingen and Julian of Norwich. Through further study of the links between and among medieval women writers we shall forge an understanding of how their minor literature evolved.

Although Porete was burned at the stake for her alleged heresy, her ideas about a feminized Trinity were not wholly unusual in the Middle Ages, nor was her concept of the annihilation of original sin. Women mystics of the Middle Ages frequently feminized God through one of the three persons of the Trinity, especially the Holy Ghost—as agent of God constructing Creation, Adam and Eve, and the Virgin Mary—or Christ Himself, the second person of the Trinity (that is, God the Father is retained but as an abstract and distant figure, replaced in emphasis by either the second or the third person, who is then enlarged through a feminized interpretation or cast or role). This feminizing tradition began as early as the time of the innovative and radical twelfth-century Saxon abbess Hildegard of Bingen (b. 1098–d. 1179?). She feminizes God through the second person of the Trinity, Christ, as an image of wisdom and love, essential to a theological core that centers on the cosmic spiritual force of *viriditas*, "regreening."[4] An apotheosis of the Virgin Mary through her motherhood of Christ, second person of the Trinity, also appears in the writings of the fourteenth-century English anchorite and mystic Julian of Norwich (ca. 1342–post 1416).[5] Interestingly, Julian's *Shewings* in the shorter version has been copied into one Carthusian manuscript along with a Middle English translation of Porete's work. Written in one hand (ca. 1450) when Julian was still alive, according to Maureen Cré, this manuscript also contains a number of contemplative works—translations of two works by Richard Rolle, a Middle English translation of Dutch Jan van Ruusbroec's *Vanden Blinckenden Steen* [The Treatise of Perfection of the Sons of God], and short mystical pieces by Rolle, Herbert Suso, Bridget of Sweden, and the anonymous author of *The Cloud of Unknowing*.[6] However, in this manuscript, as in others, *The Mirror of Simple Souls* is anonymous, which accounted for the assumption of medieval readers and editors that the author was male.[7] Because of this anonymity, the manuscript collection, probably copied and edited by a Carthusian, Cré argues, was not viewed as marked in particular by a spirituality noticeably feminine.[8] Only in 1946 did Romana Guarnieri attribute the *Mirror* to Marguerite Porete and identify this book as the cause for her burning at the stake.[9]

Porete, alone among the other continental mystics, as Barbara Newman has hinted, uniquely compares with Julian's "radically speculative approach to mystical theology."[10] Although Newman does not specify what in Porete's work applies—perhaps because Newman focuses on Julian's later revision of the *Shewings* in what is known as the Long Text in the early fifteenth century, after Wycliff had been condemned,[11] and not the shorter version of the *Shewings* (ca. 1373), several of whose provocative Lollard-like statements having been omitted in the longer version—it is Julian's annihilation of original sin in the shorter version that most closely follows Porete's. A brief discussion will enhance the concept of a developing feminized literary tradition.

Where Julian obliterates original sin is in the making of Christ as our mother in both our redemption and our return to the natural state at our creation. In line with Marguerite, Julian understands God to be divinity and Christ to name—*anempnen*—our humanity, or what she calls sensuality, likely through his mother Mary: "In the Second Person, in witt and wisdam, we have our keping as anempts our sensualite, our restoryng, and our savyng. For He is our Moder, broder, and savior."[12] Such humanity provides the basis for Christ's mercy. "Thus is Jesus our very Moder in kynde, of our first makyng; and He is our very Moder in grace, be takyng of our kynde made."[13] Therefore, through Christ, Julian boldly argues, we return to our natural state, prior to original sin: "We be bowte agen be Moderhede of mercy and grace into our kindly stede; wher that we were made be the Motherhede of kynd love; which kynd love, it never levyth us."[14] There are no intermediaries between us and Christ, and through Christ directly we receive all the sacraments, most especially, communion: "The Moder may geven hir child soken her mylke, but our pretious Moder Jesus, He May fedyn us with Himselfe, and doith full curtesly and full tenderly with the blissid sacrament that is pretious fode of very lif. And with al the swete sacraments He susteynith us ful mercifully and graciously."[15] What Julian says is a "comforte to us agens al this [synne]" in two ways, aside from the Passion and Will of Christ.[16] First, what Julian sees in the third revelation—God does all that is done—has no sin: "God doth al thing except synne, never changyng His purpose without end, for He hath made al thing in fulhede of goodness."[17] Second, when God describes sin, He declares that "Al shall be wele."[18]

Julian's spiritual universe is without original sin. She asks in a very important passage, available only in the shorter version but cut from the longer, "What may make me mare to luff myn evencristen than to see in god that he loues alle that schalle be safe, as it ware alle a saulle? And in ilke saule that schall be sayfe is a goodely wille that neuer assentyd to synne, na never schall" (Beer notes that "in this view Julian diverges from church doctrine").[19] For this reason, God loves each person on earth as well as in heaven, regardless of sin: Julian continues: "For as þer is a bestely wille in the nethere party that maye wille na goode, so is thare a goodely wille in the ouer partye that maye wille nane eville, botte euer goode, na mare than the parsones of þe blissed trinyte. And this schewyd oure lorde me in the holehed of luffe, that we stande in his sight, ȝa, that he luffeȝ vs nowe als wele whiles we ere here as he schalle do when we ere thare before his blissed face."[20] This suggests that in the unredeemed state human beings are good enough for Christ to love —before death, before redemption.

In another passage early in the *Shewings* that was cut from the later, longer version, Julian reveals herself to be conscious of her subject position as a woman and of the Pauline prohibitions against women preaching or teaching: "Botte god for bede that ȝe schulde saye or take it so that I am a techere."[21] Rather too apologetically, given the boldness of her statements, Julian momentarily reverts to the conventional female modesty topos and then subverts her confession by authorizing herself through the ultimate teacher, Christ Himself: "for I meene nouȝt soo, no I mente nevere so; for I am a womann, leued, febille and freylle. Botte I wate wele, this that I saye, I hafe it of the schewynge of hym tha(t) es souerayne techare."[22] Indeed, Julian continues, asking her auditor coyly, should she refuse to teach "Botte for I am a woman?"

Julian extends the feminized mystical theologies of both Hildegard of Bingen and Marguerite of Porete and with them extinguishes the concept of original sin as caused by a woman. If flesh were not fallen, if we were not born with original sin, then women would not be culpable, male intermediaries would not be necessary to guide the soul to God, and redemption would be afforded all of us simply through a recognition of our common goodness and virtue offered by feminized Love and Faith, Porete's "ladies of the house." The Son of God, as the second person of the Trinity, is also the Holy Spirit, or Love, recognizably female. Divinity is, indeed, female, as is the holy aristocracy that serves it.

In her Holy Church the Great, Porete creates her own feminized fantasy that, despite its mysticism, in its construction of a community of Annihilated Souls most astonishingly anticipates the legendary and saintly women who populate Christine de Pizan's early-fifteenth-century *Cité des Dames*. Further, just as Porete's Soul in that later part of the *Mirror* presents petitions to God, so also Christine de Pizan petitions the God of Love in *Epistre au dieu d'amours* [Letter to the God of Love], written May 1399, and, following her, the nine ladies in the anonymous late-fifteenth-century Middle English visionary poem, *The Assembly of Ladies,* offer petitions to Loyalty at her castle. The ladies and gentlewomen present "bills" that are motto-like, clichés suggesting the fragmentary nature of women's language or, perhaps, because in French, the language of the court and law: "Sanz que jamais" [Without ever giving cause], "Une sans chaungier" [One without changing], "Oncques puis lever" [I can never rise], Entierment vostre [Entirely yours], "C'est sanz dire" [It needs no words], "En Dieu est" [In God is {my trust}], "Sejour ensure" [Rest assured], and "Bien monest" [Well advised]. What are these, if not the hackneyed words of socially adept women? Their language is homogenous and incomplete; individuality is impossible. That issue of fragmentation and failed individual identity is personified in—even symbolized by—the questing and questioning narrator herself. The narrator has no word—no complaint—no motto, and, hence, no self. Or perhaps that *is* her "worde," wishing that she knew who and what she really was. " 'Forsoth,' quod I, 'ye shal wele know and se: / And for my word, I have none, this is trewe; / It is inough that my clothyng be blew.' "[23] After the petitions have been presented, the promise of a court hearing is assured, but in fact there is no consolation, except the wide-awake narrator's answer to the knight who has asked the title of her book, "La Semble des Dames." The consolation is the fact of sororial community, or else the process that results in the writing of the book with the same name.

Porete's *Mirror*, we might observe, in Love's use of equivocal names for the Soul anticipates *The Assembly of Ladies*. Love constitutes these names—philosophically, accidents of being—through gerundive phrases and fragmentary thoughts that definitely do not reflect logical balance and completion, such as "The Not Understood," and Porete's last name in the work, "Oblivion, Forgotten": consider "The Very Marvelous One,"

"The Not Understood," "Most Innocent of the Daughters of Jerusalem," "She upon Whom the Holy Church Is Founded," "Illuminated by Understanding," "Adorned by Love," "Living by Praise," "Annihilated in All Things through Humility," "At Peace in Divine Being through Divine Will," "She Who Wills Nothing except the Divine Will," "Filled and Satisfied without Any Lack by Divine Goodness through the Work of the Trinity."[24] This proto-existential philosophical process of the Soul's becoming in the course of the narrative offers true freedom through nonbeing—or essential being through nonbeing.

Finally, Christine herself in her *Ladvision-Christine*, remarkably like Porete in some ways, constructs an alternate University of Paris in which she becomes the pupil tutored by female *magistrae*, including Dame Philosophy.[25] Although no concrete evidence exists that Christine read Porete's *Mirror*, at least she was close enough to have seen the currently inaccessible copy of the *Mirror* owned by a convent outside Paris. She may have known of Porete through Jean Gerson, Christine's mentor and ally in the Quarrel of the *Rose*, who lauds the book of "Maria de Valenciennes" despite her mistaken revelation about the possibility of the earthly soul's union with divine love, in *De distinctione verarum revelationum a falsis* [On Distinguishing True Revelations from False] (1401).[26]

The allegorical gambit of these three works provides women direct opportunity to voice their requests to a supreme but fictional authority, whether Love, Philosophy, or Perseverance. While all petitioning appears within the venue of the university, the court, or the castle, it is Marguerite Porete who first authorizes female personifications identified with the writer in a fabulous narrative whose tropes depend upon a fantasy of an inverted church, society, and university. But she exists within an evolving feminized literary tradition, one in which dissonance and resistance shape the minor literature.

NOTES

1 Introduction: The Discursive Strategies of the Marginalized

1. Judith Butler, "Contingent Foundations: Feminism and the Question of 'Postmodernism,'" in *Feminists Theorize the Political*, ed. Judith Butler and Joan W. Scott (New York: Routledge, 1992), 12 [3–21].

2. See Raphael Patai, *The Arab Mind* (New York: Scribner's Sons, 1976), 188–90.

3. Albert Memmi, *The Colonizer and the Colonized* (Boston: Beacon Press, 1965), 129; see also Butler, "Contingent Foundations," in *Feminist Theorize the Political*, ed. Judith Butler and Joan W. Scott, 21 n9.

4. Butler, "Contingent Foundations," in *Feminist Theorize the Political*, ed. Judith Butler and Joan W. Scott, 21 n9.

5. Homi K. Bhabha, *The Location of Culture*, Routledge Classics (London and New York: Routledge, 2004), 6.

6. See Bhabha, *Location of Culture*, 50. Bhabha notes that "Forms of popular rebellion and mobilization are often most subversive and transgressive when they are created through opposition of cultural practices" (29).

7. Butler, "Contingent Foundations," in *Feminist Theorize the Political*, ed. Judith Butler and Joan W. Scott, 13.

8. Bhabha, *Location of Culture*, 3.

9. Bhabha, *Location of Culture*, 2.

10. Bhabha, *Location of Culture*, 2.

11. Elizabeth Fox-Genovese, *Within the Plantation Household* (Chapel Hill: University of North Carolina Press, 1988), 329; see also Bhabha, *Location of Culture*, 24.

12. Bhabha, *Location of Culture*, 15.

13. Gilles Deleuze and Félix Guattari, *Kafka: Toward a Minor Literature*, trans. Dana Polan, foreword by Réda Bensmaïa, Theory and History of Literature, vol. 30 (Minneapolis: University of Minnesota Press, 1986), 16–17.

14. Although the vernacular is said to be the norm for most medieval women, many did know, read, and write Latin, a language conventionally regarded as patriarchal and reserved for male ecclesiastics in the Middle Ages. See the fine anthology of texts by medieval women edited by Laurie J. Churchill,

Phyllis R. Brown, and Jane E. Jeffrey, *Women Writing Latin: From Roman Antiquity to Early Modern Europe*, 3 vols. (New York: Routledge, 2002).

15. Isidore of Seville, *Etymologies* 11.2.23, excerpted in Alcuin Blamires, Karen Pratt, and C.W. Marx, eds., *Woman Defamed and Women Defended: An Anthology of Medieval Texts* (Oxford, UK: Clarendon Press, 1992), 43. Blamires's handy anthology of excerpts allows a close reading of gender difference through etymologies that is extremely helpful for understanding contemporary feminist theory.

16. Isidore, *Etymologies* 11.2.17, excerpted in Blamires, *Woman Defamed*, 43.

17. Isidore, *Etymologies* 11.2.17, excerpted in Blamires, *Woman Defamed*, 43.

18. Isidore, *Etymologies* 11.2.23, excerpted in Blamires, *Woman Defamed*, 43.

19. Isidore, *Etymologies* 9.5.3, excerpted in Blamires, *Woman Defamed*, 44.

20. Isidore, *Etymologies* 9.5.3, excerpted in Blamires, *Woman Defamed*, 44.

21. Isidore, *Etymologies* 7.6.5, excerpted in Blamires, *Woman Defamed*, 44–45.

22. Isidore, *Etymologies* 7.6.5, excerpted in Blamires, *Woman Defamed*, 45.

23. St. Jerome, *Against Jovinian* 1 (1.7) and 2, excerpted in Blamires, *Woman Defamed*, 64, 65.

24. 1 Cor. 14 (Rheims-Douai Version of the Catholic Vulgate Bible); see St. John Chrysostom, *Homily 9*, 1 and 2, excerpted in Blamires, *Woman Defamed*, 58, 59.

25. St. John Chrysostom, *Homily 9*, 2, excerpted in Blamires, *Woman Defamed*, 59.

26. St. John Chrysostom, *Homily 9*, 3, excerpted in Blamires, *Woman Defamed*, 59.

27. St. Jerome, *Against Jovinian*, 4 (156), excerpted in Blamires, *Woman Defamed*, 62.

28. R. Howard Bloch, "Medieval Misogyny," *Representations* 20 (1987): 1 [1–24].

29. Bloch, "Medieval Misogyny," 3.

30. Bloch, "Medieval Misogyny," 6.

31. Stephen Harper, " 'So Euyl to Rewlyn': Madness and Authority in 'The Book of Margery Kempe,' " *Neuphilologische Mitteilungen* 98 (1997): 59 [53–61].

32. See Thelma S. Fenster and Claire A. Lees, eds., *Gender and Debate from the Early Middle Ages to the Renaissance* (New York and Houndmills, Basingstoke, UK: Palgrave Macmillan, 2002).

33. See, for example, Carol M. Meale, ed., *Women and Literature in Britain, 1150–1500*, 2nd edn. (Cambridge: Cambridge University Press, 1996); Laurie Finke, *Women Writing in Medieval England* (London: Longmans, 1999); Juliette Dor, Lesley Johnson, and Jocelyn Wogan-Browne, eds., *New Trends in Spirituality: The Holy Women of Liège*, Medieval Women: Texts and Contexts 2 (Turnhout, Belg.: Brepols, 1999); and, for a work more specifically focused on the spaces in which women wrote, Diane Watt, ed., *Medieval Women in Their Communities* (Toronto: University of Toronto Press, 1997).

34. See Joan M. Ferrante, *To the Glory of Her Sex: Women's Roles in the Compositions of Medieval Texts* (Bloomington and Indianapolis: Indiana University Press, 1997).

35. For medieval books written by and intended for women, see Jane H.M. Taylor and Lesley Smith, *Women and the Book: Assessing the Visual Evidence*,

British Library Studies in Medieval Culture (London: British Library; Toronto: University of Toronto Press, 1996); for book ownership by women, see Mary C. Erler, *Women, Reading, and Piety in Late Medieval England* (Cambridge: Cambridge University Press, 2002).

36. For Hrotsvit of Gandersheim, see Phyllis R. Brown, Linda A. McMillan, and Katharina M. Wilson, eds., *Hrotsvit of Gandersheim: Contexts, Identities, Affinities, and Performances* (Toronto and London: University of Toronto Press, 2004); for Anna Comnena, see Thalia Gouma-Peterson, ed., *Anna Komnene and Her Times* (New York and London: Garland/Taylor and Francis, 2000).

37. For Heloise, see Bonnie Wheeler, ed., *Listening to Heloise: The Voice of a Twelfth-Century Woman*, New Middle Ages Series (London and New York: Palgrave Macmillan/St. Martin's, 2000); for Hildegard of Bingen, see Barbara Newman, *Sister of Wisdom: St. Hildegard's Theology of the Feminine* (Berkeley and Los Angeles: University of California Press, 1987).

38. For Christine de Pizan, see Earl Jeffrey Richards, with Joan Williamson, Nadia Margolis, and Christine Reno, eds., *Reinterpreting Christine de Pizan* (Athens: University of Georgia Press, 1992); Margarete Zimmermann and Dina De Rentiis, eds., *The City of Scholars: New Approaches to Christine de Pizan* (Berlin and New York: Walter de Gruyter, 1994); Helen Solterer, *The Master and Minerva: Disputing Woman in French Medieval Culture* (Berkeley: University of California Press, 1995); Barbara Altmann and Deborah McGrady, eds., *A Casebook on Christine de Pizan* (New York: Routledge, 2003); and Angus J. Kennedy, with Rosalind Brown-Grant, James C. Laidlaw, and Catherine M. Müller, eds., *Contexts and Continuities: Proceedings of the IVth International Colloquium on Christine de Pizan (Glasgow 21–27 July 2000), Published in Honour of Liliane Dulac*, Glasgow University Medieval French Texts and Studies, 3 vols. (Glasgow: University of Glasgow Press, 2002).

39. For women visionaries and mystics, including Bridget of Sweden and Margery Kempe, see Rosalynn Voaden, *God's Words, Women's Voices: The Discernment of Spirits in the Writing of Late-Medieval Women Visionaries* (Woodbridge, Suffolk, UK, and Rochester, NY: York Medieval Press, 1999); and Amy Hollywood, *Sensible Ecstasy: Mysticism, Sexual Difference, and the Demands of History*, Religion and Postmodernism (Chicago and London: University of Chicago Press, 2001). Also, on Margery Kempe, see Lynn Staley, *Margery Kempe's Dissenting Fictions* (University Park: Pennsylvania State University Press, 1994); Karma Lochrie, *Margery Kempe and Translations of the Flesh* (Philadelphia: University of Pennsylvania Press, 1991); and John H. Arnold and Katherine J. Lewis, eds., *A Companion to "The Book of Margery Kempe"* (Woodbridge, Suffolk, UK: D.S. Brewer, 2004).

40. For aristocratic women's family letters, see John M. Klassen, trans., *The Letters of the Rožmberk Sisters: Noblewomen in Fifteenth-Century Bohemia, Library of Medieval Women* (Woodbridge, Suffolk, UK: Boydell and Brewer, 2001); and Diane Watt, ed., *The Paston Women: Selected Letters, Library of Medieval Women* (Woodbridge, Suffolk, UK: Boydell and Brewer, 2004).

41. Sharon Kinoshita, *Medieval Boundaries: Rethinking Difference in Old French Literature* (Philadelphia: University of Pennsylvania Press, 2006).

42. See Margaret W. Ferguson, *Dido's Daughters: Literacy, Gender, and Empire in Early Modern England and France* (Chicago: University of Chicago Press, 2003).

43. Susan Schibanoff, "Taking the Gold Out of Egypt: The Art of Reading as a Woman," in *Gender and Reading*, ed. Elizabeth A. Flynn and Patrocinio Schweickart (Baltimore and London: Johns Hopkins University Press, 1986), 101–2 [83–106].

44. See Pam Whitfield, "Power Plays: Relationships in Marie de France's *Lanval* and *Eliduc*," *Medieval Perspectives* 14 (1999): 242–54.

45. There are exceptions, of course; for example, both Hrotsvit of Gandersheim (ca. 935–ca. 1000) and Anna Comnena (1083–153) wrote epics: the former, in her *Primordia Coenobii Gandeshemensis* and *Carmen de Gestis Oddonis Imperatoris*, which trace the origins of her convent and the Ottonian dynasty that supported it, and the latter, in her *Alexiad*, which memorializes the rule of her own family.

46. Karen Cherewatuk and Ulrike Wiethaus, eds., *Dear Sister: Medieval Women and the Epistolary Genre* (Philadelphia: University of Pennsylvania Press, 1993).

47. Roberta Krueger, *Women Readers and the Ideology of Gender in Old French Verse Romance* (Cambridge: Cambridge University Press, 1993); and Maureen Quilligan, *The Allegory of Female Authority: Christine de Pizan's 'Cité des Dames'* (Ithaca, NY: Cornell University Press, 1991).

48. William D. Paden, ed., *The Voice of the Trobairitz: Perspectives on the Women Troubadours* (Philadelphia: University of Pennsylvania Press, 1989); Sarah Kay, *Subjectivity in Troubadour Poetry* (Cambridge: Cambridge University Press, 1990); Angelica Rieger, *Trobairitz: Der Beitrag der Frau in der altokzitanischen höfischen Lyrik: Edition des Gesamtkorpus* (Tübingen, Ger.: Max Niemeyer, 1991); and Matilda Bruckner, "Fictions of the Female Voice: The Woman Troubadour," *Speculum* 67 (1992): 865–91.

49. See Caroline Walker Bynum, *Jesus as Mother: Studies in the Spirituality of the High Middle Ages* (Berkeley: University of California Press, 1984); Bynum, *Holy Feast and Holy Fast* (Berkeley: University of California Press, 1986); Newman, *Sister of Wisdom*; Newman, *From Virile Woman to WomanChrist: Studies in Medieval Religion and Literature* (Philadelphia: University of Pennsylvania Press, 1995); Ulrike Wiethaus, ed., *Maps of Flesh and Light: The Religious Experience of Medieval Women Mystics* (Syracuse, NY: Syracuse University Press, 1993); and Elizabeth A. Petroff, *Body and Soul: Essays on Medieval Women and Mysticism* (New York and Oxford: Oxford University Press, 1994).

50. Monique Wittig, "The Mark of Gender," in *The Poetics of Gender*, ed. Nancy Miller (New York: Columbia University Press, 1986), 63–73.

51. Laurie Finke, *Feminist Theory, Women's Writing* (Ithaca, NY, and London: Cornell University Press, 1992), 9.

52. Finke, *Feminist Theory*, 9.

53. Finke, *Feminist Theory*, 11, 14–15.

54. Finke, *Feminist Theory*, 11, 22.

55. See especially Finke, *Feminist Theory*, 11, 24–25. On p. 24 Finke cites Serres. See William R. Paulson, *The Noise of Culture: Literary Texts in a World of Information* (Ithaca, NY: Cornell University Press, 1988).

56. Michel de Certeau, *The Practice of Everyday Life*, trans. Steven F. Rendall (Berkeley: University of California Press, 1984), xii, cited in Finke, *Feminist Theory*, 10.

57. Finke, *Feminist Theory*, 13.

58. M.M. Bakhtin, *The Dialogic Imagination*, ed. Michael Holquist and Caryl Emerson (Austin: University of Texas Press, 1981), 346–47. Finke discusses Bakhtin in *Feminist Theory*, 14.

59. See the theorized approach to Marie de France by Michelle A. Freeman, "Marie France's Poetics of Silence: the Implications for a Feminine *Translatio*," *PMLA* 99 (1984): 860–83. Sharon Kinoshita has summarized Freeman's approach to ellipsis in Marie and Chrétien de Troyes as an example of how this poetics works in practice: first, Marie openly dedicates her work to a male patron in contrast to Chrétien's more ironic and even subversive response to his commissions; second, Marie leaves out the essential and layers her text with polysemy and ambiguity, whereas Chrétien offers rhetorical devices such as ellipsis and preterition to point explicitly to what has been omitted; and, third, Marie's thematics of silence in *Lanval*, which resembles that in the male-authored *Conte du Graal*, offers female innovation as an opportunity for male imitation without reducing the significance of a woman writer's voice and poetics. See Sharon Kinoshita, " 'Cherchez la femme': Feminist Criticism and Marie de France's *Lai de Lanval*," *Romance Notes* 34 (1994): 267 n11 [263–73].

60. See Joan Ferrante, "Public Postures and Private Maneuvers: Roles Medieval Women Play," in *Women and Power in the Middle Ages*, ed. Mary Erler and Maryanne Kowaleski (Athens: University of Georgia Press, 1988), 213–29.

61. See E. Jane Burns, *Bodytalk: When Women Speak in Old French Literature* (Philadelphia: University of Pennsylvania Press, 1993). The misogyny evident in labeling the so-called female voice as disruptive has been outlined by Bloch in "Medieval Misogyny," 1–24.

62. See Kinoshita, "Cherchez la femme," 263–73. As an example, Kinoshita offers Marie de France's *Lanval*: "Ostensibly the most blandly conventional of literary heroes, Lanval—perhaps for that very reason—is able to reject the 'project of primogeniture' to which all but the most rebellious of literary heroines are inevitably conscripted" (272).

63. Kinoshita "Cherchez la femme," 265.

64. See Bruckner, "Fictions," 867 [865–91]. In a footnote Bruckner acknowledges two crucial works concerning the voices of women breaking the silence: Carol Gilligan, *In a Different Voice: Psychological Theory and Women's Development* (Cambridge, MA: Harvard University Press, 1982); and Mary Field Belenky, Blythe Clinchy, Nancy Goldberger, and Jill Tarule, eds., *Women's Ways of Knowing: The Development of Self, Voice, and*

Mind (New York: Basic Books, 1986). The latter theorizes feminist episte-mology as learning to move from silence to hearing the voices of others to learning to discern women's own inner voices (867 n12).

65. Bruckner, "Fictions," 868.

66. Hildegard of Bingen, *Causae et curae*, bk. 2, in *Hildegardis causae et curae*, ed. Paul Kaiser (Leipzig: Teubner, 1903), 47; for the English translation of rearranged passages, see Hildegard of Bingen, *On Natural Philosophy and Medicine, Selections from "Cause et cure,"* trans. Margret Berger, Library of Medieval Women (Woodbridge, Suffolk, UK, and Rochester, NY: D.S. Brewer, 1999), 41 [3.5].

67. Hildegard, *Causae et curae*, 143 (bk. 2); *On Natural Philosophy* 41–42, 44 (3.8, 4).

68. Hildegard, *Causae et curae*, 59 (bk. 2); *On Natural Philosophy* 43 (4).

69. Hildegard, *Causae et curae*, 60 (bk. 2); *On Natural Philosophy* 44 (4).

70. Hildegard, *Causae et curae*, 35–36 (bk. 2); *Natural Philosophy* 51–52 (5.2).

71. Hildegard, *Causae et curae*, 36 (bk. 2); *On Natural Philosophy* 52 (5.2).

72. For the original Old French, see Christine de Pizan, *La Città delle Donne*, trans. into Italian by Patricia Caraffi, ed. Earl Jeffrey Richards (Milan and Trento, IT: Luni Editrice, 1997), 40 (1.1); for the English translation, Christine de Pizan, *The Book of the City of Ladies*, trans. Earl Jeffrey Richards (1982; rev. edn. New York: Persea, 1998), 3 (1.1). Subsequent references in this paragraph come from these pages and book and chapter number.

73. Christine de Pizan, *La Città delle Donne*, 42 (1.1); *The Book of the City of Ladies*, 4 (1.1). All references in this paragraph come from these pages, book, and chapter.

74. Christine de Pizan, *La Città delle Donne*, 42 (1.1); *The Book of the City of Ladies*, 4 (1.1).

75. Christine de Pizan, *La Città delle Donne* (1.1–11); *The Book of the City of Ladies*, 3–32.

76. See, for example, Barbara Harlow, *Barred: Women, Writing, and Political Detention* (Hanover, NH: Wesleyan University Press, 1992), 75.

77. Harlow, *Barred*, 74.

78. See Christine de Pizan, *La Città delle Donne*, 460, 462, 464, 466, 468, 470, 472 (3.10); Christine de Pizan, *The Book of the City of Ladies*, 234–40 (3.10.1).

79. See Dyan Elliott, *Proving Women: Female Spirituality and Inquisitional Culture in the Later Middle Ages* (Princeton, NJ, and Oxford, UK: Princeton University Press, 2004).

2   St. Agnes and the Emperor's Daughter in Saxon Hrotsvit of Gandersheim: Feminizing the Founding of the Early Roman Church

1. See the Venerable Bede, *Ecclesiastical History of the English People*, ed. Bertram Colgrave and R.A.B. Mynors (Oxford, UK: Oxford University Press, 1969), bk. 4, chap. 20; and Aldhelm, *Carmen de virginitate*, in *Aldhelm: The Prose Works*, trans. Michael Lapidge and Michael Herren (Cambridge, and Totowa, NJ: Rowman and Littlefield, 1979).

2. See Scott Gwara, "The Transmission of the 'Digby' Corpus of Bilingual Glosses to Aldhelm's *Prosa de virginitate*," *Anglo-Saxon England* 27 (1998): 139–68.

3. See M. Teresa Tavormina, "Of Maidenhood and Maternity: Liturgical Hagiography and the Medieval Ideal of Virginity," *American Benedictine Review* 31.4 (1980): 384–99.

4. See the Venerable Bede, "Saint Bede's *Martyrologium*: A Translation with an Introduction," trans. Clarence J. Bogetto (M.A. thesis, De Paul University, 1957); George Herzfeld, ed., *An Old English Martyrology*, Early English Text Society, o.s., no. 116 (London: K. Paul, Trench, Trübner, 1900); and Ælfric, *Aelfric's Lives of Saints, Being a Set of Sermons on Saints' Days Formerly Observed by the English Church, Edited from Manuscript Julius E. VII in the Cottonian Collection, with Various Readings from Other Manuscripts*, ed. and trans. Walter W. Skeat, part 1, in vol. 1, Early English Text Society, o.s., no. 76 (London: Trübner, 1881; repr. New York: Early English Text Society/Oxford University Press, 1966). For the Old English legend of St. Agnes, "Natale sancte Agnetis, virginis," translated from Skeat's edition, see Leslie Donovan, *Women Saints' Lives in Old English Prose*, Library of Medieval Women (Woodbridge, Suffolk, UK: D.S. Brewer, 1999), 46–55.

5. Indeed, the consequences of sexual promiscuity appear as late as the fifteenth century, in Robert Henryson's fifteenth-century Middle English *Testament of Cresseid*, which depicts the fickle beloved of Troilus (and of Diomede) as afflicted with the disfiguring disease of leprosy.

6. Book 1 includes her eight legends (*Maria, Ascensio, Gongolf, Pelagius, Saint Basilius, Saint Theophilus, Dionysius*—about the first bishop of Paris—and *Saint Agnes*). In book 2 appear her plays, *Gallicanus I* and *II, Dulcitius, Callimachus, Paphnutius, Abraham*, and *Sapientia*. In book 3 appear her two epics, written in leonine hexameter, the *Carmen de Gestis Oddonis Imperatoris* and the *Primordia Coenobii Gandeshemensis*.

7. Katharina M. Wilson, introduction to *Hrotsvit of Gandersheim: A Florilegia of Her Works*, Library of Medieval Women (Cambridge, UK, and Rochester, NY: D.S. Brewer, 1998). See also the description of Hrotsvit's works in Katharina M. Wilson's anthology, *Medieval Women Writers* (Athens: University of Georgia Press, 1984), 13.

8. Hrotsvit, "Praefatio," in *Hrotsvithae opera*, ed. Helene Homeyer (Munich: Schöningh, 1970), 233–34; "Preface to the Dramas," translated by Wilson, *Hrotsvit of Gandersheim*, 41.

9. Homeyer, *Hrotsvithae opera*, 235; Wilson, *Hrotsvit of Gandersheim*, 43. See also Paul von Winterfeld, ed., *Hrotsvithae opera* (Berlin, Ger.: Weidmann, 1902), iii; Peter Dronke, *Women Writers of the Middle Ages* (Cambridge: Cambridge University Press, 1984), 57.

10. Andrea Rossi-Reder, "Embodying Christ, Embodying Nation: Ælfric's Accounts of Saints Agatha and Lucy," in *Sex and Sexuality in Anglo-Saxon England: Essays in Memory of Daniel Calder*, ed. Carol Braun Pasternack and Lisa M.C. Weston (Tempe: Arizona Center for Medieval and Renaissance Studies, 2004), 183 n1 [183–202].

11. Rossi-Reder, "Embodying Christ," in *Sex and Sexuality*, ed. Pasternack and Weston 185.

12. See Elizabeth Petroff's argument in "Eloquence and Heroic Virginity in Hrotsvit's Verse Legends," in Wilson, *Hrotsvit of Gandersheim*, 229–38.

13. The metrical *Vita* by Prudentius and one by Pope St. Damasus appear in the *Acta sanctorum*, 2:352 and 2:228. See Sister M. Gonsalva Wiegand, "The Non-dramatic Works of Hroswitha: Text, Translation, and Commentary" (Ph.D. diss., St. Louis University, 1936), 263.

14. For sources previously identified for *Gallicanus*, see Sibylle Jefferis, "Hrotsvit and the *Magnum Legendarium Austriacum*," in Katharina M. Wilson, ed., *Hrotsvit of Gandersheim: Rara Avis in Saxonia?* Medieval and Renaissance Monograph Series 7 (Ann Arbor: Medieval and Renaissance Collegium, University of Michigan, 1987), 239–52; Sandro Sticca, "The Hagiographical and Monastic Context of Hrotswitha's Plays," in Wilson, *Hrotsvit of Gandersheim*, 11, citing Walter Berschin, "*Passio* und Theater. Zur dramatischen Struktur einiger Vorlagen Hrotsvit von Gandersheim," in *The Theatre in the Middle Ages*, ed. Herman Braet, Johan Nowé, and Gilbert Tournoy (Leuven, Belg.: Leuven University Press, 1985), 9 [1–11]; and, for the sources of the two parts of *Gallicanus*, taken from the different legends of the saints, specifically, the conversion of Gallicanus and the martyrdom of John and Paul—spiritual advisers of Constantia in Hrotsvit's Latin drama *Gallicanus* sent to convert Gallicanus who are subsequently martyred twenty years later, in the reign of Julian the Apostate—in the *Acta sanctorum*, 1868, for 7 June, see Marianne Schütz-Pflugk, *Herrscher- und Märtyrer-Auffassung bei Hrotsvit von Gandersheim*, Frankfurter Historische Abhandlungen 1 (Wiesbaden, Ger.: Steiner, 1972), 38–53

15. For an edition of Hrotsvit's legend, *Passio sanctae Agnetis virginis et martyris*, and for the play, *Gallicanus I* and *II*, see Homeyer, *Hrotsvithae opera*, 204–27 and 238–63; for an edition and translation of the legend in English, see Wiegand, "The Non-dramatic Works of Hroswitha," 237–68. For an English translation of the play, see Larissa Bonfante and Alexandra Bonfante-Warren, trans., *The Plays of Hrotswitha of Gandersheim* (Oak Park, IL: Bolchazy-Carducci, 1986), 1–38.

16. For the life of St. Leoba, see Georg Waitz, ed., *Monumenta Germaniae Historica, Scriptores*, vol. 15 (Hannover, Ger.: Hahnsche, 1887), 1:127–31; and for the *Hodoeporican* of St. Willibald by Huneberc of Heidenheim, see Oswald Holder-Egger, ed., *Monumenta Germaniae Historica, Scriptores*, vol. 15 (Hannover, Ger.: Hahnsche, 1887), 1:80–117. See also Wilhelm Ferdinand Arndt, ed. and trans., *Leben des h. Bonifazius von Wilibald, der h. Leoba von Rudolf von Fulda, des abts Sturmi von Eigil, des h. Lebuin von Hucbald. Nach den ausgaben der Monumenta Germaniae übersetzt von Wilhelm Arndt*, Geschichtschreiber der deutschen Vorzeit: 8. Jahrhundert, 2 vols, 2nd edn. (Leipzig, Ger.: Dyksche, 1888). For translations, see Charles H. Talbot, trans. and ed., *The Anglo-Saxon Missionaries in Germany, Being the Lives of Saints Willibald, Boniface, Sturm, Leoba, and Libuin, Together with*

the "Hodoeporicon" of Saint Willibald and a Selection from the Correspondence of Saint Boniface (New York: Sheed and Ward, 1954).

17. See Christina Lee's important essay, about recovering the extant evidence (mostly non-English) concerning Eadgyth as Otto's wife, and Hrotsvit's particular interest in her, in "Eclectic Memories: In Search of Eadgyth," *Offa: Berichte und Mitteilungen zur Urgeschichte, Frühgeschichte und Mittelalterarchäologie* 58 (2001; published 2004): 277–85, here, 277a, 279b, 280. Gifts (likely books) given to Gandersheim on behalf of Eadgyth by the Anglo-Saxon king (her half brother) for his liturgical remembrance are noted in the mid-ninth-century Latin *Gandersheim Gospels*; a late ninth-century Latin gospel book, of St. Matthew, similarly records the names of Otto and his mother, "Mihthild" (Mathilde) (Lee, "Eclectic Memories," 280). Concerning the puzzling lack of Anglo-Saxon documentation about Eadgyth, Lee speculates that, when this daughter of Edward the Elder and his second wife, his second cousin Ælfflæd, was displaced as heir to the English throne—that is, when Edward divorced his cousin on the basis of consanguinity and married a third wife, Eadgifu—this third wife might well have expurgated mentions of her stepdaughter's (and stepson's) names in the records (283b). Lee argues that a paucity of evidence may conceal women's historical importance: "It is rather that women were concealed by the throne they wished to protect" (283b). Much of Lee's argument concerning Eadgyth derives from Saxon chronicles and annals in Latin and late vernacular (Middle High German, Bavarian, and Slavonic and Czech) literature and martyrologies, which make of Eadgyth, a saintly queen, and of her life, a legend (282ab).

18. See Homeyer, *Hrotsvithae opera*, 409, discussed in Lee, "Eclectic Memories," 280b. Lee notes that in the *Gesta Ottonis* (ca. 965), which is dedicated to Otto the Great, Hrotsvit connects Eadgyth (and her half brother Athelstan) by descent to St. Oswald. Such an ancestor would have boosted Eadgyth's (and, therefore, the emperor's) importance and simultaneously encouraged Otto's bestowal of a convent, Magdeburg, upon his bride and his building of a cathedral after her death (both dedicated to St. Maurice, whose relics were received by Athelstan) (282a). By the thirteenth century, Magdeburg revered Eadgyth as a patron saint (282a).

19. See Jane Chance, "Hrotsvit's Latin Drama *Gallicanus* and the Old English Epic *Elene*: Intercultural Founding Narratives of a Feminized Church," in *Hrotsvit of Gandersheim: Contexts, Identities, Affinities, and Performances*, ed. Katharina Wilson, Phyllis Brown, and Linda McMillan (Toronto and London: University of Toronto Press, 2004), 193–212.

20. Wilson, *Hrotsvit of Gandersheim*, 6.

21. Wilson, *Hrotsvit of Gandersheim*, 6

22. Wilson, *Hrotsvit of Gandersheim*, 6–7.

23. Wilson, *Hrotsvit of Gandersheim*, 7; see also Katharina Wilson, "Hrotsvit and *The Artes*," in *Creativity, Influence, and Imagination: The World of Medieval Women*, ed. Constance Berman, Charles Connell, and Judith Rothschild (Morgantown: University of West Virginia Press, 1985), 3–14.

24. See Bert Nagel, *Hrotsvit von Gandersheim* (Stuttgart, Ger.: Metzlersche, 1965), 43, who acknowledges such visits as reported by Bodo of Clus.

25. See Franz Dögler, "Die Ottonenkaiser und Byzanz," in *Karolingische und Ottonische Kunst: Werden, Wesen, Wirkung* [VI. Internationaler Kongress für Frühmittelalterforschung] (Wiesbaden, Ger.: F. Steiner, 1957); Rudolf Vey, *Christliches Theater im Mittelalter und Neuzeit* (Aschaffenburg, Ger.: P. Pattlock, 1960), 12; and Wilson, *Hrotsvit of Gandersheim*, 9.

26. "Natale sancte Agnetis, virginis," line 155; Skeat, *Aelfric's Lives of Saints*, 178; Donovan, *Women Saints' Lives*, 49.

27. "Natale sancte Agnetis, virginis," lines 266–76; Skeat, *Aelfric's Lives of Saints*, 184, 186; Donovan, *Women Saints' Lives*, 51.

28. "Natale Sancte Agnetis, Virginis," lines 282–84; Skeat, *Aelfric's Lives of Saints*, 186; Donovan, *Women Saints' Lives*, 51.

29. "Natale Sancte Agnetis, Virginis," lines 285–95; Skeat, *Aelfric's Lives of Saints*, 186; Donovan, *Women Saints' Lives*, 52; my emphasis.

30. See St. Ambrose, *De virginibus ad Marcellinam sororem suam* 1.4.15, *Patrologia Latina* 16:187 [187–232], translated as "Concerning Virginity, to Marcellina, His Sister," Fathers of the Church Web-site, New Advent (1997). http://www.newadvent.org/fathers/34071.htm (accessed 5 June 2006). For Ambrose's reasons for supporting virginal integrity, see Peter Brown, "Aula Pudoris: Ambrose," in *The Body and Society: Men, Women, and Sexual Renunciation in Early Christianity* (New York: Columbia University Press, 1988), 341–65. For Aldhelm's dependence on Ambrose as a source in this letter, see Michael Lapidge, "Introduction to Aldhelm's Prose *De virginitate*," in *Aldhelm: The Prose Works*, trans. Lapidge and Herren, 56 [51–58]. See also Carol Braun Pasternack's excellent essay on Aldhelm's sexualization of virginity in "The Sexual Practices of Virginity and Chastity in Aldhelm's *De virginitate*," in *Sex and Sexuality in Anglo-Saxon England*, ed. Pasternack and Weston, 93–120; this letter is discussed on 94–95.

31. For deconstruction of the concept of virginity in the Middle Ages, see the recent studies by Kathleen Coyne Kelly, in *Performing Virginity and Testing Chastity in the Middle Ages*, Routledge Research in Medieval Studies, 2 (London and New York: Routledge, 2000); and Kathleen Coyne Kelly and Marina Leslie, *Menacing Virgins: Representing Virginity in the Middle Ages and Renaissance* (Newark: University of Delaware Press; London: Associated University Presses, 1999).

32. See Barbara Newman, "Devout Women and Demoniacs in the World of Thomas of Cantimpré," in *New Trends in Feminine Spirituality: The Holy Women of Liège and Their Impact*, ed. Juliette Dor, Lesley Johnson, and Jocelyn Wogan Browne (Turnhout, Bel.: Brepols, 1999), 35–60.

33. Constantine witnesses a burning cross in the sky on the eve of an important battle and is inspired to convert to Christianity, which saves him and his men, in the Old English religious epic *Elene* (Helena, his mother, finds the True Cross in this poem, after which she converts Judas

[Quiriacus] to Christianity, that is, to his new life as "Cyriacus"). See the edition of *Elene* by George Philip Krapp and Elliott Van Kirk Dobbie, in *The Exeter Book, Anglo-Saxon Poetic Records*, vol. 3 (New York: Columbia University Press, 1936), here, lines 1062, 95; and the translation of Robert Kay Gordon, *Anglo-Saxon Poetry*, rev. edn. (London: Dent; New York: Dutton, 1954), here, 230.

34. Donovan, *Women Saints' Lives*, 52.

35. For information on the Roman cult of Vesta, see the dissertation and its abstract by Richard Everett Wright, "Vesta: A Study on the Origin of a Goddess and Her Cults," *Dissertation Abstracts International* 56 (June 1996), 4744A (University of Washington, 1995).

36. All references to Ovid derive from *Fastorum libri sex: The Fasti of Ovid*, vol. 5 of *Ovid in Six Volumes*, ed. and trans. Sir James George Frazer, 2nd edn., revised by G. Goold, Loeb Classical Library (Cambridge, MA, and London: Harvard University Press, 1977).

37. Ovid, *Fasti*, ed. Frazer, 340–41 (6.283–92).

38. Ovid, *Fasti*, ed. Frazer, 352–53 (6.460).

39. Ovid, *Fasti*, ed. Frazer, 340–41 (6.299–306).

40. For an edition of Remigius, see Remigius of Auxerre [Antissiodorensis; Autissiodorensis], *Commentum in Martianum Capellam libri I–II et III–IX*, ed. Cora E. Lutz, 2 vols. (Leiden, Neth.: E.J. Brill, 1962–65).

41. All references to Notker derive from Notker Labeo's translation of *De nuptiis Philologiae et Mercurii: In Notkers des deutschen Werke*, ed. E. H. Sehrt and Taylor Starck, vol. 2, Altdeutsche Textbibliothek, no. 37 (Halle: Max Niemeyer, 1935), 34; and *Notker latinus zum Martianus Capella*, ed. James V. King, in *Die Werke Notkers des Deutschen*, vol. 4A (Tübingen, Ger.: Max Niemeyer, 1986).

42. See the chapter on medieval commentaries on the *Fasti* and other Ovidian works discussed in Jane Chance, *Medieval Mythography*, vol. 2: *From the School of Chartres to the Court at Avignon, 1177–1350* (Gainesville, FL, and London: University Press of Florida, 2000), chap. 1.

43. *Passio*, lines 266–69; Wiegand, "The Non-dramatic Works of Hroswitha," 250, 251.

44. *Passio*, lines 306–10; Wiegand, "The Non-dramatic Works of Hroswitha," 252, 254; 253, 255.

45. Wiegand, "The Non-dramatic Works of Hroswitha," 238, 239; my emphasis.

46. *Passio*, lines 111–22; Wiegand, "The Non-dramatic Works of Hroswitha," 242, 243.

47. *Gallicanus I*, 2.3; Homeyer, *Hrotsvithae opera*, 246; Bonfante and Bonfante-Warren, *Plays of Hrotswitha*, 7.

48. *Gallicanus I*, 2–3; Homeyer, *Hrotsvithae opera*, 249; my emphasis; Bonfante and Bonfante-Warren, *Plays of Hrotswitha*, 13.

49. *Gallicanus I*, 5.6; Homeyer, *Hrotsvithae opera*, 250.

50. *Gallicanus I*, 12.6; Homeyer, *Hrotsvithae opera*, 255; Bonfante and Bonfante-Warren, *Plays of Hrotswitha*, 23.

51. *Gallicanus I*, 5.6; Homeyer, *Hrotsvithae opera*, 250; Bonfante and Bonfante-Warren, *Plays of Hrotswitha*, 15.
52. *Gallicanus I*, 9.1; Homeyer, *Hrotsvithae opera*, 252; Bonfante and Bonfante-Warren, *Plays of Hrotswitha*, 17.
53. *Gallicanus I*, 9.1; Homeyer, *Hrotsvithae opera*, 252; Bonfante and Bonfante-Warren, *Plays of Hrotswitha*, 17.
54. *Gallicanus I*, 9.1; Homeyer, *Hrotsvithae opera*, 252; Bonfante and Bonfante-Warren, *Plays of Hrotswitha*, 17.
55. *Gallicanus I*, xii.4; Homeyer, *Hrotsvithae opera*, 254; Bonfante and Bonfante-Warren, *Plays of Hrotswitha*, 22.
56. *Gallicanus I*, 12.7, Homeyer, *Hrotsvithae opera*, 255; Bonfante and Bonfante-Warren, *Plays of Hrotswitha*, 23.
57. *Gallicanus II*, 1.2; Homeyer, *Hrotsvithae opera*, 259; Bonfante and Bonfante-Warren, *Plays of Hrotswitha*, 30; my emphasis. Homeyer notes that "inerguminus" signifies "vom Teufel besessen" [possessed by the devil], 259 n.
58. *Gallicanus II*, 8.1; Homeyer, *Hrotsvithae opera*, 262; Bonfante and Bonfante-Warren, *Plays of Hrotswitha*, 36.
59. *Gallicanus II*, 9.2; Homeyer, *Hrotsvithae opera*, 263; Bonfante and Bonfante-Warren, *Plays of Hrotswitha*, 38; my emphasis.
60. Skeat, *Aelfric's Lives of Saints*, 186, Donovan, *Women Saints' Lives*, 54. Note that "Terentianus" is listed as the author of the second part of the Old English legend of Agnes, that is, on Gallicanus and Constantia, before line 296 (Skeat, *Aelfric's Lives of Saints*, 186; Donovan, *Women Saints' Lives*, 52).
61. For Hrotsvit's literary relationship with the Roman playwright Terence, see Henry E. Burgess, "Hroswitha and Terence: A Study in Literary Imitation," *Proceedings of the Pacific Northwest Conference on Foreign Languages* 19 (1968): 23–29; Kenneth De Luca, "Hrotsvit's 'Imitation' of Terence," *Classical Folia* 28 (1974): 89–102; Judith Tarr, "Terentian Elements in Hrotsvit," in Wilson, *Hrotsvit of Gandersheim*, 55–62; and, in the same collection, on *Paphnutius* as a moralized Terentian *Eunuchus*, Charlotte Thompson, "*Paphnutius* and the Cultural Vision" 111–25. See also Judith Ellen Tarr, "Holy Virgins and Wanton Women: Hrotsvitha's Terence and 'Anti-Terence,' " *Dissertation Abstracts International* 50.11 (1990): 3582A. A feminist analysis of Hrotsvit's 'anti-Terence' plays appears in Sue-Ellen Case, "Re-viewing Hrotsvit," *Theatre Journal* 35.4 (1983): 533–42.
62. *Gallicanus I*, xii.7; Homeyer, *Hrotsvithae opera*, 255; Bonfante and Bonfante-Warren, *Plays of Hrotswitha*, 23.

3   Marie De France versus King Arthur: Lanval's Gender Inversion as Breton Subversion

1. Wace, *Wace's Roman de Brut: A History of the British, Text and Translation*, ed. and trans. Judith Weiss (Exeter, UK: University of Exeter Press, 1999), 244–46 (lines 9741–72).

2. Wace, *Wace's Roman de Brut*, 243 (lines 9648–52).

3. Wace, *Wace's Roman de Brut*, 332–33 (lines 13207–12).

4. Wace, *Wace's Roman de Brut*, 270–71 (lines 10743–46).

5. See the introduction by translator William W. Kibler to Chrétien de Troyes, *Arthurian Romances* (London: Penguin; New York: Viking Penguin, 1991), 8.

6. Chrétien de Troyes, *Arthurian Romances*, 3 (*Cligés*, lines 2–3), 8–10.

7. See Walter Map, "Dissuasio Valerii ad Rufinum philosophum, ne uxorem ducat," in *Jankyn's Book of Wikked Wyves*, vol. 1: *The Primary Texts*, ed. Ralph Hanna III and Traugott Lawler (Athens and London: University of Georgia Press, 1997), 124–25.

8. Hanna and Lawler, introduction to *Jankyn's Book of Wikked Wyves*, 46, 54.

9. See Glyn S. Burgess, introduction to *Marie de France: Lais*, ed. Alfred Ewert (1944; repr. Bristol, UK: Bristol Classical Press; London: Gerald Duckworth; Newburyport, MA: Focus Information Group, 1995), v–vi.

10. See David Carlson, "The Middle English *Lanval*, the Corporal Works of Mercy, and Bibliothèque Nationale, nouv. Acq. Fr. 1104," *Neophilologus* 72 (1988): 97–106.

11. See Ernst Hoepffner, *Les lais de Marie de France* (Paris: Boivin, 1935), 71.

12. See Hoepffner, *Les lais de Marie de France*, 67; also by Hoepffner, "Pour la chronologie des *Lais* de Marie de France. I—Le lai de *Lanval*," *Romania* 59 (1933): 370 [351–70]; Richard Baum, *Recherches sur les oeuvres attribuées à Marie de France* (Heidelberg: C. Winter, 1968), 153; and W.T.H. Jackson, "The Arthuricity of Marie de France," *Romanic Review* 70 (1979): 3 [1–18].

13. Michèle Koubichkine, "A propos du *Lai de Lanval*," *Le Moyen Age: Revue d'histoire et de philologie* 78 (1972): 482 [467–88]; and Edgard Sienaert, *Les lais de Marie de France: Du conte merveilleux à la nouvelle psychologique* (Paris: H. Champion, 1984), 107.

14. David Chamberlain, "Marie de France's Arthurian *lais*: Subtle and Political," in *Culture and the King: The Social Implications of the Arthurian Legend; Essays in Honor of Valerie M. Lagorio*, ed. Martin B. Schichtman and James Carley (Albany: State University of New York Press, 1994), 15–34.

15. Sharon Kinoshita " 'Cherchez la femme': Feminist Criticism and Marie de France's *Lai de Lanval*," *Romance Notes* 34 (1994): 263 [263–73].

16. The reference to Pentecost appears in line 11. Pentecost, or Whitsunday, was the seventh Sunday after Easter, generally, forty days following, and signified the feast of the appearance of Christ after the Resurrection, or the manifestation of the Holy Ghost to the Apostles and the establishment of the Catholic Church. Arthurian romances frequently take place at Pentecost in both Chrétien de Troyes and Sir Thomas Malory. But Marie may also use this religious holiday to signify the establishment of an order alternate to that of Arthur's Round Table—the "Order" of Avalon to which Lanval will willingly subscribe. See the notes in Ewart, *Marie de France: Lais*; and Marie de France, *The Lais*, trans. Robert Hanning and Joan Ferrante (Grand Rapids, MI: Baker Books, 1978), 196. Subsequent references to the *Lais* in

the original and in translation will be cited by line number(s) parenthetically within the text.

17. On Anglo-Norman law and *Lanval*, several essays have been published that focus on Lanval's trial. One of the earliest treatments was Elizabeth A. Francis, "The Trial in *Lanval*," in *Studies in French Language and Medieval Literature Presented to Professor Mildred K. Pope by Pupils, Colleagues, and Friends* (Manchester, UK: Manchester University Press, 1939), 115–24. See also the discussion of *Lanval*'s legal parallels and terminology in Katherine Kong, "Guilty as Charged? Subjectivity and the Law in *La Chanson de Roland* and 'Lanval,'" *Essays in Medieval Studies* 17 (2001): 35–47. See also W. Rothwell's detailed analysis of the lexicology of the vocabulary in *Lanval's* trial scene, which accurately deploys the terminology of Anglo-Norman law as exhibited in documents in the language, in "The Trial Scene in *Lanval* and the Development of the Legal Register in Anglo-Norman," *Neuphilologische Mitteilungen: Bulletin de la Société Néophilologique/Bulletin of the Modern Language Society* 101.1 (2000): 17–36. The essay concludes with an appendix of Anglo-Norman legal words from various contemporary nonlegal documents. Rothwell indicates that even the Latin Assize of Clarendon of 1166 (written during Henry II's reign, when the law changed remarkably) utilizes terms from the Anglo-Norman and Middle English vernaculars that did not exist in classical Latin, (22).

18. Kong, "Guilty as Charged," 42.

19. The statement about the polarities in the (more recent) criticism on Marie de France is my own. For a bibliography on Marie before the early to mid-1990s, consult Glyn S. Burgess, *Marie de France: An Analytical Bibliography*, Research Bibliographies and Checklist 21 (London: Grant and Cutler, 1977); Burgess, *Marie de France: An Analytical Bibliography, Supplement no. 1*, Research Bibliographies and Checklist 21 (London: Grant and Cutler, 1986); and Burgess's summary of the criticism in his introduction and bibliography to *Marie de France: Lais*, ed. Ewert, v–lxxii. For an older but still helpful analysis of the critical issues in *Lanval*, in particular, see M.J. Walkley, "The Critics and *Lanval*," *New Zealand Journal of French Studies* 4 (1983): 5–23.

20. See Jeanne Wathelet-Willem, "Le mystère chez Marie de France," *Revue belge de philology et d'histoire* 39 (1969): 672 [661–86].

21. Koubichkine, "A propos du *Lai de Lanval*," 474.

22. Elizabeth Wilson Poe, "Love in the Afternoon: Courtly Play in the *Lai de Lanval*," *Neuphilologische Mitteilungen* 84 (1983): 301–10.

23. Katharina Wilson and Glenda McLeod, "Wholism and Fusion: Success in/of the *Lais* of Marie de France," *Arachnē: An Interdisciplinary Journal of the Humanities* 5 (1998): 15 [3–30].

24. See the comparison of *Lanval* with Chaucer's only Arthurian romance (often perceived as a Breton lay), the "Wife of Bath's Tale" in the *Canterbury Tales*, as well as with *Sir Gawain and the Green Knight*, in Esther C. Quinn, "Chaucer's Arthurian Romance," *Chaucer Review* 18.3 (1984): 211–13 (on *Lanval*) [211–20]. Quinn facilely sees Marie as proposing a "clear and

simple feminine perspective," with "gentle and essentially straightforward" irony; Chaucer's tale is "complex—more realistic, more fanciful, more comic, and more ambiguous," because as a masculine poet he inscribes a female narrator (212). If their differences are more compelling than their similarities, nevertheless, the beneficent fairy queen who rescues the knight in *Lanval* resembles the fairy queen who marries and instructs the knight in the "Wife of Bath's Tale." Quinn believes Chaucer may have appropriated the idea of a female view of Arthurian romance because he knew of Marie's *Lanval*: he may have read a fourteenth-century version of the fifteenth-century manuscript of Thomas Chestre's *Sir Launfal* (ca. 1400), and there also existed the shorter and earlier Middle English *Sir Landevale* (212 and 219 n6). Quinn also alleges that Chaucer may have known *Sir Gawain*, with which the "Wife of Bath's Tale" bears some relation (213). *Lanval* might compare equally well with the thirteenth-century French *Roman de Silence* by Heldris of Cornwall, given its similar reworking of Potiphar's tale in the charges of an irate queen against the girl who has assumed a man's identity and the sexual ambiguity of the protagonist in each.

25. See Kinoshita "Cherchez la femme," 268.

26. See the critical response to Kinoshita by Jacqueline Eccles, "Feminist Criticism and the Lay of *Lanval*: A Reply," *Romance Notes* 38 (1998): 285 [281–85].

27. Aristotle's definition of man (warm, wet) as superior to woman (cold, dry) because of man's contribution of form in reproduction in contrast to woman's of matter is well known; for the scientific and theological ramifications, see Joan Cadden, *Meanings of Sex Difference in the Middle Ages: Medicine, Science, and Culture* (Cambridge: Cambridge University Press, 1993), 22–24. See also Ambrose, *Paradise* 15.73, allegorizing the Fall, with the female representing the senses and the male, the mind, in *Hexameron, Paradise, and Cain and Abel*, trans. H. de Romestin, Select Library of Nicene and Post-Nicene Fathers, 2nd series, 10 (Oxford, UK: James Parker; New York: Christian Literature, 1896), 351, discussed in Alastair Blamires, ed., *Woman Defamed and Woman Defended: An Anthology of Medieval Texts* (Oxford, UK: Clarendon Press, 1992), 3.

28. See Sharon Kinoshita, "Colonial Possessions: Wales and the Anglo-Norman Imaginary in the *Lais* of Marie de France," *Medieval Boundaries: Rethinking Difference in Old French Literature* (Philadelphia: University of Pennsylvania Press, 2006), 105–32. "Yonec" illustrates the desire to escape "the harsh demands of the feudal politics of lineage," whereas "Milun proposes a new Cambro-Norman model that functions as a chivalric meritocracy" (132).

29. Kinoshita, "Cherchez la femme," 269; R. Howard Bloch, "New Philology and Old French," *Speculum* 65 (1990): 50 [38–58].

30. Burgwinkle notes, somewhat implausibly, it seems to me, that Lanval's use of the word *mestier* (line 293)—"that sort of profession"—for sex with boys during his defense of himself against Guinevere's charge of homosexuality implies an economic exchange. See William E. Burgwinkle, *Sodomy, Masculinity, and Law in Medieval Literature: France and England, 1050–1230* (Cambridge; New York: Cambridge University Press, 2004), 164.

31. R. Howard Bloch, *The Anonymous Marie de France* (Chicago and London: University of Chicago Press, 2002), 68–71.

32. Note that, at the end of Marie's collection of *Lais*, husband Eliduc and not his wife has the courtly relationship, more conventional in courtly love terms. But as long as Eliduc can, he keeps his mistress secret from his wife and his wife secret from his mistress.

33. See Carolyn Dinshaw, who also argues that younger sons, as bachelor knights dispossessed by primogeniture, practiced homoeroticism, in "A Kiss Is Just a Kiss: Heterosexuality and Its Consolations in *Sir Gawain and the Green Knight*," *Diacritics* 24 (1994): 205–26.

34. Kong acknowledges the behavior of the fairy queen as a sovereign protecting her liege: "The relationship between Lanval and the lady is contractual, and its commencement parallels fealty-swearing between a noble and his vassal. She offers terms, he accepts, she gives him a gift, they swear allegiance, embrace, and seal their agreement over a meal. She does what Arthur the king does not, thereby inserting a parallel jurisdiction, which scripts a competing intersubjectivity." See Kong, "Guilty as Charged," 41.

35. See Burgwinkle, *Sodomy, Masculinity, and Law*, 164, who, missing the point of the spiritual regeneration provided by the lady for Guigemar in his Other World voyage, notes pessimistically that "the connection between death, disappearance, and heterosexuality is ominous and alerts us once again to the signs of a persecutory mentality at work." For the meaning of *ravi* and the legal concept of *raptus* as abduction as well as rape, see Kathryn Gravdal, *Ravishing Maidens: Writing Rape in Medieval French Literature and Law* (Philadelphia: University of Pennsylvania Press, 1991).

36. See the discussion of the fairy mistress as Morgain of the "Isle of Apples," found in Geoffrey of Monmouth's *Vita Merlini*, with associations of fate through the Irish Morrígan from *Taín Bó Cualnge*, and of "Avalun" as most likely the fairy Other World, in Eithne M. O'Shakey, "The Identity of the Fairy Mistress in Marie de France's *Lai de Lanval*," *Trivium* 6 (1971): 17–25.

37. See Koubichkine, "A Propos du *Lai de Lanval*," 467–88.

38. See the discussion of alienation in *Lanval* and the role of the Celtic Other World in Tom Peete Cross, "The Celtic Elements in the Lays of *Lanval* and *Graelent*," *Modern Philology* 12 (1914–15): 642 [585–644]; Gerhart B. Ladner, "*Homo viator*: Medieval Ideas on Alienation and Order," *Speculum* 42 (1967): 233 [233–59]; and Frederick Hodgson, "Alienation and the Otherworld in *Lanval*, *Yonec*, and *Guigemar*," *Comitatus: A Journal of Medieval and Renaissance Studies* 5 (1974): 19–31.

39. For the fairy mistress motif in Celtic sources in *Lanval*, and the formal pattern it instantiates of the woman who arrives from the other world to love a mortal man, to institute a *geis* (prohibition) that he must observe, and then to punish him for violating it, see Colleen Donagher, "Socializing the Sorceress: The Fairy Mistress in *Lanval*, *Le Bel Inconnu* and *Partonopeu de Blois*," *Essays in Medieval Studies* 4 (1987): 69–90.

40. Although Burgwinkle aptly avers that "Marie's young men suffer under the pressures of chivalric knighthood and her young women must overcome their inscription as cultural commodities" (*Sodomy, Masculinity, and Law*, 150), he only identifies their condition at the beginning, not their transformation during, and at the end, of each lay.

41. Early scholars teased out four stages in the Breton lay and its analogues without, however, explicitly feminizing it: the obstruction, the encounter with an amorous fairy, the taboo and its violation, and the resolution. See G.V. Smithers, "Story-Patterns in Some Breton Lays," *Medium Aevum* 22 (1953): 61–92. For the application of this story pattern to *Lanval*, see Patrick John Ireland, "The Narrative Unity of the *Lanval* of Marie de France," *Studies in Philology* 74 (1977): 130–45.

42. See the thirteenth-century Anglo-Norman Harley 978, London, British Library. For the manuscript order of the lays and the discussion of other manuscripts, consult Burgess, introduction to Ewart, *Marie de France*, v–vi, xxxv.

43. See Pam Whitfield, "Power Plays: Relationships in Marie de France's *Lanval* and *Eliduc*," *Medieval Perspectives* 14 (1999): 242–54. Whitfield declares, "Through the exploration of these two models of female power, Marie subverts conventional thinking to create a space within medieval society for love relationships based on equality and cooperation, rather than hierarchy and competition, and thus introduces an alternative morality" (243).

44. See the summary discussion of previous research on Marie's identity by Burgess, introduction to Ewart, *Marie de France*, viii–ix, the most plausible of which are: she was, first, either Marie, abbess of Shaftesbury; or, second, Marie, abbess of Reading; or, third, Marie, daughter of Waleran II, Count of Neulan, most likely from Vexin, in France, and wife of Hugh Talbot, Baron of Cleuville; or, fourth, Marie, Countess of Boulogne and daughter of King Stephen of England and Marie de Boulogne. The latter Marie, convent-educated and abbess of Romsey in Hampshire, was also the wife of Matthew of Flanders who returned to the convent from 1168–80. The first fits best, according to Burgess, introduction to Ewart, *Marie de France*, ix–x. Laurie A. Finke and Martin B. Schichtman, crafting an argument that *Lanval* concerns a new order of female patronage, identify her patron, Count William, cited at the beginning of her *Fables*, as William Marshal, Earl of Pembroke and King Henry's marshal of England and guardian of his son, in "Magical Mistress' Tour: Patronage, Intellectual Property, and the De-semination of Wealth in Marie de France's *Lanval*," *Signs* 25 (2000): 479–503.

45. See Michelle A. Freeman, "Marie France's Poetics of Silence: The Implications for a Feminine *Translatio*," *PMLA* 99 (1984): 877–78 [860–83]. Burgess analyzes these symbolic objects in all the lays except the fifth in the collection, *Lanval*, and the tenth, *Chaitivel*, which lack them (Burgess, introduction to Ewart, *Marie de France*, xxxi–xxxii). Freeman also perceives Marie's use of understatement and elision as similarly feminist, although Kinoshita critiques Freeman's understanding of Marie's rhetorical strategy—an "odd metaphorical biologism"—as a mirror of the gendering

of male and female at work in society as a whole, that is, through "the links between textual production and sexual reproduction" ("Cherchez la femme," 266–68).

46. See Trotula, *On Treatments for Women*, in *The Book of Trotula: A Medieval Compendium of Women's Medicine*, ed. and trans. Monica Green (University Park: Penn State University Press, 2001, 2002), 89–112, mostly remedies concerning childbirth, its aftermath, and its consequences. Note the euphemism for (and translation of) the *menses* as "the flowers" (*flos*), 21. The analogy depends on the need for the tree to flower before it bears fruit, just as a woman must menstruate before conceiving and bearing a child.

47. See Judith Rice Rothschild, "A *Rapprochement* between *Bisclavret* and *Lanval*," *Speculum* 48 (1973): 81 [78–88].

48. The lines read, "Li reis parla vers sun vassal / Que jeo vus oi numer Lanval; / De *felunie* le retta / E d'un *mesfait* l'acheisuna, / D'un amur dunt il se vanta, / E ma dame s'en curuça" [The king spoke against his vassal / whom I have heard named Lanval; / he accused him of *felony*, / charged him with a *misdeed*— / a love that he had boasted of, / which made the queen angry] (lines 437–42, my emphasis). See Kong, "Guilty as Charged," 42, on Lanval's *mesdire*.

49. This pronouncement is akin to the fairy queen's lecture on *gentilesse* in Chaucer's "Wife of Bath's Tale" that also dismisses poverty as a bar to true nobility, in *The Riverside Chaucer*, ed. Larry Benson, 3rd edn. (Boston: Houghton Mifflin, 1987), lines 1109–1212.

50. See Sarah Roche-Mahdi, ed. and trans., *Silence: A Thirteenth-Century French Romance* (East Lansing, MI: Colleagues Press, 1992), lines 3935–49. For the sexual assault charges, see lines 4075–4148.

51. For this argument about Eleanor, see Margaret Aziza Pappano, "Marie de France, Aliénor d'Aquitaine, and the Alien Queen," in *Eleanor of Aquitaine: Lord and Lady*, ed. Bonnie Wheeler and John Carmi Parsons (New York: Palgrave Macmillan, 2002), 337–67. Pappano suggests that Marie functions in this lay as a historian recording orally disseminated truths for posterity (irrespective of whether Marie was Eleanor's half sister or bore some other kinship to her); Pappano declares, "Through the figure of the fairy lady, Marie holds out the alternative of female rule, control over property, and true and noble desire, perhaps even figuring Aquitaine as a sort of Avalon" (346). But a double historical perspective toward Eleanor makes this argument fit the lay only when the two queens—fairy queen and Guenevere—embody *in bono* and *in malo* glossations of Eleanor's character. Outside her own domain Eleanor was regarded negatively, as alien (thus, Aliénor), insubordinate, and sexually demanding, given her divorce from King Louis because of his monkish ways. Marie's politic ability to delineate the dangers of a disempowered foreign queen married to an English king and, simultaneously, the merits of an autonomous queen who rules her own country beneficently would explain why her *lais* pleased the ladies of the Anglo-Norman court. Denis Piramus in his *Vie Seint Edmund le Rei* (The life of Saint Edmund the king)

(ca. 1190–1200) explains that the *lais* also pleased them because they were written according to the ladies' wishes (lines 35–48). See Pappano, "Marie de France," in *Eleanor of Aquitaine*, 338–39 and 360 n8.

52. Marie translated the Latin *Tractatus de Purgatorio Sancti Patricii* into French and fables from English into French in her collection, thereby establishing a formal tripartite program of *translatio* both written and oral, if the lays are included. See the feminist discussion of her work in terms of the "myth of the wild" (a name for the female self) by Tilde A. Sankovitch, *French Women Writers and the Book: Myths of Access and Desire* (Syracuse, NY: Syracuse University Press, 1988), 15–41.

53. See Burgess, introduction to Ewart, *Marie de France*, vii. This alternate identification would date the composition of the *lais* as before 1183, or perhaps 1189. Hoepffner's chronology of their composition would place *Lanval* roughly in the middle: see his "Pour la chronologie," 351–70.

4 Marguerite Porete's Annihilation of the Character Reason in her Fantasy of an Inverted Church

1. Joanne Maquire Robinson offers several texts (in translation) in an appendix about the interrogation and censure and the 1309 Paris condemnation of Porete (including the first and fifteenth articles from the *Mirror* singled out for special blame), followed by the 1311 Council of Vienne bull "Ad Nostrum" against eight "Free Spirit" doctrines of the "Brethren" (a second bull at Vienne, "Cum de quisdam mulieribus," not included in Robinson, criticized the beguines). See *Nobility and Annihilation in Marguerite Porete's "Mirror of Simple Souls,"* SUNY Series in Western Esoteric Traditions (Albany: State University of New York Press, 2001), 109–10. But see also the full discussion by Robert E. Lerner, in *Heresy of the Free Spirit in the Later Middle Ages* (Berkeley: University of California Press, 1972), 68–78, who believes there is no evidence that this brotherhood existed; and the extant documents for both the trial against Porete and Guiard in the excellent Paul Verdeyen, "Le Procès d'inquisition contre Marguerite Porete et Guiarde de Cressonessart (1309–1310)," *Revue d'histoire ecclésiastique* 81.1–2 (1986): 47–94. Apparently the official heretical charges have not survived, although Richard Methley's glosses on his Latin translation of the Middle English version in 1491 convinced Edmund Colledge and Romana Guarnieri that Methley—a vicar at Mount Grace Charterhouse in north Yorkshire—may have seen the specific articles because of his justification of Porete's text through a figurative reading: see his glosses in Colledge and Guarnieri's "Glosses of 'M.N.' and Richard Methley to *The Mirror of Simple Souls*," *Archivio italiano per la storia della pietà* 5 (1968): 357–82. See also the discussion of the investigation as summarized in Maria Lichtmann, "Marguerite Porete's *Mirror for Simple Souls*: Inverted Reflection of Self, Society, and God," *Studia mystica* 16 (1995): 15–20 [4–29]; this article was revised and published as " 'Marguerite

Porete and Meister Eckhart: *The Mirror of Simple Souls* Mirrored," in *Meister Eckhart and the Beguine Mystics: Hadewijch of Brabant, Mechthild of Magdeburg, and Marguerite Porete,* ed. Bernard McGinn (New York: Continuum, 1994), 65–86. For gender issues in the charges, see Michael G. Sargent, "The Annihilation of Marguerite Porete," *Viator* 28 (1997): 253–79.

2. See Lerner's critique of modern scholars' positioning of Porete as part of this sect, in *Heresy of the Free Spirit,* 7–8; and Robinson, *Nobility and Annihilation,* 30.

3. See Ellen L. Babinsky's cogent discussion of other possible reasons, *Marguerite Porete's "The Mirror of Simple Souls,"* Classics of Western Spirituality (New York, NY, and Mahwah, NJ: Paulist Press, 1993), 24–26, specifically, according to Verdeyen, whom she cites, the wish of William to enforce ecclesiastical discipline and doctrinal control and maintain his authority and Philip the Fair's desire to enlist mendicant support for attacks on the Templars in return for sanctions against the beguines (Verdeyen, "Le Procès," 85).

4. See Lerner, *Heresy of the Free Spirit,* 1–2, 200–208; and John A. Arsenault, "Authority, Autonomy, and Antinominianism: The Mysticism and Ethical Piety of Marguerite Porete in *The Mirror of Simple Souls,*" *Studia Mystica,* n.s., 21 (2000): 65–94. See also Eleanor McLaughlin on the heresy of the Free Spirit: "The Heresy of the Free Spirit and Late Medieval Mysticism," *Medieval and Renaissance Spirituality* 4 (1973): 37–54. Medieval cases of the Brethren of the Free Spirit are enumerated in the first part of Romana Guarnieri, "Il movimento del Libero Spirito," *Archivio italiano per la storia della pietà* 4 (1965): 351–708, the latter half of which contains Porete's Old French *Mirror,* 513–635.

5. *Continuatio chronici Guillelmi de Nangiaco* in *Recueil des historiens des Gaules et de la France,* ed. J. Naudet and C.F. Danou (Paris: Welter, 1894), 20:601. See also Verdeyen, "Le Procès," 88, 89. All the documents relating to her trial and that of her beghard defender, Guiard de Cressinessart, have been included in Verdeyen, although the ones for Marguerite's trial were originally published by Henry C. Lea, *A History of the Inquisition in the Middle Ages,* 3 vols. (1887; repr. New York: Russell and Russell, 1955), 2:575–78; and by Paul Frédéricq, *Corpus documentorum inquisitionis haereticae pravitatis neerlandicae,* 5 vols. (Ghent: J. Vuylsteke, 1889–1906), 1:155–60, 2:63–64. See Robert E. Lerner for the documents in Guiard's trial, "An 'Angel of Philadelphia' in the Reign of King Philip the Fair: The Case of Guiard de Cressonessart," in *Order and Innovation in the Middle Ages: Essays in Honor of Joseph R. Strayer,* ed. William C. Jordan, Bruce McNab, and Teofilo F. Ruiz (Princeton: Princeton University Press, 1976), 343–64 and 529–40. See also Lerner, *Heresy of the Free Spirit,* 71.

6. Babinsky, introduction, 26. The major Middle English text, British Library Additional 37790, was notated after 1450 by James Grenehalgh, a Shene Carthusian. While Michael Northbrook, bishop of London and founder of the London Charterhouse, may have been the translator "M.N." of the Middle English Additional 37790 from the mid-late fourteenth century, the translation was made from a French text of the late thirteenth–early fourteenth century. The other two manuscripts in Middle English—Bodley

505 and St. John's College Cambridge 71—both come from the early fifteenth century and were connected with the London Charterhouse, according to Romana Guarnieri, ed., *Marguerite Porete: Le mirouer des Simples Ames*; and Paul Verdeyen, ed., *Margaretae Porete: Speculum simplicium animarum*, Corpus Christianorum: Continuatio Mediaevalis 69 (Turnhout, Belg.: Brepols, 1986), vii.

7. See Robinson, *Nobility and Annihilation*, 28. Most likely Porete was a beguine unconfined by a convent. See Lerner, 207–8, who acknowledges that her solitary and wandering nature may have made her vulnerable to accusation.

8. For the marginalization of unhoused beguines, even by Franciscans and Dominicans, see Lerner, *Heresy of the Free Spirit*, 46–53. See also the extended overview of Porete's specific case by Babinsky in her introduction to her translation, 5–26.

9. Robinson, *Nobility and Annihilation*, xi.

10. See Guarnieri and Verdeyen, *Le mirouer des Simples Ames/Speculum simplicium animarum*, 70 [chap. 19], which includes the Old French and fifteenth-century Latin editions (the latter by Carthusian Richard Methley from the Middle English translation) on facing pages; for the modern English translation by Babinsky, see *Marguerite Porete's "The Mirror of Simple Souls,"* 101. For just the early edition of the Old French text from the mid-fifteenth-century Musée Condé manuscript, see Romana Guarnieri, ed., *Marguerite Porete: Le mirouer des simples ames, in "Il movimento de Libero Spirito," Archivio italiano per la storia della pietà* (Rome: n.p., 1965): 4:513–635 [351–708]. The fifteenth-century Middle English translation is available in Marilyn Doiron, ed., "Margaret Porete: *The Mirror of Simple Souls,* A Middle English Translation," *Archivio italiano per la storia della pietà,* 5 (1968): 242–355. All references in this essay to *The Mirror of Simple Souls* are to Guarnieri's Old French in the CCCM edition and Babinsky's modern English translation. Subsequent references to page number(s) in Guarnieri and Babinsky will be cited parenthetically in text and notes by the name of the editor and/or translator with chapter and line number(s) as appropriate within brackets.

11. See Catharine Randall, "Person, Place, Perception: A Proposal for the Reading of Porete's *Mirouer des âmes simples et anéanties," Journal of Medieval and Renaissance Studies* 25 (1995): 231 [229–44]. Thus, we find for Reason (or the complex faculties of knowing), the Intellect of Reason, Discretion, and the Encumbered Reason. Of the Virtues there are Faith, Hope, and Charity. Of emotional and spiritual states (some positive and some negative), we find Fear, Modesty, Astonishment, Desire, and the Unrighteous Will. But most of the specialized personifications shed light on Love (Holy Spirit) or the Soul. Of Love and the Holy Spirit, we find Pure Courtesy, Courtesy of the Goodness of Love, Faith, the Light of Faith, the Height of the Intellect of Love, Truth, the Intellect of Divine Light, FarNear, the person of God the Father, the Holy Spirit, the Supreme Lady of Peace, and Divine Love. Of the Soul we find the Seeker, Those Who Hide, Soul-Speaks-to-Love, the Intellect, the Highest Intellect, the Soul-by-Faith, the Encumbered Soul, the Spirit, the Amazed Soul, the Unencumbered Soul,

the Annihilated Soul, the Intellect of the Annihilated Soul, the Nobility of the Unity of the Soul, the Astonished-Soul-in-Pondering-Nothing, the Satisfied Soul, the First Petition, the Second Petition, and the Light of the Soul.

12. The seven states are described briefly in the *Mirouer*, chap. 61 (Babinsky, *Mirror*, 138) and again, in greater detail, in chap.118 (Babinsky, *Mirror*, 188–94).

13. See Maria Lichtmann, "Negative Theology in Marguerite Porete and Jacques Derrida," *Christianity and Literature* 47.2 (1998): 213–27. Maria Lichtmann also describes the *Mirror* as "apophatic mysticism"—a term that was used by Michael Sells in "The Pseudo-Woman and the *Meister*: 'Unsaying' and Essentialism"—declaring that "Marguerite's mysticism is not particularly affective, ecstatic, or visionary, but actually has more in common with the apophatic mysticism of the fifth-century Syrian monk, Pseudo-Dionysius." See Lichtmann, "Marguerite Porete and Meister Eckhart," in *Meister Eckhart and the Beguine Mystics*, ed. McGinn, 65–86; and Lichtmann, "Marguerite Porete's *Mirror for Simple Souls*," 10. For Michael Sells, see "The Pseudo-Woman and the Meister: 'Unsaying' and Essentialism," in *Meister Eckhart and the Beguine Mystics*, ed. McGinn, 114–46.

14. See the title of chapter 12, for example: "Le vray entendement de ce que ce livre dit en tant de lieulx, que l'Ame Adnientie *n'a point de* voulenté" (Guarnieri, *Mirouer*, 48 [12.1–2]) [The true intellect by which this book speaks in different places, that the Annihilated Soul *possesses* no will] (Babinsky, *Mirror*, 92; my emphasis).

15. See Jean Dagens, "*Les mirouer des simples ames* et Marguerite de Navarre," in *La mystique rhénane: Colloque de Strasbourg, 16–19 Mai 1961* (Paris: Presses Universitaires de France, 1963), 281–89. Marguerite Porete has been studied in relation to other beguine mystics, beginning with Kurt Ruh, "Beguinenmystik: Hadewijch, Mechthild von Magdeburg, Marguerite Porete," *Zeitschrift für deutsches Altertum und deutsche Literatur* 106 (1977): 265–77; and also Kurt Ruh, "Gottesliebe bei Hadewijch, Mechthild von Madgdeburg und Marguerite Porete," in *Romanische Literaturbeziehungen im 19. und 20. Jahrhundert: Festschrift für Franz Rauhut zum 85. Geburtstag*, ed. Angel San Miguel, Richard Schwaderer, and Manfred Tietz (Tübingen, Ger.: Narr, 1985), 243–54. See also Catherine Monique Müller, "De l'autre côté du miroir: Pour une lecture féminine du `Mirouer' de Marguerite Porete et du `Speculum' de Marguerite d'Oingt" (Ph.D. diss., Purdue University, 1996), which was later published as *Marguerite Porete et Marguerite d'Oingt de l'autre côté du miroir*, Currents in Comparative Romance Languages and Literatures (New York: Peter Lang, 1999). Müller's ideas first appeared in Catherine M. Bothe [Müller], "Writing as Mirror in the Work of Marguerite Porete," *Mystics Quarterly* 20 (1994): 105–12.

16. Robinson, *Nobility and Annihilation*, 28.

17. While Joachim of Fiore in the late twelfth century had offered the general concept of an inner greater spiritual church—an *Ecclesia spiritualis* (Spiritual

church) as an "ideal assembly of free souls"—superseding and transforming the outer lesser actual church, the more realistic later theologian Porete was content to idealize the Holy Church the Greater as an interior community without any necessary transformation of the external Holy Church the Little. See Peter Dronke, *Women Writers of the Middle Ages: A Critical Study from Perpetua (d. 203) to Marguerite Porete (d. 1310)* (Cambridge: Cambridge University Press, 1984), 223, for the discussion of Joachim of Fiore, who saw the lesser (actual) church being superseded—transformed—by the greater (interior) church, rather than guided by it, as in the case of Porete. An earlier version of Dronke's discussion of Porete and the relationship to Joachim appeared in Peter Dronke, "Lyrical Poetry in the Work of Marguerite Porete," in *Literary and Historical Perspectives of the Middle Ages: Proceedings of the 1981 SEMA Meeting,* , ed. Patricia W. Cummins, Patrick W. Conner, and Charles W. Connell (Morgantown: West Virginia University Press, 1982), 12–13 [1–18].

18. Porete's work has also been argued as having influenced Eckhart himself, in Edmund Colledge and J.C. Marler, " 'Poverty of the Will': Ruusbroec, Eckhart and *The Mirror of Simple Souls*," in *Jan van Russbroec: The Sources, Context, and Sequels of His Mysticism*, ed. Paul Mommaers and Norbert de Paepe (Leuven: Leuven University Press, 1984), 14–47. In addition, Bernard McGinn identifies Porete as belonging to "four female Evangelists" (the others besides Marguerite being Angela of Foligno, Hadewijch of Antwerp, and Mechthild of Magdeburg) who influenced the fourteenth-century mysticism of Meister Eckhart—himself accused of heresy at the end of his life. See *Meister Eckhart and the Beguine Mystics*, which includes articles by Amy Hollywood, "Suffering Transformed: Marguerite Porete, Meister Eckhart, and the Problem of Women's Spirituality," 87–113; Lichtmann, "Marguerite Porete and Meister Eckhart," 65–86; and Sells, "The Pseudo-Woman and the Meister: 'Unsaying' and Essentialism," ed. McGinn, 114–46. See also Amy W. Hollywood, *The Soul as Virgin Wife: Mechthild of Magdeburg, Marguerite Porete, and Meister Eckhart* (Notre Dame, IN, and London: Notre Dame University Press, 1995). For Porete's relationship with Meister Eckhart, see also Luiz Felipe Pondè, "The Relation between the Concept of 'Anéantissement' in Marguerite Porete and the Concept of 'Abegescheindenheit' in Meister Eckhart: Meister Eckhart and the Béguines," in *What Is Philosophy in the Middle Ages? International Kongress für mittelalterliche Philosophie* (1997): 311–12; and Heidi Marx, "Metaphors of Imaging in Meister Eckhart and Marguerite Porete," *Medieval Perspectives* 13 (1998): 99–108.

19. Barbara Newman, *God and the Goddesses: Vision, Poetry, and Belief in the Middle Ages* (Philadelphia: University of Pennsylvania Press, 2003), 26.

20. Newman, *God and the Goddesses*, 47.

21. See, for example, Georgette Épiney-Burgard and Emilie zum Braun, *Femmes troubadours de Dieu* (Turnhout, Belg.: Brepols, 1988); and Saskia M. Murk-Jansen, "The Use of Gender and Gender-Related Imagery in Hadewijch," in *Gender and Text in the Later Middle Ages*, ed. Jane Chance,

52–68. Robinson, *Nobility and Annihilation*, also sees Porete's complex use of courtly love as an analogy for the process of annihilation, or union, with God, as similar to the metaphors of Hadewijch of Brabant and Hildegard of Bingen (102–4).

22. Randall, "Person, Place, Perception," 230 [229–44].

23. See Robert D. Cottrell, "Marguerite Porete's Heretical Discourse; Or, Deviating from the Model," *Modern Language Studies* 21 (1991): 20 [16–21], which discusses Methley's glosses on heretical text in Porete as vindicatory. Elsewhere, Cottrell focuses on Porete's use of language as icon, with poetry signifying the spirit, and ultimately her attempt to "articulate silence in language": see Robert D. Cottrell, "Marguerite Porete's *Le mirouer des ames* and the Problematics of the Written Word," *Medieval Perspectives* 1 (1986):152, 155 [151–58].

24. Kathleen Garay, " 'She Swims and Floats in Joy': Marguerite Porete, an `Heretical' Mystic of the Later Middle Ages," *Canadian Women's Studies: Les cahiers de la femme* 17.1 (1997): 19 [18–21].

25. Marleen Cré correctly perceives Porete as following Boethius's theme of "spiritual ascent" in *De consolatione Philosophiae*, but she also describes the work inaccurately as a Macrobian *oraculum*—a dream vision relayed by an oracle (it is not a dream), specifically, Lady Love: Porete "proves herself to be a master of the genre." See Marleen Cré, "Women in the Charterhouse? Julian of Norwich's *Revelations of Divine Love* and Marguerite Porete's *Mirror of Simple Souls* in British Library, MS Additional 37790," in *Writing Religious Women: Female Spiritual and Textual Practices in Late Medieval England*, ed. Denis Renevey and Christiania Whitehead (Toronto and Buffalo: University of Toronto Press, 2000), 55 [43–62].

26. See Henri d'Andeli, *The Battle of the Seven Arts*, ed. Louis J. Paëtow, Memoirs of the University of California, vol. 4, no. 1 [History, vol. 1, no. 1] (Berkeley: University of California Press, 1914), 17–18. See also Dahlberg's introduction to his translation of *The Romance of the Rose*, 2.

27. For discussion of the key manuscript, see Verdeyen, *Margaretae Porete: Speculum simplicium animarum*, vii. For other information about the manuscripts, see Michael G. Sargent, " 'Le Mirouer des simples ames' and the English Mystical Tradition," *Abendländische Mystik im Mittelalter: Symposium Kloster Engelberg 1984*, ed. Kurt Ruh (Stuttgart: J.B. Metzlersche, 1986), 443–65. Sargent acknowledges that the only other—fourteenth-century—manuscript is owned by French-speaking contemplatives outside France who do not wish to be identified or to open access to it.

28. Barbara Newman, "The Mirror and the Rose: Marguerite Porete's Encounter with the *Dieu d'Amours*," *The Vernacular Spirit* 1 (2002): 109 [105–23].

29. Newman, "Mirror and the Rose," 110.

30. See the *Rose*, lines 1425–1614 in Guillaume's portion, for the Fountain of Narcissus and the Mirror Perilous, with the crystals at the bottom of the fountain reflecting the eyes of the lover and, as the Mirror Perilous, the lady as rosebud; and in Jean's portion, lines 20525–86, esp. 20528–30, on

the holy carbuncle. All references come from Guillaume de Lorris and Jean de Meun, *The Romance of the Rose*, trans. Charles Dahlberg (Princeton, NJ: Princeton University Press, 1971). See also the discussion of mirror images in the *Rose* by Alan M.F. Gunn, *The Mirror of Love: A Reinterpretation of "The Romance of the Rose"* (Lubbock: Texas Tech Press, 1952), esp. 110–12, 116, 266–73. According to Gunn, the mirror imagery begins in Guillaume with the Fountain of Love, mirroring the garden, including the lady as rosebud, and ends in Jean with the mirror of generation, taken from the chain of mirrors in the Great Chain of Being that, with increasing distance from God, reflects less distinctly His image (267). In Jean's *Rose*, the mirror symbolizes "God's bounty," human love, generation, truth, and the allegory itself, as a "book of truth in love, an all-reflecting Mirouer aus Amoureus" (266).

31. See the study by Herbert Grabes, *The Mutable Glass: Mirror Imagery in Titles and Texts of the Middle Ages and the English Renaissance* (Cambridge: Cambridge University Press, 1982).

32. See Alan of Lille, *De planctu Naturae*, in *The Anglo-Latin Satirical Poets and Epigrammatists of the Twelfth Century*, ed. Thomas Wright, Rerum Britannicarum Medii Aevi Scriptores, vol. 2 of 2 vols. (London: Longman, 1872), 451 [429–522]; see also *The Plaint of Nature*, trans. James J. Sheridan, Medieval Sources in Translation 26 (Toronto, ON: Pontifical Institute of Mediaeval Studies, 1980), 118–19 [chap. 6; prose 3] (my emphasis).

33. See Lichtmann, "Marguerite Porete's *Mirror for Simple Souls*," 4–29, for this argument that differs so radically from that of Robinson in *Nobility and Annihilation*.

34. See the description of Oiseuse in Guillaume's *Roman*, lines 506–94.

35. See Lichtmann, "Marguerite Porete's *Mirror for Simple Souls*," 14.

36. See the intriguing argument by Müller in which the mirror is less a genre than a symbol, "De l'autre cote du miroir: Pour une lecture feminine du 'Mirouer' de Marguerite Porete et du 'Speculum' de Marguerite d'Oingt," published as *Marguerite Porete et Marguerite d'Oingt de l'autre côté du miroir*. Müller's ideas were first advanced about Porete's "mirror" of her self and of the speechless gaze of the ineffable in Bothe [Müller], "Writing as Mirror in the Work of Marguerite Porete," 105–12.

37. What is actually taking place at the end of the *Rose* has been debated recently by Karl D. Uitti, who understands the poem to celebrate growth of the self and the completion of the writing of the romance. See Karl D. Uitti, " 'Cele [qui] doit ester Rose clamee' (*Rose*, vv. 40–44): Guillaume's Intentionality," in *Rethinking the Rose: Text, Image, Reception*, ed. Kevin Brownlee and Sylvia Huot (Philadelphia: University of Pennsylvania Press, 1992), 39–64.

38. See Robinson, *Nobility and Annihilation*, 16–20.

39. See Garay, "She Swims and Floats in Joy," 19. Other scholars, for example, Ellen Louise Babinsky, "The Use of Courtly Language in *Le mirouer des simple ames anienties*," *Essays in Medieval Studies* 4 (1998): 91–106, examine *The Mirror* in terms of Neoplatonic philosophy and the relationship between soul and God therein. But note Barbara Newman, *From Virile Woman to WomanChrist*

(Philadelphia: University of Pennsylvania Press, 1993), who discusses Porete's critique of Bräutmystik (eroticized relationship of the soul to God derived from imagery in the Song of Songs) in conjunction with *fine amour* (what Newman terms *la mystique courtoise*) in Hadewijch and Mechthild (137–67).

40. Robinson, *Nobility and Annihilation*, does not go far enough, I believe, in her discussion of Porete's complex use of courtly love as an analogy for the process of annihilation, or union, with God, which she sees as similar to the metaphors of Hadewijch of Brabant and Hildegard of Bingen (102–4).

41. See Robinson's first chapter in *Nobility and Annihilation*, "Nobility as Historical Reality and Theological Motif." According to Robinson, Porete incorrectly identifies lineage as important only in attracting the lover to the beloved. Robinson also discusses nobility throughout the book in relation to Porete's doctrines of annihilation through love (chap. 2), doctrines of God, the soul, and no-thingness (chap. 3), and doctrines of nobility and annihilation (chap. 4).

42. Robinson, *Nobility and Annihilation*, xii; my emphasis.

43. I am indebted to Joshua Cooley and Jill Delsigne for their papers on the literary Marguerite Porete, specifically, Cooley's "Marguerite Porete's *Mirror of Simple Souls* as Gendered Debate," delivered at the Texas Medieval Association conference meeting at Houston, 13 October 2005, and Delsigne's " 'Entendez la glose': Painting Subversion in *Guigemar* and *Le mirouer des Simples Ames*," delivered at the Forty-First International Conference on Medieval Studies, Western Michigan University, May 4–7, 2006. Cooley traces the gendered narrative of a masculinized (but female) Reason's changes and eventual "death" and resurrection; Delsigne argues for Porete's use of fable as conveying truth literally rather than allegorically—allegory representing the academic fondness for figurative meaning interpreted by means of scholastic gloss. In this practice, argues Delsigne, Porete thus resembles Marie de France a century earlier, in her creation of the fresco on which Guigemar's imprisoned beloved gazes that depicts the burning of Ovid's book by Venus. See also, for a study of Augustinian figurative reading, Robert D. Cottrell, *The Grammar of Silence: A Reading of Marguerite de Navarre's Poetry* (Washington, DC: Catholic University of America Press, 1986), 12–15.

44. See Jerome Taylor, introduction to his translation of *The Didascalicon of Hugh of St Victor: A Medieval Guide to the Arts* (New York and London: Columbia University Press, 1961), 4.

45. For the original, see Hugh of St. Victor, *Didascalicon* 1.3, in *Hugo van Sankt Viktor. Didascalicon de studio legendi: Studienbuch*, ed. and trans. German by Thilo Offergeld (Freiberg and New York: Herder, 1997); trans. Taylor, 49 (my emphasis).

46. See Alan of Lille, *Anticlaudianus*, in *The Anglo-Latin Satirical Poets and Epigrammatists of the Twelfth Century*, ed. Thomas Wright, Rerum Britannicarum Medii Aevi Scriptores, vol. 2 of 2 vols. (London: Longman, 1872), 369 (6.2) [268–428]; also *Anticlaudianus, or The Good and Perfect Man*, trans. James J. Sheridan (Toronto, ON: Pontifical Institute of Mediaeval Studies, 1973), 160 (6.119–20).

47. Winthrop Wetherbee, for example, notes that "The *homo novus* exists in Prudentia herself once mind, will, and speech have become congruent again with the dignity implied by man's upright carriage." See *Platonism and Poetry in the Twelfth Century: The Literary Influence of the School of Chartres* (Princeton, NJ: Princeton University Press, 1972), 218.

48. Both Guillaume de Lorris and Jean de Meun were associated with the Orléans region, from whose schools so many humanistic scholars sprang; Jean de Meun likely left Orléans for Paris. See Henri d'Andeli, *The Battle of the Seven Arts*, ed. Louis J. Paëtow, Memoirs of the University of California, vol. 4, no. 1 [History, vol. 1, no. 1] (Berkeley: University of California Press, 1914), 17–18. See also Dahlberg's introduction to his translation of *The Romance of the Rose*, 2. Alan of Lille probably trained at Paris.

49. See the discussions of this fable in Fulgentius's *Mitologiae* in Jane Chance, *Medieval Mythography*, vol. 1: *From Roman North Africa to the School of Chartres, AD 433–1177* (Gainesville and London: University Press of Florida, 1994), 103; and in Fulgentius, the Third Vatican Mythographer, Alexander Neckam, and John Ridewall, in *Medieval Mythography*, vol. 2: *From the School of Chartres to the Court at Avignon, 1177–1350* (Gainesville and London: University Press of Florida, 2000), 287, 151–52, 198, 287–91, and 293, respectively.

50. See Fulgentius, *Mitologiae* 11.1, in Fulgentius, *Opera*, ed. Rudolf Helm (1898; repr. Stuttgart: B.G. Teubner, 1970), 17.

51. Third Vatican Mythographer, proem to *De diis gentium et illorum allegoriis*, in *Scriptores rerum mythicarum latini tres Romae nuper reperti*, ed. Georgius Henricus Bode (1834; repr. Hildesheim: Georg Olms, 1968), 152.

52. Babinsky notes that Porete's exemplum concerns the courtly tale of Candace and Alexander the Great (*Mirror*, 223 n2).

53. See the thirteenth-century British Library MS Harley 3487, *De anima*, lines 350–53, in René Gauthier, "Le traité *De anima et de potencies eius* d'un maître dès artes (vers 1225)," *Revue des sciences philosophiques et théologiques* 66 (1982): 45 [3–86]; see also the discussion of this passage in Chance, *Medieval Mythography*, 2:153.

54. From the *Roman d'Alexander* by Alexander of Bernay. See Emilie zum Brunn and Georgette Épiney-Burgard, *Women Mystics in Medieval Europe*, trans. Sheila Hughes (New York: Paragon, 1989), 153. Alexander is also mentioned in the *Rose;* see the discussion in Newman, "The Mirror and the Rose," 112.

55. Porete defines *engin* as "la substance de l'Ame" [the operation of the soul], with *cognoissance* (understanding) being the *somme de l'Ame* (height of the Soul) (Guarnieri, *Mirouer*, 300 [110.13–14], Babinsky, *Mirror*, 182). Babinsky notes that this definition appears in the Latin but not in the Old French (229 n97). Babinsky's "skill"—*engin* in Old French, from the Latin *ingenium*—is that natural ability from which intellect springs: "C'est ung engin soubtil don't entendement naist" (Guarnieri, *Mirouer*, 298 [110.13]; Babinsky, *Mirror*, 182). The Latin reads, "Hic ingenium subtile est substantia animae, et intellectus est operatio animae, et notitia est summa animae, quae notitia est de substantia et intellectu" (Verdeyen, *Speculum*, 301

[110,10–13]. A better reading (from the Latin) would have memory or common sense or imagination as the foundation of the soul, intellectual ability as the working of the soul, and understanding as the height of the soul. However, *ingenium* meant "invention," "genius," close to "imagination" or "inventiveness" (or memory), in medieval scholastic references: see Alan of Lille's *Plaint of Nature*, in which Genius, priest of Nature, inscribes on parchment images, including Plato with his *ingenium*, trans. James J. Sheridan, Medieval Sources in Translation 26 (Toronto: Pontifical Institute of Mediaeval Studies, 1980), as discussed by Jane Chance Nitzsche, *The Genius Figure in Antiquity and the Middle Ages* (New York and London: Columbia University Press, 1975), 112. In Middle English, *kynde wit(te)* comes closest: "natural ability," "common sense."

56. See Cooley, "Marguerite Porete's *Mirror of Simple Souls* as Gendered Debate." Reason never seems to follow the train of Love's thought, interrupts her, repeats herself, and asks repeatedly, "Ah, for God's sake,…what can that mean?"

57. Hugh of St. Victor, *Didascalicon* 1.3, in Offergeld, *Didascalicon de studio legendi: Studienbuch*, 122; Taylor, *Didascalicon*, 49–50.

58. Robinson suggests that for Porete the soul and God share nobility as defined by the chivalric (masculine) virtues of largesse, courtesy, and courage and imagined as if the king resided in a manor desired by the noble (Robinson, *Nobility and Annihilation*, 79).

59. See Porete's *Mirror*, trans. Babinsky, chap. 84, "How the Unencumbered Soul in Her Four Aspects Ascends into Sovereignty and Lives Unencumbered by Divine Life."

60. Robinson argues against the characterizations of Porete's pride by editor Edmund Colledge ("stubborn, willful determination") and by scholar Barbara Newman ("hauteur") as only "apparent elitism" in that Porete merely segregates noble souls from those who are base (Robinson, *Nobility and Annihilation*, 99); for Porete, "nobility is a means to an end, not an end in itself" (Robinson, *Nobility and Annihilation*, 104). Further, Robinson acknowledges a similar elitism in Hildegard and Hadewijch—and Bernard of Clairvaux (Robinson, *Nobility and Annihilation*, 102–3). But then Robinson undercuts her own argument through her suspicion that exactly that elitism stopped Porete from deploying that familiar modesty topos of the "lowly woman" found in other women writers. Robinson suggests that Porete viewed herself as an equal to other male authorities and for this reason admonishes ecclesiasts for their ignobility, which no doubt enhanced the irritation of church officials (Robinson, *Nobility and Annihilation*, 106).

61. See Cottrell, "Marguerite Porete's Heretical Discourse," 20, who declares that Porete refuses to identify the female self as Christ's bride.

62. For example, in a version of the medieval family allegory, the Unencumbered or Annihilated Soul is "dame des Vertuz" [lady of the Virtues], "fille de Deité" [daughter of Deity], "seure de Sapience" [sister of Wisdom], and "espouse d'Amour" [bride of Love] (Guarnieri, *Mirouer*, 246 [87.3–4];

Babinsky, *Mirror*, 162; my emphasis). According to Robinson, Porete's mysticism differs from Bräutmystik or Minnemystik; instead, Robinson argues, it shares in Wesenmystik—the mysticism of being—*unitas indistinctionis*, "the union of indistinction," *unio sine distinctione*, or *differentia* (Robinson, *Nobility and Annihilation*, 79).

63. Babinsky, *Mirror*, 229 n93.

64. Robinson explains that the body and soul, originally united at the creation of Adam, were divorced by sin (*Nobility and Annihilation*, 65). Therefore, the body cannot be considered defective, as we can see from Jesus Christ's humanity, through the Virgin (65). It is the soul that originates in nothingness; the body itself cannot be considered as having agency in the Fall. Instead, the will of Adam bears greatest culpability in the Fall (69).

65. Robinson argues that the Holy Spirit (love) equals in importance God the Father and the Son (Wisdom) in creating and taking care of the soul in Porete's Trinitarian doctrine (*Nobility and Annihilation*, 61). See also Randall, "Person, Place, Perception," 229–44, for her discussion of Porete's Trinity as a "thoughtful dialogue with church doctrine" (230), in particular, Jesus as a figuration of Love.

66. Written on the first page was "De conventu Magdalenes prope Aurellianis," according to Verdeyen, vii.

67. Babinsky, *Mirror*, 227 n58.

68. Robinson, *Nobility and Annihilation*, 51; see also chap. 3, "God, the Soul, and No-thingness."

5 Unhomely Margery Kempe and St. Catherine of Siena: "Comunycacyon" and "Conuersacion" as Homily

1. See an *in bono* treatment of the sobs in Sandra J. McEntire, "Walter Hilton and Margery Kempe: Tears and Compunction," in *Mysticism: Medieval and Modern*, ed. Valerie M. Lagorio, Salzburg Studies in English Literature, 92.20 (Salzburg: Institut für Anglistik und Amerikanistik, Universität of Salzburg, 1986), 49–57; and Kathy Lavezzo, "Sobs and Sighs between Women: The Homoerotics of Compassion in *The Book of Margery Kempe*," in *Premodern Sexualities*, ed. Louise Fradenberg and Carla Freccero (New York and London: Routledge, 1996), 175–98.

2. See, for example, Liliana Sikorska, " 'Hir Not Lettyrd': The Use of Interjections, Pragmatic Markers and When-Clauses in *The Book of Margery Kempe*," in *Placing Middle English in Context*, ed. Irma Taavitsainen, Terttu Nevalainen, Päivi Pahta, and Matti Rissanen (Berlin and New York: Mouton de Gruyter, 2000), 391–410; and Fiona Somerset, "Excitative Speech: Theories of Emotive Response from Richard Fitzralph to Margery Kempe," in *The Vernacular Spirit: Essays on Medieval Religious Literature*, ed. Renate Blumenfeld-Kosinski, Duncan Robertson, and Nancy Bradley Warren (New York, NY: Palgrave, 2002), 59–79.

3. See Carole Slade, "Alterity in Union: The Mystical Experience of Angela of Foligno and Margery Kempe," *Religion and Literature* 23 (Autumn, 1991): 109–26.

4. For a thoughtful examination of the white clothes, see Gunnel Cleve, "Semantic Dimensions in Margery Kempe's 'Whyght Clothys,' " *Mystics Quarterly* 12 (1986): 162–70; and Mary C. Erler, "Margery Kempe's White Clothes," *Medium Aevum* 62 (1993): 78–83.

5. There are numerous early analyses of Kempe's hysteria and madness; for a recent example, see Richard Lawes, "Psychological Disorder and the Autobiographical Impulse in Julian of Norwich, Margery Kempe and Thomas Hoccleve," in *Writing Religious Women: Female Spiritual and Textual Practices in Late Medieval England*, ed. Denis Renevey and Christiania Whitehead (Toronto: University of Toronto Press, 2000), 217–43; and Becky R. Lee, "The Medieval Hysteric and the Psychedelic Psychologist: A Revaluation of the Mysticism of Margery Kempe in the Light of the Transpersonal Psychology of Stanislav Grof," *Studia mystica* 23 (2002): 102–26.

6. See Mary Hardiman Farley, "Her Own Creature: Religion, Feminist Criticism, and the Functional Eccentricity of Margery Kempe," *Exemplaria* 11 (1999): 1, 5–6 [1–21]. In addition, see Stephen Harper, " 'So Euyl to Rewlyn': Madness and Authority in *The Book of Margery Kempe*," *Neuphilologische Mitteilungen* 98 (1997): 53–61, who notes Kempe suffered from bouts of "mania and melancholia, the two principal forms of madness recognized in late medieval textbooks. In terms of medieval medicine, Margery is insane" (56); and Roy Eriksen, "Sacred Art and the Artful Conversion of Margery Kempe," *Nordlit: Arbeidstidsskrift i litteratur* 6 (Fall 1999): 15–29.

7. See Lawes, "Psychological Disorder," in *Writing Religious Women*, ed. Renevey and Whitehead, 230.

8. The scribe in book 1 may have been her son; this book may have been rewritten by a different priest with a better command over English, who also added to it ten chapters. For the first scribe as Kempe's son, see Lynn Staley, ed., *The Book of Margery Kempe*, Middle English Series (Kalamazoo, MI: Western Michigan University, 1996), chap. 89. Subsequent citations will appear within the text indicated by parentheses and chapter and page number(s). *The Book* has been translated, among others, by B.A. Windeatt (London: Penguin, 1985), which is used in this chapter where appropriate and cited in the text by page number(s) within parentheses. For a discussion of the son's ineptitude, which may have resulted in the confused chronology, displaced locations, and so forth, see Samuel Fanous, "Measuring the Pilgrim's Progress: Internal Emphases in *The Book of Margery Kempe*," in *Writing Religious Women*, ed. Renevey and Whitehead, 158 [177–95].

9. Hope E. Allen, Prefatory Note, *The Book of Margery Kempe*, ed. Sanford B. Meech, Original Series, 212 (London: Early English Text Society, 1940), lxiv.

10. See Denis Renevey, "Margery's Performing Body: The Translation of Late Medieval Discursive Religious Practices," in *Writing Religious Women*, ed. Renevey and Whitehead, 209 [197–216].

11. Cynthia Ho, "Margery Reads Exempla," *Medieval Perspectives* 8 (1993): 143–52.

12. For the female self and authentic voice in Kempe, see, for example, Janel M. Mueller, "Autobiography of a New 'Creatur': Female Spirituality, Selfhood, and Authorship in *The Book of Margery Kempe*," in *The Female Autograph*, ed. Domna C. Stanton (New York: New York Literary Forum, 1984), 63–75; Karma Lochrie, "*The Book of Margery Kempe*: The Marginal Woman's Quest for Literary Authority," *Journal of Medieval and Renaissance Studies* 16 (1986): 33–55, revised as chapter 3 of Karma Lochrie, *Margery Kempe and Translations of the Flesh* (Philadelphia: University of Pennsylvania Press, 1991), 97–134; Sandra J. McEntire, "The Journey into Selfhood: Margery Kempe and Feminine Spirituality," in *Margery Kempe: A Book of Essays*, ed. Sandra J. McEntire, Garland Medieval Casebooks, vol. 4 (New York: Garland, 1992), 51–69; Sarah Beckwith, "Problems of Authority in Late Medieval English Mysticism: Language, Agency, and Authority in *The Book of Margery Kempe*," *Exemplaria* 4 (1992): 172–99; Peter Dorsey, "Women's Autobiography and the Hermeneutics of Conversion," *A/B: Auto/Biography Studies* 8 (1993): 72–90; and Cheryl Glenn, "Reexamining *The Book of Margery Kempe*: A Rhetoric of Autobiography," in *Reclaiming Rhetorica: Women in Rhetorical Tradition*, ed. Andrea Lunsford (Pittsburgh: University of Pittsburgh Press, 1995), 53–71.

13. See Lynn Staley, *Margery Kempe's Dissenting Fictions* (University Park: Pennsylvania State University Press, 1994).

14. See Suzanne L. Craymer, "Margery Kempe's Imitation of Mary Magdalene and the 'Digby Plays,' " *Mystics Quarterly* 19 (1993): 173–81; Mary Magdalene, by Susan Eberley, "Margery Kempe, St. Mary Magdalene, and Patterns of Contemplation," *Downside Review* 107 (1989): 209–33; and the Wife of Bath, by Janet Wilson, "Margery and Alisoun: Women on Top," in *Margery Kempe*, ed. McEntire,, 233–37.

15. See Denise L. Despres, "Franciscan Spirituality: Margery Kempe and Visual Meditation," *Mystics Quarterly* 11 (1985): 12–18; and Denise L. Despres, "The Meditative Art of Scriptural Interpretation in *The Book of Margery Kempe*," *Downside Review* 106 (1988): 253–63.

16. See Joel Fredell, "Margery Kempe: Spectacle and Spiritual Governance," *Philological Quarterly* 75 (1996): 137–66.

17. See Diana R. Uhlman, "The Comfort of Voice, the Solace of Script: Orality and Literacy in *The Book of Margery Kempe*," *Studies in Philology* 91 (1994): 50–69.

18. See Martin L. Warren, *Asceticism in the Christian Transformation of Self in Margery Kempe, William Thorpe, and John Rogers*, Studies in Religion and Society, vol. 60 (Lewiston, NY: E. Mellen Press, 2003).

19. See, for example, the important study by Farley, "Her Own Creature: Religion, Feminist Criticism, and the Functional Eccentricity of Margery Kempe," 1–21.

20. For a comparison with Mary of Oignies and Christina Mirabilis, see Patricia Deery Kurtz, "Mary of Oignies, Christine the Marvelous, and Medieval

Heresy," *Mystics Quarterly* 14 (1988): 186–96; with Elizabeth of Spalbeck and Christina Mirabilis, see John A. Erskine, "Margery Kempe and Her Models: The Role of the Authorial Voice," *Mystics Quarterly* 15 (1989): 75–85.

21. See Alexandra Barratt, "Margery Kempe and the King's Daughter of Hungary," in *Margery Kempe*, ed. McEntire : 189–201.

22. For the comparison with Julian of Norwich, see Karin Boklund-Lagopoulos, "Visionary Discourse: Julian of Norwich and Margery Kempe," *Yearbook of English Studies* (Aristotle University of Thessaloniki) 3 (1991–92): 27–43; and Lynn Staley Johnson, "The Trope of the Scribe and the Question of Literary Authority in the Works of Julian of Norwich and Margery Kempe," *Speculum* 66 (1991): 820–38; for Julian, St. Birgitta, and the Wife of Bath, see Julia Bolton Holloway, "Bride, Margery, Julian, and Alice: Bridget of Sweden's Textual Community in Medieval England," in *Margery Kempe*, ed. McEntire, 203–33; for St. Birgitta, see Nanda Alexis Hoppenwasser, "The Human Burden of the Prophet: St. Birgitta's *Revelations* and *The Book of Margery Kempe*," *Medieval Perspectives* 8 (1993): 153–62.

23. See Slade, "Alterity in Union," 109–26.

24. See Ute Stargardt, "The Beguines of Belgium, the Dominican Nuns of Germany, and Margery Kempe," in *The Popular Literature of Medieval England*, ed. Thomas Heffernan (Knoxville: University of Tennessee Press, 1985), 277–313.

25. See Beverly Boyd, "Wyclif, Joan of Arc, and Margery Kempe," *Fourteenth Century English Mystics Newsletter* 12.3 (Sept. 1986): 112–18.

26. See Brian W. Gastle, "Breaking the Stained Glass Ceiling: Mercantile Authority, Margaret Paston, and Margery Kempe," *Studies in the Literary Imagination* 36.1 (Spring 2003): 123–47.

27. See Thomas of Cantimpré, *Life of Christina Mirabilis*, trans. Margot H. King (Toronto, ON: Peregrina Press, 1997), 14 [chap. 9]; 4 [chap. 1].

28. See also Cristina Mazzoni, *Angela of Foligno's Memorial, Translated from Latin with Introduction, Notes, and Interpretive Essay*, Library of Medieval Women (Cambridge, UK: D.S. Brewer, 1999), 26–27, 37.

29. See Thomas de Cantimpré, *Life of Christina Mirabilis*, 14 (shackled with iron chains), 18 (leg broken with a cudgel), 19 (bound in a dungeon) [chaps. 9, 17–18].

30. Barbara Newman, "Possessed by the Spirit: Devout Women, Demoniacs, and the Apostolic Life in the Thirteenth Century," *Speculum* 73 (1998): 733–86.

31. Thomas of Cantimpré, *Life of Christina Mirabilis*, 12, 16, 18. For an example of the counsel of Margery's inner voice, see Margery's relation to the vicar of how the Lord dallies in her soul, in Staley, *Book of Margery Kempe*, 50–51; Windeatt, 75 [chap. 17].

32. See Raymond of Capua (Raimundus Vineis, de Capua), *Here beginneth the Lyf of Saynt Katherin of senis the Blessed Virgin; The revelacions of Saynt Elysabeth the Kynges doughter of hungarye*, ed. William Caxton (London: Wynken de Worde, from William Caxton's plates, 1493?); and the more readily available

edition by C. Hortsmann, " 'The lyf of saint Katherin of Senis,' nach dem Drucke W. Caxtons (ca. 1493) mitgeteilt," *Archiv für das Studium der neueren Sprachen und Litteraturen* 76 (1886): 33–112, 265–314, 353–400. All references are to the Horstmann edition, by page, book, and chapter, and the Lamb translation, where appropriate, by page, book, and chapter.

33. Lochrie, "*The Book of Margery Kempe*: The Marginal Woman's Quest for Literary Authority," 42–47 [33–55].

34. Wendy Harding, "Body into Text: *The Book of Margery Kempe*," *Feminist Approaches to the Body in Medieval Literature*, ed. Linda Lomperis and Sarah Stanbury, New Cultural Studies Series (Philadelphia: University of Pennsylvania Press, 1993), 175–76 [167–87]. See also Gunnel Cleve, "Margery Kempe's 'Dalyawns' with the Lord," in *Neophilologica Fennica: Société*, ed. Leena Kahlas-Tarkka (Helsinki: Société neophilologique de Helsinki, 1987), 10–21.

35. *Oxford English Dictionary*, 2nd edn., s.v. "conversation."

36. See Nadeane Trowse, "The Exclusionary Potential of Genre: Margery Kempe's Transgressive Search for a Deniable Pulpit," in *The Rhetoric and Ideology of Genre: Strategies for Stability and Change*, ed. Richard Coe, Lorelei Lingard, and Tatiana Teslenko (Creskill, NJ: Hampton Press, 2002), 341–53.

37. Guidini's memorial appears in two publications, the "Memorie di Ser Cristofano di Galgano Guidini da Siena, scritte da lui medesimo nel secolo XIV," ed. Carlo Milanesi, *Archivio storico italiano*, series 1, vol. 4 [1842]: 25–48, and P. Innocenzo Taurisano, *I fioretti di S. Caterina da Siena* (Rome: F. Ferrari, 1922), 105–26; 2nd edn. (1927), 111–34.

38. The Horstmann edition of de Worde/Caxton's *Lyf* does not contain the *Revelations* of St. Elisabeth of Hungary. Eight known copies exist of the de Worde/Caxton edition; twelve others are owned privately but their whereabouts are unknown. See Seymour de Ricci, *A Census of Caxtons*, Illustrated Monographs of the Bibliographical Society, no. 15 (Oxford: Oxford University Press, 1909), 122; for the description of this book, see pp. 113–14 (no. 106), described as "96 ff.: a^{8b}-p^6 q^4 43 (and 44) lines. 214x150 mm. Printed about 1493." There were only five books printed by de Worde from Caxton's types, of which this was one.

39. For Thomas of Gascoigne's role in translating the *Life of St. Birgitta*, see William Patterson Cumming, ed., *The Revelations of Saint Birgitta, Edited from the Garrett MS Princeton University Library Deposit 1397*, Early English Text Society, o.s., no. 178 (London: Humphrey Milford/Oxford University Press, 1929 [for 1928]), xxx.

40. For the manuscript, see Catharine R. Borland, *A Descriptive Catalogue of the Western Mediaeval Manuscripts in Edinburgh University Library* (Edinburgh: University of Edinburgh Press/ T. and A. Constable, 1916), 142–43. As to what Latin source existed in Britain from which a Middle English translation might have come, Hodgson has surmised that the Latin translation now at University of Edinburgh (MS 87) must have been written by Cristofano di Galgano Guidini and not by Raymond of Capua, as the catalogue

descriptions indicate: see Phyllis Hodgson and Gabriel M. Liegey, editors of the Middle English version of Catherine of Siena's *Dialogo*, *The Orcherd of Syon*, vol. 1: Text, Early English Text Society, vol. 258 (London: Oxford University Press, 1966), vii; see also Phyllis Hodgson, "*The Orcherd of Syon* and the English Mystical Tradition (Sir Israel Gollancz Memorial Lecture, Read 1 July 1964)," *Proceedings of the British Academy* 50 (1964): 231 [229–43]. Because Guidini first translated the *Dialogo* into Latin, in 1389, his translation is considered to be closer to the original Italian than some of the later translations. Hodgson's argument makes sense because Raymond died before completing the third translation (Stefano Maconi's was second), of which only the first five and the last two chapters exist, and therefore it is unlikely that MS 87, of the entire *Dialogus*, was in fact written by Raymond. University of Edinburgh 87 has not been edited; it was of English provenance and is written by at least three scribes. Hodgson also posits either a Carthusian or a Dominican channel for the transmission of this MS, in "*Orcherd of Syon* and the English Mystical Tradition," 231. William Flete, the English Austin Minor hermit close to Catherine, lived in Italy and may have transmitted some of these copies to his house in England: see Michael B. Hackett, "Catherine of Siena and William of England," in *Proceedings of the Patristic, Medieval, and Renaissance Conference* 6 (1981): 29–47.

41. See Hodgson, "*The Orcherd of Syon* and the English Mystical Tradition," 229.
42. For an edition of the Witham Charterhouse library listing, see E. Margaret Thompson, *The Carthusian Order in England* (London: Society for Promoting Christian Knowledge; New York and Toronto: Macmillan, 1930), 32.
43. Most significantly, in 1517, four years after the disastrous battle at Flodden, in which many Scottish lords lost their lives, a convent devoted to St. Catherine of Siena was founded by James the Fifth in Edinburgh at Sciennes (pronounced "Sheens" as a corruption of the Latin "Senis" for "Siena," or of the French "Siennes"); there is speculation that a nunnery had actually been given in the later fifteenth century, by Lady Saint Clair, Countess of Caithness and wife of Sinclair of Roslyn, and lands and a priest obtained at that earlier date. See George Chalmers, *Caledonia: Or, an Account, Historical and Topographic, of North Britain, from the Most Ancient to the Present Times*, 3 vols. (London: Paisley /A. Gardner, 1807–24), 2:761.
44. See especially Margaret Deanesly, *The Incendium Amoris of Richard Rolle* (1915; repr. Norwood, Pennsylvania: Norwood Editions, 1977), 91–130, which discusses and contains many of the documents relating to its founding; and David Knowles, *The Religious Orders in England*, vol. 2 of 2 vols.: *The End of the Middle Ages* (Cambridge: Cambridge University Press, 1955), 2:171–81, for information regarding its founding. King Henry V, who laid the foundation stone, supported the Abbey and St. Bridget throughout his life, mentioning his prayers to her in his will and owning one of her relics: see James H. Wylie, *The Reign of Henry the Fifth*, vol. 1 of 3 vols. (Cambridge: Cambridge University Press, 1914), 219–20. To a sympathetic "King Henry" (whether the Fourth or the Fifth is unclear) Stefano Maconi had also sent Catherinian

"material," but apparently not his transcription of her *Dialogue*, according to Thomas Caffarini; this information comes from William B. Hackett and is cited in Hodgson, "*The Orcherd of Syon* and the English Mystical Tradition," 231 n2.

45. See Michael Aston, *Monasteries* (London: B. T. Batsford, 1993), 141–42, which includes a diagram of all these locations.

46. See John Henry Blunt, ed., *The Myroure of oure Ladye containing a Devotional treatise on Divine Service, with a Translation of the Offices Used by the Sisters of the Brigittine Monastery of Sion, at Isleworth, during the Fifteenth and Sixteenth Centuries*, EETS 19 (London: Early English Text Society, 1873), xi. The "Pardon of Syon" was mentioned in John Audelay's 1426 poem, "A Salutation to St. Bridget."

47. Sir Georges James Aungier, *The History and Antiquities of Syon Monastery: The Parish of Isleworth, and the Chapelry of Hounslow/Compiled from Public Records, Ancient Manuscripts, Ecclesiastical and other Authentic Documents* (London: J.B. Nichols and Son, 1840), 29.

48. Anthony Goodman, *Margery Kempe and Her World* (London and New York: Pearson Education, 2002), 116.

49. Goodman, *Margery Kempe*, 118.

50. Goodman, *Margery Kempe*, 120–21.

51. See Sanford B. Meech and Hope E. Allen, introduction to *The Book of Margery Kempe*, xxxii–xxxvff.

52. See also the "Catalogue of Sion Library" compiled by Bishop Tanner, British Library Additional MS 6261, fols. 153–56; and Mary Bateson, *Catalogue of the Library of Syon Monaster, Isleworth* (Cambridge: Cambridge University Press, 1898), appendix 1; and Christopher de Hamel, "The Library: The Medieval Manuscripts of Syon Abbey, and Their Dispersal," *Syon Abbey: The Library of the Bridgettine Nuns and Their Peregrinations after the Reformation* (Arundel Castle: The Roxburghe Club, 1991), 48–158. According to de Hamel, there are records of more than 1400 books catalogued at Syon (48), with more books printed for Syon than for any other monastery in England (101). For the impact of St. Bridget in fifteenth-century England, see F. R. Johnston, "The Cult of St. Bridget of Sweden in Fifteenth-Century England," M.A. thesis, University of Manchester, 1948; and for the uses of her manuscripts, see Roger Ellis, " 'Flores ad fabricandam…coronam': An Investigation into the Uses of the *Revelations* of St. Bridget of Sweden in Fifteenth-Century England," *Medium Aevum* 51 (1982): 163–86. Ann M. Hutchison, "Devotional Reading in the Monastery and the Late Medieval Household," in *De Cella in Seculum: Religious and Secular Life and Devotion in Late Medieval England*, ed. Michael G. Sargent (Bury St. Edmunds, Suffolk: D. S. Brewer, 1989), 215–27, discusses the role of Syon Abbey in guiding the reading of its nuns and other women. For a survey of fifteenth-century book production, see H. S. Bennett, *English Books and Readers 1475 to 1557, Being a Study of the History of the Book Trade from Caxton to the Incorporation of the Stationers' Company*, 2nd edn. (Cambridge: University Press, 1970).

53. Cited in Blunt, *Myroure*, ix. The manuscript on which the edition is based (MS Aberdeen University W.P.R. 4. 18) is dated 1460–1500 and according to Blunt originally belonged to one of the sisters, Elizabeth Mounton (vii).

54. "Rycharde Suttun esquyer Stewarde of the Monastery of Syon" is described by translator "Dane Jamys" as "fyndynge this ghostely tresure these dyologes and reuelacyons of the newe seraphycall spouse of cryste Seynte Katheryne of Sene in a corner by it selfe wyllynge of his great charyte it sholde come to lyghte that many relygyous and devoute soules myght be releued and haue comforte thereby." See *Orchard of Syon* (1519), 3. According to Bateson's *Catalogue of the Library of Syon Monastery* and the 1526 Cambridge Corpus Christi MS 141, there was a copy of the *Reuelaciones catherine de senis vm aliis* (copied by William the Englishman?), donated by Curzon (probably David Curson, Monk of Syon in 1537, declares Aungier, *History and Antiquities of Syon Monastery*, 90, 428, 436); there was also a copy of the *Vita sancte Katerine de Senis* (from which a translation might have come) donated by Lawis (probably John, deacon, who died in 1477). The identity of brother "Dane James," who may not have even translated the text but who may only have been a helper, cannot be known, according to Sister Mary Denise, "The *Orchard of Syon*: An Introduction," *Traditio* 14 (1958): 291–34, but he may have been a Carthusian at Sheen (where "Dan" was commonly used), an English Dominican friar for whom "your brother" was a helper, or a Syon brother himself.

55. See Hodgson, "*The Orcherd of Syon* and the English Mystical Tradition," 236.

56. St. Birgitta, *Opera Minora I; Regvla Salvatoris*, ed. Sten Eklund, The Royal Academy of Letters, History, and Antiquities (Stockholm: Almqvist and Wiksell International, 1975), 102–3.

57. I am indebted to Sister Julia Bolton Holloway for information about the orchards in the early houses; see also Roger Ellis, "*Viderunt eam Filie Syon*": *The Spirituality of the English House of a Medieval Contemplative Order from its Beginnings to the Present Day*, Analecta Cartusiana 68 (Salzburg, Aus.: Institut für Anglistik und Amerikanistik, 1984), plates 47 and 48, 185–90.

58. Horstmann, The *lyf of saint Katherin of Senis*, 38 [1.1].

59. Horstmann, The *lyf of saint Katherin of Senis*, 41 [1.2]; see also 42 for similar desires on her part.

60. Horstmann, The *lyf of saint Katherin of Senis*, 45 [1.3].

61. Horstmann, The *lyf of saint Katherin of Senis*, 45 [1.3].

62. Horstmann, The *lyf of saint Katherin of Senis*, 50 [1.4].

63. Horstmann, The *lyf of saint Katherin of Senis*, 50 [1.4].

64. Horstmann, The *lyf of saint Katherin of Senis*, 60 [1.7]; 83–84 [1.12].

65. Staley, *Book of Margery Kempe*, 22 [chap. 1].

66. See Jacques de Vitry, *The Life of Marie d'Oignies*, trans. Margot H. King, in *Two Lives of Marie d'Oignies*, 4th edn. (Toronto, ON: Peregrina Publishing, 1998), 58–60 [1.16–18].

67. On her "hysterical personality organization," see Clarissa W. Atkinson, *Mystic and Pilgrim: The Book and the World of Margery Kempe* (Ithaca: Cornell University Press, 1983), 208.

68. Horstmann, The *lyf of saint Katherin of Senis*,, 106 [2.5]; my emphasis.

69. Lamb, *Life of St. Catherine of Siena*, 151.

70. Horstmann, The *lyf of saint Katherin of Senis*, 85 [2.1]; my emphasis.

71. See Karen Scott, "*Io Catarina*': Ecclesiastical Politics and Oral Culture in the Letters of Catherine of Siena," in *Dear Sister: Medieval Women and the Epistolary Genre*, ed. Karen Cherewatuk and Ulrike Wiethaus (Philadelphia: University of Pennsylvania Press, 1993), 87–121; and also her dissertation, "Not Only with Words, but with Deeds: The Role of Speech in Catherine of Siena's Understanding of Her Mission" (Ph.D. diss., University of California-Berkeley, 1989).

72. See Georges Barthouil, "Boccacce et Catherine de Sienne (la dixième journée du *Decameron*: Noblesse ou subversion?)," *Italianistica* 7 (1982): 249–76.

73. See Suzanne Noffke, trans., *Dialogue of St. Catherine of Siena* (New York, Ramsay, and Toronto: Paulist Press, 1980).

74. Because of Catherine's impact on the church and society, during the later years of this decade William Flete, the English Austin Minor (a member of Catherine's *familia* originally from Fleet, in Lincolnshire, not far from Norfolk and Cambridge), was instrumental in making the case to the English to support Urban VI during the Great Schism: "[H]e is true Pope, as has been made known to God's servants in revelations, inspirations and prayers," particularly those of Catherine. In one letter copied and circulated throughout England (between 1378 and 1380), William talks about all classes trying to kiss Catherine's hand; he also asks, "*Are men to follow women, or be guided by their counsels?*" and in praise of valiant women, in a passage on the Book of Proverbs, describes the battlefield as God's church and "the vineyard which she has planted in her blood is the same Church, so afflicted to-day with the abuses of pride and pomp, ambition and simony"; see Aubrey Gwynn, *The English Austin Friars in the Time of Wyclif* (London: Oxford University Press/Humphrey Milford, 1940), 177, 178. In 1382 William delivered an important sermon in Siena on the doctrines of St. Catherine, one of many he presented that year in Italy. For William's sermon about God's gift of Catherine to the papacy, and in particular to Urban VI, in the battle against simony and other vices during the Babylonian Captivity, see Siena, Biblioteca communale MS T. ii. 7, fols. 17–29. See Gwynn, 193, 240, for William's support of the pope in 1378, in letters circulated from convent to convent and used as a base in the sixteen *demonstrationes* of the *Rationes Anglorum* (the English decided to support Urban VI at the Parliament of Gloucester in October 1378, but the document was not finished until summer of 1380; see Gwynn, 246–47). William's letters (Gwynne, 177, 178), one addressed to or copied by Adam Stocton, an English friar, can be found in Trinity College-Dublin MS A.5.3, fols. 179–86 and Royal MS 7. E. X, fols. 85–87.

75. Lamb, *Life of St. Catherine of Siena*, 304 [3.1].

76. Horstmann, The *lyf of saint Katherin of Senis*,, 360 [3.1]; Lamb, *Life of St. Catherine of Siena*, 304.

77. Horstmann, The *lyf of saint Katherin of Senis*,, 360 [3.1].

78. Despite the work's seeming lack of organization, according to Hodgson, "The [symbol] which spans the whole *Orcherd* and gives its unity is the great apocalyptic symbol of the Bridge. The opening vision of *Piers Plowman* has comparable vastness and sublimity, but it is surpassed in dynamic force by the Bridge, which through its manifold interpretation is essentially a symbol of movement—the Way, the Truth, the Life. This is the Bridge of God's mercy," in "*The Orcherd of Syon* and the English Mystical Tradition," 240. The chapter divisions were not Catherine's—the "Book" was dictated in ecstasy, according to Guidini, who helped transcribe it (see "Memorie di Ser Cristofano di Galgano Guidini," 37), and issued as one long narrative, then edited by Catherine, and only divided into 167 chapters by later disciples. In 1579, when it came to be fashionable to write treatises, editors divided the work into four parts: Onorio Farrio noted the importance of the word "trattato" named in the chapter headings for the first four and inserted "Treatise" in large capitals up to the next heading with "trattato" (see Cavallini's preface to her critical edition, *Il dialogo*, xiv). Thus, the most important part, of the eight noted by Noffke—prologue (chaps. 1–2), the way of perfection (3–12), dialogue (13–25), the bridge (26–87), tears (88–87), truth (98–109), the mystic body of Holy Church (110–34), Divine Providence (135–53), obedience (154–65), and conclusion (166–67)—is that on the bridge (26–87): "the central and most important part of the whole book, developed in several sections" (Noffke, *Dialogue*, 15).

79. See the Hodgson, *Orcherd of Syon*, 74–75 [2.3]; the original used is Catherine of Siena, *Il dialogo della Divina Provvidenza ovvero Libro della divina dottrina*, ed. Giuliana Cavallini (Rome: Edizioni cateriniane, 1968), chap. 29; Noffke, *Dialogue*, 69.

80. Hodgson, *Orcherd*, 84 [3.4]; Catherine of Siena, *Dialogo*, chap. 35; Noffke, *Dialogue*, 76; Cristofano di Galgano Guidini(?), trans. (from the Italian into Latin), "Liber Divine Doctrine S. Catherine Senensis," MS 87 [Borland] (Edinburgh, University of Edinburgh Library), fol. 40v.

81. Hodgson, *Orcherd*, 63 [2.3]; chap. 23 of Catherine of Siena, *Dialogo*, chap. 23; Noffke, *Dialogue*, 60.

82. Hodgson, *Orcherd*, 64 [2.3]; Catherine of Siena, *Dialogo*, 30.

83. Hodgson, *Orcherd*, 64–65 [2.3]; Catherine of Siena, *Dialogo*, 61; my emphasis.

84. Hodgson, *Orcherd*, 69 [2.2]; Catherine of Siena, *Dialogo* [chap. 26]; Noffke, *Dialogue*, 65.

85. Hodgson, *Orcherd*, 69; Noffke, *Dialogue*, 65. The second reference is to Catherine of Siena, *Dialogo*, chap. 35; Noffke, *Dialogue*, 77, but it does not appear in *Orcherd*.

86. Hodgson, *Orcherd*, 70 [2.2]; Catherine of Siena, *Dialogo*, chap. 27; Noffke, *Dialogue*, 65.

87. Hodgson, *Orcherd*, 71 [2.2]; Catherine of Siena, *Dialogo*, chap. 27; Noffke, *Dialogue*, 66; in Guidini, the Latin translator twice uses words related to fabrication, *lapides fabricati* and *fabricando suo sanguine*, fol. 30r.

88. Hodgson, *Orcherd*, 97 [2.5]; Catherine of Siena, *Dialogo*, chap. 42; Noffke, *Dialogue*, 86; my emphasis.

89. Hodgson, *Orcherd*, 362–63 [6.4]; Catherine of Siena, *Dialogo*, chap. 148; Noffke, *Dialogue*, 311.

90. Hodgson, *Orcherd*, 69 [2.2]; Catherine of Siena, *Dialogo*, chap. 26.

91. See Wynken de Worde, *The Orcherde of Syon*, trans. Dane Jamys (London: Wynken de Worde, 1519), M f.qr; and the prologue, Hodgson, *Orcherd*, 18.

92. de Worde, *Orcherde*, 2r. In fact, both the original work and the translation appear to be structured as if a dialogue, through the reiterated pattern of petition-answer-thanksgiving, according to Cavallini, cited in Noffke, *Dialogue*, xiii. Noffke identifies the structural principle as one of layering of arguments so that "even seemingly incompatible metaphors become inexplicably joined" (15).

93. Horstmann, The *lyf of saint Katherin of Senis*, 37 [1.1].

94. Horstmann, The *lyf of saint Katherin of Senis*, 37 [1.1].

95. Horstmann, The *lyf of saint Katherin of Senis*, 83 [1.11].

96. Horstmann, The *lyf of saint Katherin of Senis*, 86 [2.1].

97. The "Epistolae duae de canonizatione sanctae Brigidae," Oxford, Bodleian MS Hamilton 7, fol. 229 (also found in a Lincoln Cathedral MS), apparently composed after Easton's imprisonment by Urban VI, sometime between 1389–91 (the date of the Canonization Commission), is discussed by F.R. Johnston, "The Cult of St. Bridget of Sweden in Fifteenth-Century England" (M.A. thesis, University of Manchester, 1948), 150–53. Easton also acknowledges the participation of women in the establishment of the Church and the appearance of Christ *corporaliter* to holy women after the Resurrection and at other times.

98. Horstmann, The *lyf of saint Katherin of Senis*, 86 [2.1].

99. Horstmann, The *lyf of saint Katherin of Senis*, 86 [2.1].

100. Easton, "Epistolae duae de canonizatione sanctae Brigidae," fol. 232.

101. Lamb, *Life of St. Catherine of Siena*, 256–57 [2.10]; 284; 303.

102. The matter of the writing and revision of the *Dialogue* and Catherine's role in the same has been discussed and debated by scholars but not fully and finally resolved. Two years before her death, according to Raymond of Capua's *Legenda Major* 3.3, she dictated to her secretaries a book of dialogue between a soul, who asks four questions, and God, who answers with many truths. Earlier still, in October of 1377, she had written to Raymond a letter that seemed to describe the organizational frame of the book, involving four petitions to God—for church reform, for the whole world, for Raymond's spiritual welfare, and for an uncertain unnamed sinner (that is, herself). For the parallels between letter 272 and the *Dialogue*, see Eugenia Dupré-Theseider, "Sulla composizione del 'Dialogo' di Santa Caterina da Siena," *Giornale storico della letteratura italiana* 117 (1941): 161–202. Because there is no original manuscript of the *Dialogue*, modern editors have had to choose among the transcriptions by her disciples, Barduccio Canigiani, Stefano Maconi, and Neri di Landoccio de Pagliaresi, among whom Barduccio Canigiani has been singled out as having written the manuscript bearing signs of fewest interpolations and changes and therefore closest to

the "original" (see Noffke, introduction to her translation of the *Dialogue*, 19). This manuscript, 292 of the Biblioteca Casanatense in Rome, would have been written before 8 December, 1382 (the date of Barduccio's death); most important, there are passages in which the first person accusative pronoun "me" has been crossed out in the phrase "me, Dio e uomo" (chaps. 110–11), when God the Father identifies the Eucharist as "me, God and man." See B. Motzo, "Per un'edizione critica delle opere di S. Caterina da Siena," *Annali della Facoltà di filosofia e lettere della Università di Cagliari* (1930–31): 111–41. Whatever the reason for the crossings-out, they suggest the manuscript is the closest to the original (according to Motzo, the other manuscripts do not contain the pronoun at all). Also, interpolations found in other manuscripts are not found in this manuscript. See Noffke, *Dialogue*, 19. Whether Catherine wrote her book in her own hand at any time is not at issue; Tommaso Antonio Caffarini of Siena admits that he was told by Stefano Maconi that Maconi saw her writing herself "several pages of the book which she herself composed in her own dialect," in *Libellus de supplemento: Legende prolixe virginis beate Catherine de Senis*, ed. Giuliana Cavallini and Imelda Foralosso (Rome: Edizioni Cateriniane, 1974) [1.1.9].

103. Mary Morse sees Margery as a "conversion exemplar of a woman who has not attracted herself to any monastic rule, resists ecclesiastical regulation of the conversion process for herself and for others who might emulate her," in " 'Tak and Bren Hir': Lollardy as Conversion Motif in *The Book of Margery Kempe*," *Mystics Quarterly* 29 (Mar.–June. 2003): 27 [24–44]. Morse believes, in addition, that Margery's *Book* 2 follows St. Augustine's "conversion hermeneutic of spiritual autobiography" (26).

104. See Dorsey, "Women's Autobiography," 82.

105. Interestingly, both women had manuscripts copied and annotated at the Carthusian charterhouse at Mount Grace Priory, not far from Northallerton, Yorkshire, and in 1501 Wynken de Worde printed a seven-page quarto pamphlet of extracts with Margery's name listed; the only copy is housed at Cambridge University Library. Henry Pepwell reprinted these extracts in 1521 in a mystical collection, a Catholic anthology intended as an anti-Luther campaign, because he perceived Margery as a "devout anchoress." See the discussion in Jennifer Summit, *Lost Property: The Woman Writer and English Literary History, 1380–1589* (Chicago: University of Chicago Press, 2000), 126–38.

106. Windeatt, *Book*, 20. See Edmund Colledge and Romana Guarnieri, "Glosses of 'M.N.' and Richard Methley to the *Mirror of Simple Souls*," *Archivio italiano per la storia della pietà* 5 (1968): 357–82.

107. Dorsey, "Women's Autobiography," 82 [72–90].

108. Christine de Pizan cites this very Gospel text in *Cité des Dames* 1.10.6 as an example of God placing language in the mouths of women in order to serve Him. See Earl Jeffrey Richards, trans., *"The Book of the City of Ladies" by Christine de Pizan*, rev. edn. (New York: Persea, 1998), 30.

6 Conclusion. Toward a Minor Literature: Julian of Norwich's Annihilation of Original Sin

1. See Jane Chance, "Classical Myth and Gender in the *Letters* of 'Abelard' and 'Heloise': Gloss, Glossed, Glossator," in *Listening to Heloise: The Voice of a Twelfth-Century Woman*, ed. Bonnie Wheeler, New Middle Ages Series (New York: St. Martin's Press, 2000), 161–85.

2. See Jane Chance, "Gender Subversion and Linguistic Castration in Fifteenth-Century English Translations of Christine de Pizan," in *Violence against Women in Medieval Texts*, ed. Anna Walecka Roberts (Gainesville: University Press of Florida, 1998), 161–94. A fuller focus on the English treatment of Christine's works appears in Laurie A. Finke, "The Politics of the Canon: Christine de Pizan and the Fifteenth-Century Chaucerians," *Exemplaria* (2006), at http://www.english.ufl.edu/exemplaria/SD/Finke.htm, accessed 31 May 2006.

3. See also Jane Chance's discussions of female authorship in "The Floure and the Leafe," "The Assembly of Ladies," and "Assembly of Gods," in "Christine de Pizan as Literary Mother: Women's Authority and Subjectivity in 'The Floure and the Leafe' and 'Assembly of Ladies,' " *The City of Scholars: New Approaches to Christine de Pizan*, ed. Margarete Zimmermann and Dina de Rentiis, European Cultures: Studies in Literature and the Arts (Berlin and New York: Walter de Gruyter, 1994), 245–59; and Jane Chance's introduction to her edition of *Assembly of Gods, or the Banquet of Resoun and Sensualyte*, Middle English Texts Series (Kalamazoo, MI: Medieval Institute Publications/Western Michigan University, 1999), 2–17 [1–26].

4. See the studies of Barbara Newman on Hildegard's feminization of divinity through the Virgin Mary, for example, her critical edition of St. Hildegard of Bingen, *Symphonia: A Critical Edition of the Symphonia Armonie Celestium Revelationum* (Ithaca, NY: Cornell University Press, 1988).

5. For Jesus as mother in Julian of Norwich, see the groundbreaking study by Caroline Walker Bynum that introduced women mystics and this theological concept to the academy: *Jesus as Mother: Studies in the Spirituality of the High Middle Ages* (Berkeley and London: University of California Press, 1982). In part, the wound of Christ represents woman's wound, literally and figuratively sexual, in that she was punished by Eve's role in the Fall with the pain of childbirth. The wound leads to Mary, in that Mary gave birth to Christ, but in so doing she ameliorated Eve's sin and offered humankind the opportunity for redemption. Illustrations of Christ's wound in medieval religious books occasionally present this wound as sexual. See Flora Lewis, "The Wound in Christ's Side and the Instruments of the Passion: Gendered Experience and Response," in *Women and the Book: Assessing the Visual Evidence*, ed. Jane H.M. Taylor and Lesley Smith, British Library Studies in Medieval Culture (London: British Library Press; Toronto, ON: University of Toronto Press, 1996), 204–23. Lewis argues that these illustrations of Christ's wounds "cannot be disassociated from present-day use of female genital imagery," in part because the books in which they appear are intended for

female patrons and therefore have meditative significance in which the viewer is invited to unite with Christ in order to understand the Passion, as if the viewer were male and Christ, female (regardless of their actual sexes) (215). In the long version of Julian, after the fourteenth revelation, she stresses the wound in Christ's side as the gateway to Godhead and heaven, which seems to represent His own femininity and which He loves as a lover does his beloved:

> The moder may leyn the child tenderly to her brest, but our tender Moder Jesus, He may homely leden us into His blissed brest be His swete open syde, and shewyn therin party of the Godhede and the joyes of hevyn with the gostly sekirnes of endless bliss. And that He shewid in the tenth [revelation], gevyng the same understondyng this swete word wher He seith, Lo, how I lovid the, beholdand into His side, enjoyand.

See Georgia Ronan Crampton, ed., *The Shewings of Julian of Norwich*, Middle English Texts Series (Kalamazoo, MI: Consortium for the Teaching of the Middle Ages, 1993), 124 [chap. 60]. For a translation of the shorter version only, which includes a portion of the longer text, see Frances Beer, ed., *Julian of Norwich's Revelations of Divine Love, The Shorter Version, ed. from B.L. Add. MS 37790* (Heidelberg, Germany: Carl Winter Universitätsverlag, 1978), 66.

6. See Cré, "Women in the Charterhouse? Julian of Norwich's *Revelations of Divine Love* and Marguerite Porete's *Mirror of Simple Souls* in British Library, MS Additional 37790," 61 n40 [43–62]. On Porete and the *Cloud of Unknowing*, see Geneviève Lachaussée, "L'influence du *Miroir des simples âmes anéanties* du Marguerite Porete sur la pensée de l'auteur anonyme du *Nuage d'inconnaissance*," *Recherches de théologie et philosophie médiévales = Forschungen zur Theologie und Philosophie des Mittelalters* 64 (1997): 385–99.

7. Cré, "Women in the Charterhouse? Julian of Norwich's *Revelations of Divine Love* and Marguerite Porete's *Mirror of Simple Souls* in British Library, MS Additional 37790," 50–51.

8. Cré, "Women in the Charterhouse? Julian of Norwich's *Revelations of Divine Love* and Marguerite Porete's *Mirror of Simple Souls* in British Library, MS Additional 37790," 43–44.

9. See the research in support of this discovery in R. Guarnieri, "*Lo specchio delle anime semplici* e Margharita Poirette," *L'Osservatore Romano* 141 (16 June 1946): 3.

10. Barbara Newman, *God and the Goddesses: Vision, Poetry, and Belief in the Middle Ages* (Philadelphia: University of Pennsylvania Press, 2003), 223.

11. Nicholas Watson has argued for this significant date, later than the usually acknowledged one of 1393, in "The Composition of Julian of Norwich's *Revelation of Love*," *Speculum* 68 (1993): 637–83; also, see Nicholas Watson, "Censorship and Cultural Change in Late Medieval England: Vernacular Theology, the Oxford Translation Debate, and Arundel's Constitutions of 1409," *Speculum* 70 (1995): 822–64.

12. See Crampton, *Shewings*, 121 [chap. 58].

13. Crampton, *Shewings*, 123 [chap. 59].

14. Crampton, *Shewings*, 123 [chap. 60].

15. Crampton, *Shewings*, 124 [chap. 60].

16. Crampton, *Shewings*, 72 [chap. 27].

17. Crampton, *Shewings*, 53 [chap. 11].

18. Crampton, *Shewings*, 72 [chap. 27].

19. For the edition of the shorter version in Middle English, see Edmund Colledge and James Walsh, eds., *A Book of Showings to the Anchoress Julian of Norwich*, 2 vols., Studies and Texts 35 (Toronto, ON: Pontifical Institute of Medieval Studies, 1978), 1:254 [chap. 17]. Beer politely (in that she disagrees with the translator) refers the reader to Julian of Norwich, *Revelations of Divine Love*, trans. Clifton Wolters (Harmondsworth, UK: Penguin, 1966), 37, which argues that this passage derives from Julian's understanding that wrath does not form part of God's love. Beer suggests that divine love for Julian signifies a "wholeness"; the individual soul, accordingly, bears a likeness to God (see Beer, *Revelations*, 48 [chap. 16] and n46).

20. Colledge, *Book of Showings*, 1:254–55 [chap. 17]. Colledge notes that the closest equivalent of "bestely wille" in the Middle English Dictionary is "best(el)i" body, in contrast to the spiritual body, a Lollard version of 1 Corinthians 15:44 (1:254 n10).

21. See Colledge, *Book of Showings*, 1:222 [chap. 6], who confirms that the passage is nowhere in the longer version (n40). See Beer's interpretive essay, " 'All Shall Be Well': The Political Implications," in Beer, *Revelations*, 71–80; and Rita Mae Bradley, "Christ the Teacher in Julian's *Showings*: The Biblical and Patristic Traditions," in *The Medieval Mystical Tradition in England*, ed. Marion Glasscoe, vol. 2 (Exeter, UK: Exeter University Press, 1982).

22. See Colledge, *Book of Showings*, 1:222 [chap. 6].

23. See *The Assembly of Ladies*, in *The Floure and the Leafe; The Assembly of Ladies; The Isle of Ladies*, ed. Derek Pearsall (Kalamazoo, MI: Medieval Institute Publications, 1990), lines 311–13.

24. Guarnieri, *Mirouer*, 34–36 [10.7–19]; Babinsky, *Mirror*, 88. In chapter 10, Porete enumerates twelve names suggestive of the fragmentary nature of feminized being on the journey toward annihilation and union with God.

25. See Christine de Pizan, *The Vision* 3.1, trans. Glenda McLeod and Charity Cannon Willard (Woodbridge, Suffolk, UK: Boydell and Brewer, 2005); also Christine de Pizan, *Le livre de l'advision Cristine*, ed. Christine Reno and Liliane Dulac (Paris: Honoré Champion, 2001). On the magisterial metaphors in *L'advision-Christine*, see Jane Chance, "Speaking *in propria persona*: Authorizing the Subject as a Political Act in Late Medieval Feminine Spirituality," in *New Trends in Feminine Spirituality: The Holy Women of Liége and their Impact*, ed. Juliette Dor, Lesley Johnson, and Jocelyn Wogan-Browne (Turnhout: Brepols, 1999), 277–83 [266–90].

26. See Jean Gerson, *De distinctione verarum revelationum a falsis* in *Oeuvres complètes*, ed. Palémon Glorieux, 10 vols. (Paris: Desclée, 1961–73), 3:36–56, at 51–52. Gerson's original reads: "Argumentum hujus rei est in quodam libello incredibili pene subtilitate ab una foemina composito, quae Maria de

Valenciennes dicebatur; haec agit de praerogativa et eminentia dilectionis divinae, ad quam si quis devenerit fit secundum eam ab omni lege praeceptorum solutus, adducens pro se illud ab Apostolo [sic] sumptum: Caritatem habe, et fac quod vis." For Gerson her fallacy is that she was speaking of pilgrims on earth instead of souls in heaven—the very criticism of embodiment leveled by her interrogators before her burning: "vix altius quicquam de divina fruitione. Quoad aliqua, dici potuerat; sed fallebat eam sua tumiditas animi tantae passioni dilectionis immixta."

WORKS CITED

Ælfric, Abbot of Eynsham. *Aelfric's Lives of Saints, Being a Set of Sermons on Saints' Days Formerly Observed by the English Church, Edited from Manuscript Julius E. VII in the Cottonian Collection, with Various Readings from Other Manuscripts.* Ed. Walter W. Skeat. Early English Text Society, o.s., no. 76. London: Trübner, 1881. Repr. New York: Early English Text Society/Oxford University Press, 1966.

Alan of Lille. *Anticlaudianus.* In *The Anglo-Latin Satirical Poets and Epigrammatists of the Twelfth Century.* Ed. Thomas Wright. Rerum Britannicarum Medii Aevi Scriptores. 268–428. Vol. 2 of 2 vols. London: Longman, 1872.

———. *Anticlaudianus; Or The Good and Perfect Man.* Trans. James J. Sheridan. Toronto: Pontifical Institute of Medieval Studies, 1973.

———. *De planctu Naturae.* In *The Anglo-Latin Satirical Poets and Epigrammatists of the Twelfth Century.* Ed. Thomas Wright. Rerum Britannicarum Medii Aevi Scriptores. 429–522. Vol. 2 of 2 vols. London: Longman, 1872.

———. *The Plaint of Nature.* Trans. James J. Sheridan. Medieval Sources in Translation 26. Toronto: Pontifical Institute of Mediaeval Studies, 1980.

Aldhelm, of Malmesbury. *The Prose Works.* Trans. Michael Lapidge and Michael Herren. Cambridge and Totowa, NJ: Rowman and Littlefield, 1979.

Allen, Hope Emily. Prefatory Note. In *The Book of Margery Kempe.* Ed. Sanford B. Meech, with notes and appendices by Meech and Allen. Early English Text Society, o.s., no. 212. London: Oxford University Press, 1940.

Altmann, Barbara, and Deborah McGrady, eds. *A Casebook on Christine de Pizan.* New York: Routledge, 2003.

Ambrose, St. "Concerning Virginity, to Marcellina, His Sister." Trans. Fathers of the Church Web-site. New Advent (1997). http://www.newadvent.org/fathers/34071.htm (accessed 5 June 2006).

———. *De virginibus ad Marcellinam sororem suam. Patrologia Latina* 16:187–232.

Arndt, Wilhelm Ferdinand, ed. and trans. *Leben des h. Bonifazius von Wilibald, der h. Leoba von Rudolf von Fulda, des abts Sturmi von Eigil, des h. Lebuin vonHucbald. Nach den ausgaben der Monumenta Germaniae übersetzt von Wilhelm Arndt.* Geschichtschreiber der deutschen. 2 vols. 2nd edn. Leipzig, Ger.: Dyksche, 1888.

Arnold, John H., and Katherine J. Lewis, eds. *A Companion to "The Book of Margery Kempe."* Woodbridge, Suffolk, UK: D.S. Brewer, 2004.

Arsenault, John A. "Authority, Autonomy, and Antinominianism: The Mysticism and Ethical Piety of Marguerite Porete in *The Mirror of Simple Souls.*" *Studia Mystica,* n.s., 21 (2000): 65–94.

Aston, Michael. *Monasteries*. London: B.T. Batsford, 1993.

Atkinson, Clarissa W. *Mystic and Pilgrim: The Book and the World of Margery Kempe*. Ithaca, NY: Cornell University Press, 1983.

Aungier, Georges James. *The History and Antiquities of Syon Monastery: The Parish of Isleworth, and the Chapelry of Hounslow / Compiled from Public Records, Ancient Manuscripts, Ecclesiastical and other Authentic Documents*. London: J.B. Nichols and Son, 1840.

Babinsky, Ellen L. "The Use of Courtly Language in *Le mirouer des simple ames anienties*." *Essays in Medieval Studies* 4 (1998): 91–106.

———, trans. *Marguerite Porete's "The Mirror of Simple Souls."* Classics of Western Spirituality. New York, NY, and Mahwah, NJ: Paulist Press, 1993,

Bakhtin, M.M. *The Dialogic Imagination*. Ed. Michael Holquist and Caryl Emerson. Austin: University of Texas Press, 1981.

Barratt, Alexandra. "Margery Kempe and the King's Daughter of Hungary." In *Margery Kempe: A Book of Essays*. Ed. Sandra J. McEntire, 189–201. New York: Garland, 1992.

Barthouil, Georges. "Boccacce et Catherine de Sienne (la dixième journée du *Decameron*: Noblesse ou subversion?)." *Italianistica* 7 (1982): 249–76.

Bateson, Mary, ed. *Catalogue of the Library of Syon Monastery, Isleworth*. Cambridge: Cambridge University Press, 1898.

Beckwith, Sarah. "Problems of Authority in Late Medieval English Mysticism: Language, Agency, and Authority in *The Book of Margery Kempe*." *Exemplaria* 4 (1992): 172–99.

Bede, the Venerable, St. *Ecclesiastical History of the English People*. Ed. and trans. Bertram Colgrave and R.A.B. Mynors. Oxford: Clarendon Press, 1969.

———. "Saint Bede's *Martyrologium*: A Translation with an Introduction." Trans. Clarence J. Bogetto. M.A. thesis, De Paul University, 1957.

Beer, Frances, ed. *Julian of Norwich's Revelations of Divine Love: The Shorter Version, Edited from B.L. Add. MS 37790*. Heidelberg, Ger.: Carl Winter Universitätsverlag, 1978.

Belenky, Mary Field, Blythe Clinchy, Nancy Goldberger, and Jill Tarule, eds. *Women's Ways of Knowing: The Development of Self, Voice, and Mind*. New York: Basic Books, 1986.

Bennett, H.S. *English Books and Readers 1475–1557, Being a Study of the History of the Book Trade from Caxton to the Incorporation of the Stationers' Company*. 2nd edn. Cambridge: Cambridge University Press, 1970.

Berschin, Walter. "*Passio* und Theater: Zur dramatischen Struktur einiger Vorlagen Hrotsvit von Gandersheim." In *The Theatre in the Middle Ages*. Ed. Herman Braet, Johan Nowé, and Gilbert Tournoy, 1–11. Leuven, Belg.: Leuven University Press, 1985.

Bhabha, Homi K. *The Location of Culture*. London and New York: Routledge Classics, 2004.

Birgitta, St. *Opera Minora I; Regvla Salvatoris*. Ed. Sten Eklund. Royal Academy of Letters, History, and Antiquities. Stockholm: Almqvist and Wiksell International, 1975.

Blamires, Alastair, ed. *Woman Defamed and Woman Defended: An Anthology of Medieval Texts*. Oxford, UK: Clarendon Press, 1992.

Bloch, R. Howard. *The Anonymous Marie de France*. Chicago and London: University of Chicago Press, 2002.

———. "Medieval Misogyny." *Representations* 20 (1987): 1–24.

———. "New Philology and Old French." *Speculum* 65 (1990): 38–58.

Blunt, John Henry, ed. *The Myroure of Oure Lady Containing a Devotional Treatise on Divine Service, with a Translation of the Offices Used by the Sisters of the Brigittine Monastery of Sion, at Isleworth, during the Fifteenth and Sixteenth Centuries*, Early English Text Society, e.s., 19. London: N. Trübner, 1873.

Boklund-Lagopoulos, Karin. "Visionary Discourse: Julian of Norwich and Margery Kempe." *Yearbook of English Studies* (Aristotle University of Thessaloniki) 3 (1991–92): 27–43.

Bogetto, Clarence J., trans. "Saint Bede's *Martyrologium*: A Translation with an Introduction." M.A. thesis, DePaul University, 1957.

Borland, Catharine R. *A Descriptive Catalogue of the Western Mediaeval Manuscripts in Edinburgh University Library*. Edinburgh: University of Edinburgh Press/T. and A. Constable, 1916.

Bothe, Catherine M. *See* Müller, Catherine Monique [Bothe].

Boyd, Beverly. "Wyclif, Joan of Arc, and Margery Kempe." *Fourteenth Century English Mystics Newsletter* 12.3 (Sept. 1986): 112–18.

Brown, Peter. *The Body and Society: Men, Women, and Sexual Renunciation in Early Christianity*. New York: Columbia University Press, 1988.

Brown, Phyllis R., Linda A. McMillan, and Katharina M. Wilson, eds. *Hrotsvit of Gandersheim: Contexts, Identities, Affinities, and Performances*. Toronto and London: University of Toronto Press, 2004.

Bruckner, Matilda. "Fictions of the Female Voice: The Woman Troubadour." *Speculum* 67 (1992): 865–91.

Butler, Judith. "Contingent Foundations: Feminism and the Question of 'Postmodernism.'" In *Feminists Theorize the Political*. Ed. Judith Butler and Joan W. Scott, 3–21. New York: Routledge, 1992.

Burgess, Glyn S. *Marie de France: An Analytical Biography*. Research Bibliographies and Checklist 21. London: Grant and Cutler, 1977.

———. *Marie de France: An Analytical Biography, Supplement no. 1*. Research Bibliographies and Checklist 21. London: Grant and Cutler, 1986.

Burgess, Henry E. "Hroswitha and Terence: A Study in Literary Imitation." *Proceedings of the Pacific Northwest Conference on Foreign Languages* 19 (1968): 23–29.

Burgwinkle, William E. *Sodomy, Masculinity, and Law in Medieval Literature: France and England, 1050–1230*. Cambridge, and New York: Cambridge University Press, 2004.

Burns, Jane E. *Bodytalk: When Women Speak in Old French Literature*. Philadelphia: University of Pennsylvania Press, 1993.

Bynum, Caroline Walker. *Holy Feast and Holy Fast*. Berkeley: University of California Press, 1986.

Bynum, *Jesus as Mother: Studies in the Spirituality of the High Middle Ages*. Berkeley: University of California Press, 1984.

Cadden, Joan. *Meanings of Sex Difference in the Middle Ages: Medicine, Science, and Culture*. Cambridge: Cambridge University Press, 1993.

Carlson, David. "The Middle English *Lanval*, the Corporal Works of Mercy, and Bibliothèque Nationale, nouv. Acq. Fr. 1104." *Neophilologus* 72 (1988): 97– 106.

Case, Sue-Ellen. "Re-viewing Hrotsvit." *Theatre Journal* 35.4 (1983): 533–42.

Catherine of Siena. *Dialogo, The Orcherd of Syon*, vol. 1. Ed. Phyllis Hodgson and Gabriel M. Liegey. Early English Text Society, vol. 258. London: Oxford University Press, 1966.

———. *Il dialogo della Divina Provvidenza ovvero Libro della divina dottrina*. Ed. Giuliana Cavallini. Rome: Edizioni cateriniane, 1968.

———. *Dialogue of St. Catherine of Siena*. Trans. Suzanne Noffke. New York: Paulist Press, 1980.

———. *The Orcherde of Syon*. Trans. Dane Jamys. London: Wynken de Worde, 1519.

Cavallini, Guiliana, and Imelda Foralosso, eds. *Libellus de supplemento: Legende prolixe virginis beate Catherine de Senis*. Rome: Edizioni cateriniane, 1974.

Certeau, Michel de. *The Practice of Everyday Life*. Trans. Steven F. Rendall. Berkeley: University of California Press, 1984.

Chalmers, George. *Caledonia, or, An Account, Historical and Topographic, of North Britain, from the Most Ancient to the Present Times*. 3 vols. London: Paisley/A. Gardner, 1807–24.

Chamberlain, David. "Marie de France's Arthurian *Lais*: Subtle and Political." In *Culture and the King: The Social Implications of the Arthurian Legend; Essays in Honor of Valerie M. Lagorio*. Ed. Martin B. Schichtman and James Carley, 15–34. Albany: State University of New York Press, 1994.

———. "Musical Imagery and Musical Learning in Hrotsvit." In *Hrotsvit of Gandersheim: Rara Avis in Saxonia?* Ed. Katharina M. Wilson, 79–97. Ann Arbor: Medieval and Renaissance Collegium, University of Michigan, 1987.

Chance, Jane, ed. *The Assembly of Gods, or the Banquet of Resoun and Sensualyte: Le Assemble de Deus, or Banquet of Gods and Goddesses, with the Discourse of Reason and Sensuality*. Middle English Texts Series. Kalamazoo, MI: Medieval Institute Publications/Western Michigan University, 1999.

———. "Christine de Pizan as Literary Mother: Women's Authority and Subjectivity in 'The Floure and the Leafe' and 'Assembly of Ladies.'" In *The City of Scholars: New Approaches to Christine de Pizan*. Ed. Margarete Zimmermann and Dina de Rentiis, 245–59. European Cultures: Studies in Literature and the Arts. Berlin and New York: Walter de Gruyter, 1994.

———. "Classical Myth and Gender in the *Letters* of 'Abelard' and 'Heloise': Gloss, Glossed, Glossator." In *Listening to Heloise: The Voice of a Twelfth-Century Woman*. Ed. Bonnie Wheeler, 161–85. New Middle Ages Series. New York: St. Martin's Press, 2000.

———. "Gender Subversion and Linguistic Castration in Fifteenth-Century English Translations of Christine de Pizan." In *Violence against Women in Medieval Texts*. Ed. Anna Walecka Roberts, 161–94. Gainesville: University Press of Florida, 1998.

——. *The Genius Figure in Antiquity and the Middle Ages.* New York and London: Columbia University Press, 1975.

——. "Hrotsvit's Latin Drama *Gallicanus* and the Old English Epic *Elene*: Intercultural Founding Narratives of a Feminized Church." In *Hrotsvit of Gandersheim: Contexts, Identities, Affinities, and Performances.* Ed. Katharina Wilson, Phyllis Brown, and Linda McMillan, 193–212. Toronto: University of Toronto Press, 2004.

——. *Medieval Mythography.* Vol. 1, *From Roman North Africa to the School of Chartres, AD 433–1177.* Gainesville and London: University Press of Florida, 2000.

——. *Medieval Mythography.* Vol. 2, *From the School of Chartres to the Court Avignon, 1177–1350.* Gainesville and London: University Press of Florida, 1994.

——. "Speaking *in propria persona*: Authorizing the Subject as a Political Act in Late Medieval Feminine Spirituality." In *New Trends in Feminine Spirituality: The Holy Women of Liége and their Impact.* Ed. Juliette Dor, Lesley Johnson, and Jocelyn Wogan-Browne, 266–90. Turnhout: Brepols, 1999.

——. *Woman as Hero in Old English Literature.* Syracuse, NY: Syracuse University Press, 1986.

Chaucer, Geoffrey. *The Riverside Chaucer.* Ed. Larry Benson. 3rd edn. Boston: Houghton Mifflin, 1987.

Cherewatuk, Karen, and Ulrike Wiethaus, eds. *Dear Sister: Medieval Women and the Epistolary Genre.* Philadelphia: University of Pennsylvania Press, 1993.

Chrétien de Troyes. *Arthurian Romances.* Trans. William W. Kibler. London: Penguin; New York: Viking Penguin, 1991.

Christine de Pizan. *The Book of the City of Ladies.* Trans. Earl Jeffrey Richards. New York: Persea, 1982. Rev. edn. New York: Persea, 1998.

——. *La Città delle Dame.* Trans. Patricia Caraffi into Italian. Ed. Earl Jeffrey Richards. Milan and Trento, IT: Luni Editrice, 1997.

——. *Le livre de l'advision Christine.* Ed. Christine Reno and Liliane Dulac. Paris: H. Champion, 2001.

——. *The Vision of Christine.* Trans. Glenda McLeod and Charity Cannon Willard. Library of Medieval Women. Woodbridge, Suffolk, UK: Boydell and Brewer, 2005.

Churchill, Laurie J., Phyllis R. Brown, and Jane E. Jeffrey. *Women Writing Latin: From Roman Antiquity to Early Modern Europe.* 3 vols. New York: Routledge, 2002.

Cleve, Gunnel. "Margery Kempe's 'Dalyawns' with the Lord." *Neophilologica Fennica: Société.* Ed. Leena Kahlas-Tarkka, 10–21. Helsinki: Société Neophilologique de Helsinki, 1987.

——. "Semantic Dimensions in Margery Kempe's 'Whyght Clothys.' " *Mystics Quarterly* 12 (1986): 162–70.

Colledge, Edmund, and J.C. Marler. " 'Poverty of the Will': Ruusbroec, Eckhart, and *The Mirror of Simple Souls.*" In *Jan van Ruusbroec: The Sources, Context, and Sequels of His Mysticism.* Ed. Paul Mommaers and Norbert de Paepe, 14–47. Leuven, Belg.: Leuven University Press, 1984.

Colledge, Edmund, and Romana Guarnieri. "Glosses of 'M.N.' and Richard Methley to the *Mirror of Simple Souls.*" *Archivio italiano per la storia della pietà* 5 (1968): 357–82.

Cooley, Joshua. "Marguerite Porete's *Mirror of Simple Souls* as Gendered Debate." Paper presented at the Texas Medieval Association Conference, Houston, TX, 13 October 2005.

Cottrell, Robert D. *The Grammar of Silence: A Reading of Marguerite de Navarre's Poetry*. Washington, DC: Catholic University of America Press, 1986.

———. "Marguerite Porete's Heretical Discourse; Or, Deviating from the Model." *Modern Language Studies* 21 (1991): 16–21.

Craymer, Suzanne L. "Margery Kempe's Imitation of Mary Magdalene and the 'Digby Plays.' " *Mystics Quarterly* 19 (1993): 173–81.

Cré, Marleen. "Marguerite Porete's *Le mirouer des simples ames* and the Problematics of the Written Word." *Medieval Perspectives* 1 (1986): 151–58.

———. "Women in the Charterhouse? Julian of Norwich's *Revelations of Divine Love* and Marguerite Porete's *Mirror of Simple Souls* in British Library, MS Additional 37790." In *Writing Religious Women: Female Spiritual and Textual Practices in Late Medieval England*. Ed. Denis Renevey and Christiania Whitehead, 43–62. Toronto and Buffalo: University of Toronto Press, 2000.

Cross, Tom Peete. "The Celtic Elements in the Lays of *Lanval* and *Graelent*." *Modern Philology* 12 (1914–15): 585–644.

Cumming, William Patterson, ed. *The Revelations of Saint Birgitta, Edited from the Garrett MS Princeton University Library Deposit 1397*. Early English Text Society, o.s., 178. London: Humphrey Milford/Oxford University Press, 1929 [for 1928].

Dagens, Jean. "*Le mirouer des simples ames* et Marguerite de Navarre." In *La mystique rhénane: Colloque de Strasbourg, 16–19 mai 1961*, 281–89. Paris: Presses Universitaires de France, 1963.

Deanesly, Margaret. *The Incendium Amoris of Richard Rolle*. 1915; repr. Norwood, PA: Norwood Editions, 1977.

de Hamel, Christopher. "The Library: The Medieval Manuscripts of Syon Abbey, and Their Dispersal." In *Syon Abbey: The Library of the Bridgettine Nuns and Their Peregrinations after the Reformation*, 48–158. Otley, UK: Roxburghe Club, 1991.

Deleuze, Gilles, and Feliz Guattari. *Kafka: Toward a Minor Literature*. Trans. Dana Polan. Foreword by Réda Bensmaïa. Theory and History of Literature, vol. 30. Minneapolis: University of Minnesota Press, 1986.

Delsigne, Jill. " 'Entendez la glose': Painting Subversion in *Guigemar* and *Le Mirouer des Simples Ames*." 41st International Conference on Medieval Studies. Western Michigan University, Kalamazoo, MI, 4 May 2006.

De Luca, Kenneth. "Hrotsvit's 'Imitation' of Terence." *Classical Folia* 28 (1974): 89–102.

de Romestin, H., trans. *Hexameron, Paradise, and Cain and Abel*. Select Library of Nicene and Post-Nicene Fathers, 2nd ser., 10. Oxford: James Parker; New York: Christian Literature, 1896.

Despres, Denise L. "Franciscan Spirituality: Margery Kempe and Visual Meditation." *Mystics Quarterly* 11 (1985): 12–18.

———. "The Meditative Art of Scriptural Interpretation in *The Book of Margery Kempe*." *Downside Review* 106 (1988): 253–63.

Dinshaw, Carolyn. "A Kiss Is Just a Kiss: Heterosexuality and Its Consolations in *Sir Gawain and the Green Knight*." *Diacritics* 24 (1994): 205–26.

Doiron, Marilyn, ed. "Margaret Porete: *The Mirror of Simple Souls*, A Middle English Translation." *Archivio italiano per la storia della pietà* 5 (1968): 242–355.

Donagher, Colleen. "Socializing the Sorceress: The Fairy Mistress in *Lanval, Le Bel Inconnu*, and *Partonopeu de Blois*." *Essays in Medieval Studies* 4 (1987): 69–90.

Donovan, Leslie, trans. *Women Saints' Lives in Old English Prose*. Library of Medieval Women. Woodbridge, Suffolk, UK: D.S. Brewer, 1999.

Dor, Juliette, Lesley Johnson, and Jocelyn Wogan-Browne, eds. *New Trends in Spirituality: The Holy Women of Liège*. Medieval Women: Texts and Contexts 2. Turnhout, Belg.: Brepols, 1999.

Dorsey, Peter. "Women's Autobiography and the Hermeneutics of Conversion." *A/B: Auto/Biography Studies* 8 (1993): 72–90.

Dronke, Peter. "Lyrical Poetry in the Work of Marguerite Porete." In *Literary and Historical Perspectives of the Middle Ages: Proceedings of the 1981 Southeastern Medieval Association Meeting*. Ed. Patricia W. Cummins, Patrick W. Conner, and Charles W. Connell, 1–18. Morgantown: West Virginia University Press, 1982.

———. *Women Writers of the Middle Ages: A Critical Study from Perpetua (d. 203) to Marguerite Porete (d. 1310)*. Cambridge: Cambridge University Press, 1984.

Dupré-Theseider, Eugenia. "Sulla composizione del 'Dialogo' di santa Caterina da Siena." *Giornale storico della letteratura italiana* 117 (1941): 161–202.

Easton, Adam. "Epistolae duae de canonizatione sanctae Brigidae." MS Hamilton 7. Oxford. Bodleian Library. Fols. 229, 231.

Eberley, Susan. "Margery Kempe, St. Mary Magdalene, and Patterns of Contemplation." *Downside Review* 107 (1989): 209–33.

Eccles, Jacqueline. "Feminist Criticism and the Lay of *Lanval*: A Reply." *Romance Notes* 38 (1998): 281–85.

Elliot, Dyan. *Proving Women: Female Spirituality and Inquisitional Culture in the Later Middle Ages*. Princeton, NJ, and Oxford, UK: Princeton University Press, 2004.

Ellis, Roger. " 'Flores ad fabricandam…coronam': An Investigation into the Uses of the *Revelations* of St. Bridget of Sweden in Fifteenth-Century England." *Medium Aevum* 51 (1982): 163–86.

———. *"Viderunt eam filie Syon": The Spirituality of the English House of a Medieval Contemplative Order from Its Beginnings to the Present Day*. Analecta Cartusiana 68. Salzburg, Aus.: Institut für Anglistik und Amerikanistik, 1984.

Épiney-Burgard, Georgette, and Emilie zum Braun. *Femmes troubadours de Dieu*. Turnhout, Belg.: Brepols, 1988.

Eriksen, Roy. "Sacred Art and the Artful Conversation of Margery Kempe." *Nordlit: Arbeidstidsskrift litteratur* 6 (Fall 1999): 15–29.

Erler, Mary C. "Margery Kempe's White Clothes." *Medium Aevum* 62 (1993): 78–83.

———. *Women, Reading, and Piety in Late Medieval England*. Cambridge: Cambridge University Press, 2002.

Erskine, John A. "Margery Kempe and Her Models: The Role of the Authorial Voice." *Mystics Quarterly* 15 (1989): 75–85.

Evangeliarum et constitutiones sororum ordinis predicatorum. MS 150 (Borland). University of Edinburgh Library.

Fanous, Samuel. "Measuring the Pilgrim's Progress: Internal Emphases in *The Book of Margery Kempe*." In *Writing Religious Women: Female Spiritual and Textual Practices in Late Medieval England*. Ed. Denis Renevey and Christiania Whitehead, 177–95. Toronto: University of Toronto Press, 2000.

Farley, Mary Hardiman. "Her Own Creature: Religion, Feminist Criticism, and the Functional Eccentricity of Margery Kempe." *Exemplaria* 11 (1999): 1–21.

Fenster, Thelma S., and Claire A. Leeds, eds. *Gender and Debate from the Early Middle Ages to the Renaissance*. New York and Houndmills, Basingstoke, UK: Palgrave Macmillan, 2002.

Ferguson, Margaret W. *Dido's Daughters: Literacy, Gender, and Empire in Early Modern England and France*. Chicago: University of Chicago Press, 2003.

Ferrante, Joan M. "Public Postures and Private Maneuvers: Roles Medieval Women Play." In *Women and Power in the Middle Ages*. Ed. Mary Erler and Maryanne Kowaleski, 213–29. Athens: University of Georgia Press, 1988.

———. *To the Glory of Her Sex: Women's Roles in the Compositions of Medieval Texts*. Bloomington and Indianapolis: Indiana University Press, 1997.

Finke, Laurie. *Feminist Theory, Women's Writing*. Ithaca, NY, and London: Cornell University Press, 1992.

———. *Women Writing in Medieval England*. London: Longmans, 1999.

Finke, Laurie, and Martin B. Schichtmann. "Magical Mistress' Tour: Patronage, Intellectual Property, and the De-Semination of Wealth in Marie de France's *Lanval*." *Signs* 25 (2000): 479–503.

Flete, William [Anglicus, the Englishman]. Letters. MS A.5.3. Fols. 179–86. Trinity College Library, Dublin.

———. Letters. Royal MS 7. E. X. Fols. 85–87. British Library, London.

———. Sermon, Narrative, Epistle, and Prologue to the Life of St. Catherine. Canonici MS 205. Fols. 1–6v. Bodleian Library, Oxford.

Fox-Genovese, Elizabeth. *Within the Plantation Household*. Chapel Hill: University of North Carolina Press, 1988.

Francis, Elizabeth A. "The Trial in Lanval." In *Studies in French Language and Medieval Literature Presented to Professor Mildred K. Pope, by Pupils, Colleagues, and Friends*, 115–24. Manchester, UK: Manchester University Press, 1939.

Fredell, Joel. "Margery Kempe: Spectacle and Spiritual Governance." *Philological Quarterly* 75 (1996): 137–66.

Frédéricq, Paul. *Corpus documentorum inquisitionis haereticae pravitatis neerlandicae*. 5 vols. Ghent: J. Vuylsteke, 1889–1906.

Freeman, Michelle A. "Marie France's Poetics of Silence: The Implication for a Feminine *Translatio*." *PMLA* 99 (1984): 860–83.

Fulgentius. *Opera*. Ed. Rudolph Helm. 1898. Repr., Stuttgart, Ger.: B.G. Teubner, 1970.

Garay, Kathleen. " 'She Swims and Floats in Joy': Marguerite Porete, an 'Heretical' Mystic of the Later Middle Ages." *Canadian Women's Studies. Les cahiers de la femme* 17.1 (1997): 18–21.

Gauthier, René. "Le traité *De anima et de potencies eius* d'un maître dès artes (vers 1225)." *Revue des sciences philosophiques et théologiques* 66 (1982): 3–86.

Gerson, Jean. *De distinctione verarum revelationum a falsis*. In *Oeuvres complètes*. Ed. Palémon Glorieux, 3:36–56. 10 vols. Paris: Desclée, 1961–73.

Gilligan, Carol. *In a Different Voice: Psychological Theory and Women's Development*. Cambridge, MA: Harvard University Press, 1982.

Glasscoe, Marion, ed. *The Medieval Mystical Tradition in England*. Vol. 2. Exeter, UK: University of Exeter Press, 1982.

Glenn, Cheryl. "Re-examining *The Book of Margery Kempe*: A Rhetoric of Autobiography." In *Reclaiming Rhetorica: Women in Rhetorical Tradition*. Ed. Andrea Lunsford, 53–71. Pittsburgh, PA: University of Pittsburgh Press, 1995.

Goodman, Anthony. *Margery Kempe and Her World*. London and New York: Pearson Education, 2002.

Gordon, Robert Kay, trans. *Anglo-Saxon Poetry*. Rev. edn. London: Dent; New York: Dutton, 1954.

Gouma-Peterson, Thalia, ed. *Anna Komnene and Her Times*. New York and London: Garland/Taylor and Francis, 2000.

Grabes, Herbert. *The Mutable Glass: Mirror Imagery in Titles and Texts of the Middle Ages and the English Renaissance*. Cambridge: Cambridge University Press, 1982.

Gravdal, Kathryn. *Ravishing Maidens: Writing Rape in Medieval French Literature and Law*. Philadelphia: University of Philadelphia Press, 1991.

Guarnieri, Romana, "Il movimento de Libero Spirito." *Archivio italiano per la storia della pietà* 4 (1965): 351–708.

———. "*Lo specchio delle anime semplici* e Margharita Poirette." *L'Osservatore Romano* 141 (16 June 1946): 3.

———. ed. *Marguerite Porete: Le mirouer des simples ames*. In "Il movimento de Libero Spirito." *Archivio italiano per la storia della pietà* 4 (1965): 513–635.

Guidini, Cristofano di Galgano. "Liber Divine Doctrine S. Catherine Senensis." MS 87 (Borland). University of Edinburgh Library.

Guillaume de Lorris and Jean de Meun. *The Romance of the Rose*. Trans. Charles Dahlberg. Princeton, NJ: Princeton University Press, 1971.

Guillelmus de Nangiaco. *Continuatio chronici Guillelmi de Nangiaco*. In *Recueil des historiens des Gaules et de la France*. Ed. J. Naudet and C.F. Danou, 20:601. Paris: Welter, 1894.

Gunn, Alan M.F. *The Mirror of Love: A Reinterpretation of "The Romance of the Rose."* Lubbock: Texas Tech University Press, 1952.

Gwara, Scott. "The Transmission of the 'Digby' Corpus of Bilingual Glosses to Aldhelm's *Prosa de Virginitate*." *Anglo-Saxon England* 27 (1998): 139–68.

Gwynn, Aubrey. *The English Austin Friars in the Time of Wyclif*. London: Oxford University Press/Humphrey Milford, 1940.

Hackett, Michael B. "Catherine of Siena and William of England." *Proceedings of the Patristic, Medieval, and Renaissance Conference* 6 (1981): 29–47.

Hanna, Ralph, III, and Traugott Lawler, eds. *Jankyn's Book of Wikked Wyves*. Vol. 1, *The Primary Texts*. Athens and London: University of Georgia Press, 1997.

Harding, Wendy. "Body into Text: *The Book of Margery Kempe*." In *Feminist Approaches to the Body in Medieval Literature*. Ed. Linda Lomperis and Sarah Stanbury, 167–87. New Cultural Studies Series. Philadelphia: University of Pennsylania Press, 1993.

Harlow, Barbara. *Barred: Women, Writing, and Political Detention.* Hanover, NH: Wesleyan University Press, 1992.

Harper, Stephen. " 'So Euyl to Rewlyn': Madness and Authority in *The Book of Margery Kempe.*" *Neuphilologische Mitteilungen* 98 (1997): 53–61.

Henri d'Andeli. *The Battle of the Seven Arts.* Ed. Louis J. Paëtow. Memoirs of the University of California, vol. 4, no. 1. [History, vol. 1, no. 1.] Berkeley: University of California Press, 1914.

Herzfeld, George, ed. *An Old English Martyrology.* Early English Text Society, o.s., no. 116. London: K. Paul, Trench, Trübner, 1900.

Hildegard of Bingen. *Hildegardis causae et curae.* Ed. Paul Kaiser. Leipzig, Ger.: Teubner, 1903.

———. *On Natural Philosophy and Medicine, Selections from "Cause et Cure."* Trans. Margret Berger. Library of Medieval Women. Woodbridge, Suffolk, UK, and Rochester, NY: D.S. Brewer, 1999.

———. *Symphonia: A Critical Edition of the Symphonia Armonie Celestium Revelationum.* Ed. Barbara Newman. Ithaca, NY: Cornell University Press, 1988.

Ho, Cynthia. "Margery Reads Exempla." *Medieval Perspectives* 8 (1993): 143–52.

Hodgson, Frederick. "Alienation and the Otherworld in *Lanval, Yonec,* and *Guigemar.*" *Comitatus: A Journal of Medieval and Renaissance Studies* 5 (1974): 19–31.

Hodgson, Phyllis. "*The Orcherd of Syon* and the English Mystical Tradition (Sir Israel Gollancz Memorial Lecture, Read 1 July 1964)." *Proceedings of the British Academy* 50 (1964): 229–43.

Hoepffner, Ernst. *Les lais de Marie de France.* Paris: Boivin, 1935.

———. "Pour la chronologie des *Lais* de Marie de France. I—Le lai de *Lanval.*" *Romania* 59 (1933): 351–70.

Holloway, Julia Bolton. "Bride, Margery, Julian, and Alice: Bridget of Sweden's Textual Community in Medieval England." In *Margery Kempe: A Book of Essays.* Ed. Sandra J. McEntire, 189–201. New York: Garland, 1992.

Hollywood, Amy W. *Sensible Ecstasy: Mysticism, Sexual Difference, and the Demands of History.* Religion and Postmodernism. Chicago and London: University of Chicago Press, 2001.

———. *The Soul as Virgin Wife: Mechthild of Magdeburg, Marguerite Porete, and Meister Eckhart.* Notre Dame, IN, and London: Notre Dame University Press, 1995.

———. "Suffering Transformed: Marguerite Porete, Meister Eckhart, and the Problem of Women's Spirituality." In *Meister Eckhart and the Beguine Mystics: Hadewijch of Brabant, Mechthild of Magdeburg, and Marguerite Porete.* Ed. Bernard McGinn, 87–113. New York: Continuum, 1994.

Hoppenwasser, Nanda Alexis. "The Human Burden of the Prophet: St. Birgitta's *Revelations* and *The Book of Margery Kempe.*" *Medieval Perspectives* 8 (1993): 153–62.

Hortsmann, C. " 'The lyf of saint Katherin of Senis,' nach dem Drucke W. Caxtons (ca. 1493) mitgeteilt." *Archiv für das Studium der neuern Sprachen und Litteraturen* 76 (1886): 33–112, 265–314, 353–400.

Hrotsvit of Gandersheim. *Hrotsvithae opera.* Ed. Helene Homeyer. Munich: Schöningh, 1970.

———. *Hrotsvit of Gandersheim: A Florilegia of Her Works.* Trans. Katharina M. Wilson. Library of Medieval Women. Cambridge, and Rochester, NY: D.S. Brewer, 1998.

—————. *The Plays of Hrotswitha of Gandersheim.* Trans. Larissa Bonfante and Alexandra Bonfante-Warren. Oak Park, IL: Bolchazy-Carducci, 1986.

Hugh of St. Victor. *Hugo van Sankt Viktor. Didascalicon de studio legendi: Studienbuch /* Ed. and trans. into German by Thilo Offergeld. Fontes Christiani, vol. 27. Freiberg and New York: Herder, 1997.

—————. *The Didascalicon of Hugh of St. Victor: A Medieval Guide to the Arts.* Trans. Jerome Taylor. New York and London: Columbia University Press, 1961.

Huneberc of Heidenheim. *Hodoeporicon.* In *Monumenta Germaniae Historica, Scriptores.* Ed. Oswald Holder-Egger, 1:80–117. Hannover, Ger.: Hahn, 1887.

Hutchison, Ann M. "Devotional Reading in the Monastery and the Late Medieval Household." In *De Cella in Seculum: Religious and Secular Life and Devotion in Late Medieval England.* Ed. Michael G. Sargent, 215–27. Bury St. Edmunds, Suffolk, UK: D.S. Brewer, 1989.

Internationaler Kongress für Frühmittelalterforschung, VI (Mainz, 1954). *Karolingische und Ottonische Kunst: Werden, Wesen, Wirkung.* Wiesbaden: F. Steiner, 1957.

Ireland, Patrick John. "The Narrative Unity of the *Lanval* of Marie de France." *Studies in Philology* 74 (1977): 130–45.

Jackson, W.T.H. "The Arthuricity of Marie de France." *Romance Review* 70 (1979): 1–18.

Jacques de Vitry. *The Life of Marie d'Oignies.* Trans. Margot H. King. In *Two Lives of Marie d'Oignies,* 58–60. 4th edn. Toronto: Peregrina Publishing, 1998.

Jefferis, Sibylle. "Hrotsvit and the *Magnum Legendarium Austriacum.*" In *Hrotsvit of Gandersheim: Rara Avis in Saxonia?* Ed. Katharina M. Wilson, 239–52. Ann Arbor: Medieval and Renaissance Collegium, University of Michigan, 1987.

Johnson, Lynn Staley. *See* Staley, Lynn.

Johnston, F.R. "The Cult of St. Bridget of Sweden in Fifteenth-Century England." M.A. thesis, University of Manchester, 1948.

Julian of Norwich. *A Book of Showings to the Anchoress Julian of Norwich.* Ed. Edmund Colledge and James Walsh. 2 vols. Studies and Texts 35. Toronto: Pontifical Institute of Medieval Studies, 1978.

—————. *Julian of Norwich's Revelations of Divine Love: The Shorter Version, Edited from B.L. Add. MS 37790.* Ed. Frances Beer. Heidelberg, Ger.: Carl Winter Universitätsverlag, 1978.

—————. *Revelations of Divine Love.* Trans. Clifton Wolters. Harmondsworth, UK: Penguin, 1966.

—————. *The Shewings of Julian of Norwich.* Ed. Georgia Ronan Crampton. Middle English Texts Series. Kalamazoo, MI: Consortium for the Teaching of the Middle Ages, 1993.

Kay, Sarah. *Subjectivity in Troubadour Poetry.* Cambridge: Cambridge University Press, 1990.

Kelly, Kathleen Coyne. *Performing Virginity and Testing Chastity in the Middle Ages.* Routledge Research in Medieval Studies 2. London and New York: Routledge, 2000.

Kelly, Kathleen Coyne, and Marina Leslie. *Menacing Virgins: Representing Virginity in the Middle Ages and Renaissance.* Newark: University of Delaware Press; London: Associated University Press, 1999.

Kempe, Margery. *The Book of Margery Kempe.* Ed. Lynn Staley. Middle English Series. Kalamazoo: Western Michigan University, 1996.

———. *The Book of Margery Kempe.* Trans. B.A. Windeatt. London: Penguin, 1985.

Kennedy, Angus J., Rosalind Brown-Grant, James C. Laidlaw, and Catherine M. Müller, eds. *Contexts and Continuities: Proceedings of the IVth International Colloquium on Christine de Pizan (Glasgow 21–27 July 2000), Published in Honour of Liliane Dulac.* 3 vols. Glasgow University Medieval French Texts and Studies. Glasgow: University of Glasgow Press, 2002.

Kinoshita, Sharon. " 'Cherchez la femme': Feminist Criticism and Marie de France's *Lai de Lanval.*" *Romance Notes* 34 (1994): 263–73.

———. *Medieval Boundaries: Rethinking Difference in Old French Literature.* Philadelphia: University of Pennsylvania Press, 2006.

Knowles, David. *The Religious Orders in England.* Vol. 2, *The End of the Middle Ages.* Cambridge: Cambridge University Press, 1955.

Kong, Katherine. "Guilty as Charged? Subjectivity and the Law in *La Chanson de Roland* and 'Lanval.' " *Essays in Medieval Studies* 17 (2001): 35–47.

Koubichkine, Michèle. "A propos du *Lai de Lanval.*" *Le Moyen Age: Revue d'histoire et de philologie* 78 (1972): 467–88.

Krapp, George Philip, and Elliott Van Kirk Dobbie, eds. *Elene.* In *The Vercelli Book,* vol. 2 of *The Anglo-Saxon Poetic Records.* New York: Columbia University Press, 1936.

Krueger, Roberta. *Women Readers and the Ideology of Gender in Old French Verse Romance.* Cambridge: Cambridge University Press, 1993.

Kurtz, Patricia Deery. "Mary of Oignies, Christine the Marvelous, and Medieval Heresy." *Mystics Quarterly* 14 (1988): 186–96.

Lachaussée, Geneviève. "L'influence du *Miroir des simples âmes anéanties* du Marguerite Porete sur la pensée de l'auteur anonyme du *Nuage d'inconnaissance.*" *Recherches de théologie et philosophie médiévales = Forschungen zur Theologie und Philosophie des Mittelalters* 64 (1997): 385–99.

Ladner, Gerhart B. "*Homo viator:* Medieval Ideas on Alienation and Order." *Speculum* 42 (1967): 233–59.

Lamb, George, trans. *The Life of St. Catherine of Siena.* London: Harvill Press, 1960.

Lapidge, Michael. "Introduction to Aldhelm's Prose *De virginitate.*" In *Aldhelm: The Prose Works.* Trans. Michael Lapidge and Michael Herren, 51–58. Cambridge, UK: D.S. Brewer, 1979.

Lavezzo, Kathy. "Sobs and Sighs between Women: The Homoerotics of Compassion in *The Book of Margery Kempe.*" In *Premodern Sexualities.* Ed. Louise Fradenberg and Carla Freccero, 175–98. New York and London: Routledge, 1996.

Lawes, Richard. "Psychological Disorder and the Autobiographical Impulse in Julian of Norwich, Margery Kempe and Thomas Hoccleve." In *Writing Religious Women: Female Spiritual and Textual Practices in Late Medieval England.* Ed. Denis Renevey and Christiania Whitehead. Toronto: University of Toronto Press, 2000. 217–43.

Lea, Henry C. *A History of the Inquisition in the Middle Ages.* 3 vols. 1887. New York: Russell and Russell, 1955.

Lee, Becky R. "The Medieval Hysteric and the Psychedelic Psychologist: A Revaluation of the Mysticism of Margery Kempe in the Light of the Transpersonal Psychology of Stanislav Grof." *Studia mystica* 23 (2002): 102–26.

Lee, Christina. "Eclectic Memories: In Search of Eadgyth." *Offa Berichte und Mitteilungen zur Urgeschichte, Frühgeschichte und Mittelalterarchäologie* 58 (2001; pub. 2004): 277–85.

Leoba, St. *Vita.* In *Monumenta Germaniae Historica, Scriptores.* Ed. Georg Waitz, 1:127–31. Hannover, Ger.: Hahnsche, 1887.

Lerner, Robert E. "An 'Angel of Philadelphia' in the Reign of King Philip the Fair: The Case of Guiard de Cressonessart." In *Order and Innovation in the Middle Ages: Essays in Honor of Joseph R. Strayer.* Ed. William C. Jordan, Bruce McNab, and Teofilio F. Ruiz, 343–64 and 529–40. Princeton: Princeton University Press, 1976.

———. *Heresy of the Free Spirit in the Later Middle Ages.* Berkeley: University of California Press, 1972.

Lewis, Flora. "The Wound in Christ's Side and the Instruments of the Passion: Gendered Experience and Response." In *Women and the Book: Assessing the Visual Evidence.* Ed. Jane H.M. Taylor and Lesley Smith, 204–23. British Library Studies in Medieval Culture. London: British Library Press; Toronto: University of Toronto Press, 1996.

Lichtmann, Maria. "Marguerite Porete and Meister Eckhart: *The Mirror of Simple Souls* Mirrored." In *Meister Eckhart and the Beguine Mystics: Hadewijch of Brabant, Mechthild of Magdeburg, and Marguerite Porete.* Ed. Bernard McGinn, 65–86. New York: Continuum, 1994.

———. "Marguerite Porete's *Mirror for Simple Souls*: Inverted Reflection of Self, Society, and God." *Studia mystica* 16 (1995): 4–29.

———. "Negative Theology in Marguerite Porete and Jacques Derrida." *Christianity and Literature* 47.2 (1998): 213–27.

Lochrie, Karma. "*The Book of Margery Kempe*: The Marginal Woman's Quest for Literary Authority." *Journal of Medieval and Renaissance Studies* 16 (1986): 33–55.

———. *Margery Kempe and Translations of the Flesh.* Philadelphia: University of Pennsylvania Press, 1991.

Marie de France. *The Lais.* Trans. Robert Hanning and Joan Ferrante. Grand Rapids, MI: Baker Books, 1978.

———. *Marie de France: Lais.* Ed. Alfred Ewert. 1944. Repr. Bristol, UK: Bristol Classical Press; London: Gerald Duckworth; Newbury Port, MA: Focus Information Group, 1995.

Marx, Heidi. "Metaphors of Imaging in Meister Eckhart and Marguerite Porete." *Medieval Perspectives* 13 (1998): 99–108.

Mazzoni, Cristina. *Angela of Foligno's Memorial, Translated from Latin with Introduction, Notes, and Interpretive Essay.* Library of Medieval Women. Cambridge, UK: D.S. Brewer, 1999.

McEntire, Sandra J. "The Journey into Selfhood: Margery Kempe and Feminine Spirituality." In *Margery Kempe: A Book of Essays.* Ed. Sandra J. McEntire, 51–69. Garland Medieval Casebooks, vol. 4. New York: Garland, 1992.

———. "Walter Hilton and Margery Kempe: Tears and Compunction." In *Mysticisim: Medieval and Modern.* Ed. Valerie M. Lagorio, 49–57. Salzburg

Studies in English Literature, 92:20. Salzburg: Institut für Anglistik und Amerikanistik, Universität of Salzburg, 1986.

McLaughlin, Eleanor. "The Heresy of the Free Spirit and Late Medieval Mysticism." *Medieval and Renaissance Spirituality* 4 (1973): 37–54.

Meale, Carol M., ed. *Women and Literature in Britain, 1150–1500.* 2nd edn. Cambridge: Cambridge University Press, 1996.

Memmi, Albert. *The Colonizer and the Colonized.* Boston: Beacon Press, 1965.

Milanesi, Carlo, ed. "Memorie di Ser Cristofano di Galgano Guidini da Siena, scritte di medesimo nel secolo XIV." *Archivio storico italiano,* series 1, 4 (1842): 25–48.

Morse, Mary. " 'Tak and Bren Hir': Lollardy as Conversion Motif in *The Book of Margery Kempe.*" *Mystics Quarterly* 29 (Mar.–June 2003): 24–44.

Motzo, B. "Per un'edizione critica delle opere di S. Caterina da Siena." *Annali della Facoltà di filosofia e lettere della Università di Cagliari* (1930–31): 111–41.

Mueller, Janel M. "Autobiography of a New 'Creatur': Female Spirituality, Selfhood, and Authorship in *The Book of Margery Kempe.*" In *The Female Autograph.* Ed. Domna C. Stanton, 63–75. New York: New York Literary Forum, 1984.

Müller, Catherine Monique [Bothe]. "De l'autre côté du miroir: Pour une lecture feminine du 'Mirouer' de Marguerite Porete et du 'Speculum' de Marguerite d'Oingt." Ph.D. diss., Purdue University, 1996.

———. *Marguerite Porete et Marguerite d'Oingt de l'autre côté du miroir.* Currents in Comparative Romance Languages and Literatures. New York: Peter Lang, 1999.

———. "Writing as Mirror in the Work of Marguerite Porete." *Mystics Quarterly* 20 (1994): 105–12.

Murk-Jansen, Saskia M. "The Use of Gender and Gender-Related Imagery in Hadewijch." In *Gender and Text in the Later Middle Ages.* Ed. Jane Chance, 52–68. Gainesville, FL: University Press of Florida, 1996.

Nagel, Bert. *Hrotsvit von Gandersheim.* Stuttgart, Ger.: Metzlersche, 1965.

Newman, Barbara. "Devout Women and Demoniacs in the World of Thomas Cantimpré." In *New Trends in Feminine Spirituality: The Holy Women of Liège and Their Impact.* Ed. Juliette Dor, Lesley Johnson, and Jocelyn Wogan Browne, 35–60. Turnhout, Belg.: Brepols, 1999.

———. *From Virile Woman to WomanChrist.* Philadelphia: University of Pennsylvania Press, 1993.

———. *God and the Goddesses: Vision, Poetry, and Belief in the Middle Ages.* Philadelphia: University of Pennsylvania Press, 2003.

———. "The Mirror and the Rose: Marguerite Porete's Encounter with the *Dieu d'Amours.*" *Vernacular Spirit* 1 (2002): 105–23.

———. "Possessed by the Spirit: Devout Women, Demoniacs, and the Apostolic Life in the Thirteenth Century." *Speculum* 73 (1998): 733–86.

———. *Sister of Wisdom: St. Hildegard's Theology of the Feminine.* Berkeley and Los Angeles: University of California Press, 1987.

Nitzsche, Jane Chance. *See* Chance, Jane.

Notker Labeo. *De nuptiis Philologiae et Mercurii.* In *Notkers des deutschen Werke.* Ed. E.H. Sehrt and Taylor Starck. Vol. 2 of 2 vols. Altdeutsche Textbibliothek, no. 37. Halle, Ger.: Max Niemeyer, 1935.

————. *Die Werke Notkers des Deutschen*. Vol. 4A. Ed. James V. King. Tübingen, Ger.: Max Niemeyer, 1986.

O'Shakey, Eithne M. "The Identity of the Fairy Mistress in Marie de France's *Lai de Lanval*." *Trivium* 6 (1971): 17–25.

Ovid. *Ovid in Six Volumes*. Ed. and trans. James George Frazer. 2nd edn. Rev. by G. Goold. Loeb Classical Library. Cambridge, MA, and London: Harvard University Press, 1977.

Paden, William D., ed. *The Voice of the Trobairitz: Perspectives on the Women Troubadours*. Philadelphia: University of Pennsylvania Press, 1989.

Pappano, Margaret Aziza. "Marie de France, Aliénor d'Aquitaine, and the Alien Queen." In *Eleanor of Aquitaine: Lord and Lady*. Ed. Bonnie Wheeler and John Carmi Parsons, 337–67. New York: Palgrave Macmillan, 2002.

Pasternack, Carol Braun. "The Sexual Practices of Virginity and Chastity in Aldhelm's *De virginitate*." In *Sex and Sexuality in Anglo-Saxon England: Essays in Memory of Daniel Gillmore Calder*. Ed. Carol Braun Pasternack and Lisa M.C. Weston, 93–120. Medieval and Renaissance Texts and Studies, vol. 277. Tempe: Arizona Center for Medieval and Renaissance Studies, 2004.

Paston, Margaret. *The Paston Women: Selected Letters*. Trans. Diane Watt. Woodbridge, Suffolk, UK: Boydell and Brewer, 2004.

Patai, Raphael. *The Arab Mind*. New York: Scribner's Sons, 1976.

Petroff, Elizabeth A. *Body and Soul: Essays on Medieval Women and Mysticism*. New York and Oxford: Oxford University Press, 1994.

————. "Eloquence and Heroic Virginity in Hrotsvit's Verse Legends." In *Hrotsvit of Gandersheim: Rara Avis in Saxonia?* Ed. Katharina M. Wilson, 229–38. Ann Arbor: Medieval and Renaissance Collegium, University of Michigan, 1987.

Poe, Elizabeth Wilson. "Love in the Afternoon: Courtly Play in the *Lai de Lanval*." *Neuphilologische Mitteilungen* 84 (1983): 301–10.

Pondè, Luiz Felipe. "The Relation between the Concept of 'Anéantissement' in Marguerite Porete and the Concept of 'Abegescheindenheit' in Meister Eckhart: Meister Eckhart and the Béguines." *What Is Philosophy in the Middle Ages? International Kongress für mittelalterliche Philosophie* (1997): 311–12.

Porete, Marguerite. *Marguerite Porete: Le mirouer des simples ames*. Ed. Romana Guarnieri. In "Il movimento del Spirito Libero." *Archivio italiano per la storia della pietà* 4 (1965): 513–635.

————. *Margaretae Porete: Speculum simplicium animarum*. Ed. Paul Verdeyen. Corpus Christianorum: Continuatio Medievalis 69. Turnhout, Belg.: Brepols, 1986.

————. *Marguerite Porete's "The Mirror of Simple Souls."* Trans. Ellen L. Babinsky. Classics of Western Spirituality. New York, NY, and Mahwah, NJ: Paulist Press. Marguerite Porete.

Quilligan, Maureen. *The Allegory of Female Authority: Christine de Pizan's "Cité des Dames."* Ithaca, NY: Cornell University Press, 1991.

Quinn, Esther C. "Chaucer's Arthurian Romance." *Chaucer Review* 18.3 (1984): 211–20.

Randall, Catharine. "Person, Place, Perception: A Proposal for the Reading of Porete's *Mirouer des âmes simples et anéanties*." *Journal of Medieval and Renaissance Studies* 25 (1995): 229–44.

Raymond of Capua (Raimundus de Vineis, de Capua). *Here beginneth the Lyf of Saynt Katherin of senis the Blessed Virgin; The revelacions of Saynt Elysabeth the Kynges doughter of hungarye.* Trans. from the Latin. Ed. William Caxton. London: Wynken de Worde, from William Caxton's Plates, 1493?.

———. "Legenda major." Canonici miscellaneous 205. Fols. 7r–75v. Bodleian Library, Oxford.

Renevey, Denis, and Christiania Whitehead, eds. *Writing Religious Women: Female Spiritual and Textual Practices in Late Medieval England.* Toronto: University of Toronto Press, 2000.

Ricci, Seymour de. *A Census of Caxtons.* Illustrated Monographs of the Bibliographical Society, no. 15. Oxford: Oxford University Press, 1909.

Richards, Earl Jeffrey, Joan Williamson, Nadia Margolis, and Christine Reno, eds. *Reinterpreting Christine de Pizan.* Athens: University of Georgia Press, 1992.

Rieger, Angelica. *Trobairitz: Der Beitrag der Frau in der altokzitanischen höfischen Lyrik: Edition des Gesamtkorpus.* Tübingen, Ger.: Max Niemayer, 1991.

Robinson, Joanne Maquire. *Nobility and Annihilation in Marguerite Porete's "Mirror of Simple Souls."* SUNY Series in Western Esoteric Traditions. Albany: State University of New York Press, 2001.

Roche-Mahdi, Sarah, ed. and trans. *Silence: A Thirteenth-Century French Romance.* East Lansing, MI: Colleagues Press, 1992.

Rossi-Reder, Andrea. "Embodying Christ, Embodying Nation: Ælfric's Accounts of Saints Agatha and Lucy." In *Sex and Sexuality in Anglo-Saxon England.* Ed. Carol Braun Pasternack and Lisa M.C. Weston, 183–202. Medieval and Renaissance Texts and Studies, vol. 277. Tempe: Arizona Center for Medieval and Renaissance Studies, 2004.

Rothschild, Judith Rice. "A *Rapprochement* between *Bisclavret* and *Lanval.*" *Speculum* 48 (1973): 78–88.

Rothwell, W. "The Trial Scene in *Lanval* and the Development of the Legal Register in Anglo-Norman." *Neuphilologische Mitteilungen* 101.1 (2000): 17–36.

Rožmberk, Perchta. *The Letters of the Rožmberk Sisters: Noblewomen in Fifteenth Century Bohemia.* Trans. John M. Klassen. Library of Medieval Women. Woodbridge, Suffolk, UK: Boydell and Brewer, 2004.

Ruh, Kurt. "Beguinenmystik: Hadewijch, Mechthild von Magdeburg, Marguerite Porete." *Zeitschrift für deutsches Altertum und deutsche Literatur* 106 (1977): 265–77.

———. "Gottesliebe bei Hadewijch, Mechthild von Magdeburg und Marguerite Porete." In *Romanische Literaturbeziehungen im 19 und 20. Jahrhundert: Festschrift für Franz Rauhut zum 85. Geburtstag.* Ed. Angel San Miguel, Richard Schwaderer, and Manfred Tietz, 243–54. Tübingen, Ger.: Narr, 1985.

Sankovitch, Tilde A. *French Women Writers and the Book: Myths of Access and Desire.* Syracuse, NY: Syracuse University Press, 1988.

Sargent, Michael G. "The Annihilation of Marguerite Porete." *Viator* 28 (1997): 250–79.

———. " 'Le Mirouer des simples ames' and the English Mystical Tradition." In *Abendländische Mystik im Mittelalter: Symposium Kloster Engelberg 1984.* Ed. Kurt Ruh, 443–65. Stuttgart, Ger.: J.B. Metzlersche, 1986.

Schibanoff, Susan. "Taking the Gold out of Egypt: The Art of Reading as a Woman." In *Gender and Reading.* Ed. Elizabeth A. Flynn and Patrocinio

Schweickart, 83–106. Baltimore, MD, and London: Johns Hopkins University Press, 1986.

Schütz-Pflugk, Marianne. *Herrscher- und Märtyrer-Auffassung be Hrotsvit von Gandersheim.* Wiesbaden, Ger.: Steiner, 1972.

Scott, Karen. " '*Io Catarina*': Ecclesiastical Politics and Oral Culture in the Letters of Catherine of Siena." In *Dear Sister: Medieval Women and the Epistolary Genre.* Ed. Karen Cherewatuk and Ulrike Wiethaus, 87–121. Philadelphia: University of Pennsylvania Press, 1993.

———. "Not Only with Words, but with Deeds: The Role of Speech in Catherine of Siena's Understanding of Her Mission." Ph.D. diss., University of California-Berkeley, 1989.

Sells, Michael. "The Pseudo-Woman and the Meister: 'Unsaying' and Essentialism." In *Meister Eckhart and the Beguine Mystics: Hadewijch of Brabant, Mechthild of Magdeburg, and Marguerite Porete.* Ed. Bernard McGinn, 114–46. New York: Continuum, 1994.

Sienaert, Edgard. *Les lais de Marie de France: Du conte merveilleux à la nouvelle psychologique.* Paris: H. Champion, 1984.

Sikorska, Liliana. " 'Hir Not Lettyrd': The Use of Interjections, Pragmatic Markers and When-Clauses in *The Book of Margery Kempe*." In *Placing Middle English in Context.* Ed. Irma Taavitsainen, Terttu Nevalainen, Päivi Pahta, and Matti Rissanen, 391–410. Topics in English Linguistics 35. Berlin and New York: Mouton de Gruyter, 2000.

Slade, Carole. "Alterity in Union: The Mystical Experience of Angela of Foligno and Margery Kempe." *Religion and Literature* 23 (Autumn 1991): 109–26.

Smithers, G.V. "Story-Patterns in Some Breton Lays." *Medium Aevum* 22 (1953): 61–92.

Solterer, Helen. *The Master and Minerva: Disputing Women in French Medieval Culture.* Berkeley: University of California Press, 1995.

Somerset, Fiona. "Excitative Speech: Theories of Emotive Response from Richard Fitzralph to Margery Kempe." In *The Vernacular Spirit: Essays on Medieval Religious Literature.* Ed. Renate Blumenfeld-Kosinski, Duncan Robertson, and Nancy Bradley Warren, 59–79. New York: Palgrave, 2002.

Staley, Lynn. *Margery Kempe's Dissenting Fictions.* University Park: Pennsylvania State University Press, 1994.

———. "The Trope of the Scribe and the Question of Literary Authority in the Works of Julian of Norwich and Margery Kempe." *Speculum* 66 (1991): 820–38.

Stargardt, Ute. "The Beguines of Belgium, the Dominican Nuns of Germany, and Margery Kempe." In *The Popular Literature of Medieval England.* Ed. Thomas Heffernan, 277–313. Knoxville: University of Tennessee Press, 1985.

Sticca, Sandro. "The Hagiographical and Monastic Context of Hrotswitha's Plays." In *Hrotsvit of Gandersheim: Rara Avis in Saxonia?* Ed. Katharina M. Wilson, 1–34. Ann Arbor: Medieval and Renaissance Collegium, University of Michigan, 1987.

Summit, Jennifer. *Lost Property: The Woman Writer and English Literary History, 1380–1589.* Chicago: University of Chicago Press, 2000.

Talbot, Charles H., trans. and ed. *The Anglo-Saxon Missionaries in Germany, Being the Lives of Saints Willibald, Boniface, Sturm, Leoba, and Libuin, Together with the "Hodoeporicon" of Saint Willibald and a Selection from the Correspondence of Saint Boniface.* New York: Sheed and Ward, 1954.

Tanner, Bishop. "Catalogue of Sion Library." Additional MS 6261. Fols. 153–56. British Library, London.

Tarr, Judith Ellen. "Holy Virgins and Wanton Women: Hrotsvitha's Terence and 'Anti Terence.'" *Dissertation Abstracts International* 50.11 (1990): 3582A.

———. "Terentian Elements in Hrotsvit." In *Hrotsvit of Gandersheim: Rara Avis in Saxonia?* Ed. Katharina M. Wilson, 55–62. Ann Arbor: Medieval and Renaissance Collegium, University of Michigan, 1987.

Taurisano, P. Innocenzo. *I fioretti di S. Caterina da Siena.* 2nd edn. Rome: F. Ferrari, 1927.

Tavormina, Teresa M. "Of Maidenhood and Maternity: Liturgical Hagiography and the Medieval Ideal of Virginity." *American Benedictine Review* 31.4 (1980): 384–99.

Taylor, Jane H.M., and Lesley Smith. *Women and the Book: Assessing the Visual Evidence.* British Library Studies in Medieval Culture. London: British Library; Toronto: University of Toronto Press, 1996.

Third Vatican Mythographer. *De diis gentium et illorum allegoriid.* In *Scriptores rerum mythicarum latini tres Romae nuper reperti*, ed. Georgius Henricus Bode, ed., 1834. Repr., Hildesheim: Georg Olms, 1968.

Thomas de Cantimpré. *The Life of Christina Mirabilis.* Trans. Margot H. King. Toronto: Peregrina Press, 1997.

Thompson, Charlotte. "*Paphnutius* and the Cultural Vision." In *Hrotsvit of Gandersheim: A Florilegia of Her Works.* Ed. Katharina Wilson, 111–25. Library of Medieval Women. Cambridge, UK, and Rochester, NY: D.S. Brewer, 1998.

Thompson, E. Margaret. *The Carthusian Order in England.* London: Society for Promoting Christian Knowledge; New York and Toronto: Macmillan, 1930.

Trotula. *The Book of Trotula: A Medieval Compendium of Women's Medicine.* Ed. and trans. Monica Green. University Park: Penn State University Press, 2001, 2002.

Trowse, Nadeane. "The Exclusionary Potential of Genre: Margery Kempe's Transgressive Search for a Deniable Pulpit." In *The Rhetoric and Ideology of Genre: Strategies for Stability and Change.* Ed. Richard Coe, Lorelei Lingard, and Tatiana Teslenko, 341–53. Creskill, NJ: Hampton Press, 2002.

Uhlman, Diana R. "The Comfort of Voice, the Solace of Script: Orality and Literacy in *The Book of Margery Kempe*," *Studies in Philology* 91 (1994): 50–69.

Uitti, Karl D. "'Cele [qui] doit ester Rose clamee' (*Rose*, vv.40–44): Guillaume's Intentionality." In *Rethinking the Rose: Text, Image, Reception.* Ed. Kevin Brownlee and Sylvia Huot, 39–64. Philadelphia: University of Pennsylvania Press, 1992.

Verdeyen, Paul. "Le procès d'inquisition contre Marguerite Porete et Guiarde de Cressonessart (1309–1310)." *Revue d'histoire ecclésiastique* 81.1–2 (1986): 47–94.

Vey, Rudolf. *Christliches Theater im Mittelalter und Neuzeit.* Aschaffenburg, Ger.: P. Pattlock, 1960.

Voaden, Rosalynn. *God's Words, Women's Voices: The Discernment of Spirits in the Writing of Late-Medieval Women Visionaries.* Woodbridge, Suffolk, UK, and Rochester, NY: York Medieval Press, 1999.

Wace. *Wace's Roman de Brut: A History of the British, Text and Translation*. Ed. and trans. Judith Weiss. Exeter, UK: University of Exeter Press, 1999.

Walkley, M.J. "The Critics and *Lanval*." *New Zealand Journal of French Studies* 4 (1983): 5–23.

Warren, Martin L. *Asceticism in the Christian Transformation of Self in Margery Kempe, William Thorpe, and John Rogers*. Studies in Religion and Society, vol. 60. Lewiston, NY: E. Mellen Press, 2003.

Wathelet-Willem, Jeanne. "Le mystère chez Marie de France." *Revue belge de philologie et d'histoire* 39 (1969): 661–86.

Watson, Nicholas. "Censorship and Cultural Change in Late Medieval England: Vernacular Theology, the Oxford Translation Debate, and Arundel's *Constitutiones* of 1409." *Speculum* 70 (1995): 822–64.

———. "The Composition of Julian of Norwich's *Revelation of Love*." *Speculum* 68 (1993): 637–83.

Watt, Diane, ed. *Medieval Women in Their Communities*. Toronto: University of Toronto Press, 1997.

Wetherbee, Winthrop. *Platonism and Poetry in the Twelfth Century: The Literary Influence of the School of Chartres*. Princeton, NJ: Princeton University Press, 1972.

Wheeler, Bonnie, ed. *Listening to Heloise: The Voice of a Twelfth-Century Woman*. New Middle Ages Series. London and New York: Palgrave Macmillan/St. Martin's, 2000.

Whitfield, Pam. "Power Plays: Relationships in Marie de France's *Lanval* and *Eliduc*." *Medieval Perspectives* 14 (1999): 242–54.

Wiegand, Sister M. Gonsalva. "The Non-dramatic Works of Hroswitha: Text, Translation, and Commentary." Ph.D. diss., St. Louis University, 1936.

Wiethaus, Ulrike, ed. *Maps of Flesh and Light: The Religious Experience of Medieval Women Mystics*. Syracuse, NY: Syracuse University Press, 1993.

Wilson, Janet. "Margery and Alisoun: Women on Top." In *Margery Kempe: A Book of Essays*. Ed. Sandra J. McEntire, 233–37. Garland Medieval Casebooks, vol. 4. New York: Garland, 1992.

Wilson, Katharina M., "Hrotsvit and *The Artes*." In *Creativity, Influence, and Imagination: The World of Medieval Women*. Ed. Constance Berman, Charles Connell, and Judith Rothschild. Morgantown,: University of West Virginia, 1985. 3–14.

———, trans. *Hrotsvit of Gandersheim: A Florilegia of Her Works*. Library of Medieval Women. Cambridge, UK, and Rochester, NY: D.S. Brewer, 1998.

———, ed. *Medieval Women Writers*. Athens: University of Georgia Press, 1984.

Wilson, Katharina M., and Glenda McLeod. "Wholism and Fusion: Success in/of the *Lais* of Marie de France." *Arachnē: An Interdisciplinary Journal of the Humanities* 5 (1998): 3–30.

Winterfeld, Paul von, ed. *Hrotsvithae opera*. Berlin: Weidmann, 1902.

Wittig, Monique. "The Mark of Gender." In *The Poetics of Gender*. Ed. Nancy Miller, 63–73. New York: Columbia University Press, 1986.

Wright, Richard Everett. "Vesta: A Study on the Origin of a Goddess and Her Cults." *Dissertation Abstracts International* 56 (1996) 4744A (University of Washington, 1995).

Wylie, James H. *The Reign of King Henry the Fifth*. Vol. 1 of 3 vols. Cambridge: Cambridge University Press, 1914.

Zimmermann, Margarete, and Dina De Rentiis, eds. *The City of Scholars: New Approaches to Christine de Pizan*. Berlin and New York: Walter de Gruyter, 1994.

Zum Brunn, Emilie, and Georgette Épiney-Burgard. *Women Mystics in Medieval Europe*. Trans. Sheila Hughes. New York: Paragon, 1989.

INDEX

active/passive as gendered binary, 5–6

Agatha, St., 23

agency: agency/nonagency as gendered binary, 13; conversion and agency of women, 25; de Pizan and, 13; emulation of Christ and female agency, 25; Eve as agent in fall of man, 5; female as healer, 55; as madness or irrationality in women, 6–7; Porete and female, 68

Agnes, St.: Ælfric's depiction of, 18, 23, 24–25, 28–31, 34; as anti-Vesta, 34–36; as bride of Christ, 34; Constantia linked to, 18, 24–25, 27, 29, 34–36, 38–39; as exemplar of virginity, 18, 23, 26, 28–29, 31; hagiography of, 23–24; as healer, 18–19, 23–24, 25, 34–36, 37; Hrotsvit's depiction of, 18, 25–27, 31, 34–39; as linking mechanism in Hrotsvit's work, 25; martyrdom of, 29; as *salvator*, or emulator of Christ, 19, 23, 25, 34

Alan of Lille, 20, 73, 78–79, 81

Albericus of London, 79–80

Aldhelm, 23–24

Ælfric, 18, 23–29, 34, 37, 38

the alien: Hrotsvit's and appropriation of cultural, 18, 28, 127; Kempe as wandering and displaced, 103–4; Lanval as, 19, 45, 47–48, 51, 56–57, 59; Marie de France as exile or, 16, 55, 59; supernatural as, 16; women as more likely to be, 16; xenophobia and, 43, 45, 56–58, 128

allegory: de Pizan and, 8, 14–15; mysticism and, 70, 72–73; pagan gods deployed by male authors in, 79–80; Porete and, 64–67, 72–73, 76–77, 133, 160 n43; religious *vs.* dream vision and, 70. *See also* personification

Allen, Hope Emily, 100

alterity: ambivalence and, 101–2; Catherine of Siena, 125; Christ as bridge across difference, 21, 108, 118; colonialism and construction of, 1; eccentricity and, 104–5; empowerment of, 125–26; as emulation of Christ, 105; gender difference and, 108–9, 110–11, 114–15, 121–22; as heroic, 54; Kempe and, 110–12, 125; madness as marker of, 31; the Other as transformative agent, 55–56, 121–22; as sanctified, 20–21; speech as bridge between Self and Other, 125–26; spirituality and, 20–21, 104–5, 110, 112, 121–22; the supernatural as Other, 16, 53; treason and, 56–58; unhomeliness and, 100. *See also* the alien; unhomeliness

Ambrose, St., 23

Angela of Foligno, 68, 101